Analyzing Foreign Policy

Analyzing Foreign Policy

Derek Beach

First published 2012 by
PALGRAVE MACMILLAN

Palgrave Macmillan in the UK is an imprint of Macmillan Publishers Limited, registered in England, company number 785998, of Houndmills, Basingstoke, Hampshire RG21 6XS.

Palgrave Macmillan in the US is a division of St Martin's Press LLC, 175 Fifth Avenue, New York, NY 10010.

Palgrave Macmillan is the global academic imprint of the above companies and has companies and representatives throughout the world.

Palgrave® and Macmillan® are registered trademarks in the United States, the United Kingdom, Europe and other countries

ISBN 978–0–230–23738–4 hardback
ISBN 978–0–230–23739–1 paperback

This book is printed on paper suitable for recycling and made from fully managed and sustained forest sources. Logging, pulping and manufacturing processes are expected to conform to the environmental regulations of the country of origin.

A catalogue record for this book is available from the British Library.

A catalog record for this book is available from the Library of Congress.

To my students at the University of Aarhus whose challenging comments and questions have made this a much better book

Brief Contents

Contents

List of Illustrative Material

Figures

Tables

Boxes

List of Abbreviations

BATNA	best alternative to a negotiated agreement
CFSP	Common Foreign and Security Policy
COW	Correlates of War
EU	European Union
FPA	Foreign Policy Analysis
GDP	gross domestic product
IR	International Relations
PD	prisoner's dilemma
RAM	Rational Actor Model
SOPs	standard operating procedures
WMD	weapons of mass destruction

Chapter 1

Introduction: Analyzing Foreign Policy

Why did the Soviet Union choose to relinquish control peacefully of the Eastern bloc of countries in 1989? Do democracies adopt more peaceful foreign policies than authoritarian states? Why did the United States become embroiled in the Vietnam War despite President Johnson's clear intention of keeping US involvement to a minimum? What is the impact of globalization upon the foreign policy of states? Do interest groups like the Israeli lobby influence US foreign policy and, if so, how? Does the European Union (EU) have a foreign policy identity that matches its status as a great economic power? Are leaders rational during grave international crises? These are the types of questions scholars attempt to tackle when analyzing foreign policy.

The purpose of this book is to provide students with a set of theoretical tools to analyze foreign policy, broadly understood. Employing both International Relations (IR) theories and more specific theories from the sub-discipline of Foreign Policy Analysis (FPA), I will develop a theoretical toolbox that can be used to:

- Explain what states want in foreign policy.
- Understand how states take decisions on foreign policy issues and how the process itself matters.
- Analyze what states do in different areas of foreign policy (security, diplomacy, economic).
- Assess whether we are currently witnessing a transformation in the very nature of foreign policy.

In this introductory chapter I first discuss how we can define the term 'foreign policy', before introducing the theoretical toolkit to be developed throughout the book.

Defining 'foreign policy'

This book deals with theories that can be used to analyze foreign policy. Yet the term 'foreign policy' itself is deceptively difficult to define. As with most concepts in political science and IR that attempt to understand key aspects of a very complicated reality, there is considerable debate about how we should define 'foreign policy'. All of our decisions about how we should define the term have benefits and tradeoffs that it is important to be aware of, as they restrict or expand the focus of our inquiry.

What becomes clear when one reviews the literature is that scholars are often speaking about different phenomena when they define 'foreign policy'. Christopher Hill has defined it as 'the *sum* of external relations conducted by an independent actor (usually a state) in international relations' (Hill 2003: 3, my italics). However, defining policy as the sum of external actions results in analysis that only explains broad trends in foreign policies and not individual actions and decisions. Foreign policy according to White is 'government *activity* conducted with relationships between state and other actors, particularly other states, in the international system' (White 1989: 1, my italics). Yet, as White admits, this definition does not include other forms of collective actors like the EU that also conduct foreign policy activities. Rosenau offers an even simpler definition of it as the external *behavior* of states (Rosenau 1971: 95). Brecher contends that what we should study are foreign policy *decisions* and not just measurable behavior (Brecher 1972: 15).

These competing definitions illustrate that there are a number of choices that must be made when we define the concept 'foreign policy'. First, how should we define the 'foreign' aspect of foreign policies? Many domestic policies such as farm subsidies or environmental legislation (especially by larger states) have external impacts upon other states. But are legislators making foreign policy when they are debating farm subsidies? Here the definition of White above is helpful. Note that foreign policies in this definition are *explicitly directed* toward other external actors.

The term 'policy' is also very slippery. Should we define a foreign policy as the *sum* of external actions directed toward a specific actor as Hill does? Or can we also include *specific* actions in our definition of foreign policy? Is a 'policy' the goal the action was *intended* to achieve or the actual result of the action as it was implemented? We know from public policy-making that the way that a law is implemented in practice is seldom a faithful reflection of what law-makers intended. In foreign policy, a famous example that illustrates the difference between intended and actual implemented policy is the case of US foreign policy toward Iraq in the run-up to the Iraqi invasion of Kuwait in August 1990. US ambassador to Iraq April Glaspie sent quite ambiguous signals to Saddam Hussein; for example telling him that the US had 'no opinion on the Arab–Arab conflicts, like your border disagreement with Kuwait' (*New York Times*, September 23, 1990). Saddam

Hussein mistakenly perceived this to mean that it was US foreign policy to not respond forcefully to an invasion of Kuwait by Iraq (Yetiv 2004: 22–3); an interpretation that did not reflect the policy that was intended in Washington. Was the 'foreign policy' of the US toward Iraq what was intended by US decision-makers? Or should it be measured as the actions that took place? Given the difficulty of measuring intentionality, should we then only focus upon 'actions' or 'behavior' as policy – as argued by Rosenau and others? An alternative solution is to follow Brecher, who argues that we should study 'decisions', given that taking a decision implies a degree of intentionality. However, there are also numerous problems with restricting our attention to decisions. One key problem is that most foreign policy decisions take place behind closed doors, meaning that we often are unable to measure empirically whether a decision has actually taken place (at least until the point in time when archives are opened).

Finally, should we define foreign policy as the external actions of *states*, or open up the possibility that other collective actors such as the EU have foreign policies? The EU, despite not being a legal state, does undertake common foreign policy actions toward its neighbors. Further, in federal systems such as the US, individual states like California also have foreign relations with neighboring countries. In this book I do however limit the scope of collective actors to public authorities, denying that private collective actors such as multinational companies have 'foreign policies'. Instead, these firms have what can be defined as relations with public authorities or other private companies.

The definition of foreign policy in this book is both broad and pragmatic and is as follows:

> Foreign policy is both the broad trends of behavior and the particular actions taken by a state or other collective actor as directed toward other collective actors within the international system. Foreign policy actions can be undertaken using a variety of different instruments, ranging from adopting declarations, making speeches, negotiating treaties, giving other states economic aid, engaging in diplomatic activity such as summits, and the use of military force.

What is the analysis of foreign policy?

FPA is an important sub-discipline of the study of IR. I will argue that what sets FPA apart from the broader study of IR is the *scope* of what is to be explained (see Figure 1.1). Although IR encompasses the foreign policy actions of individual states, the range of phenomena studied within IR is much broader. IR scholarship does investigate interstate relations conducted through foreign policies, but it also looks

Figure 1.1   *The scope of Foreign Policy Analysis and International Relations scholarship*

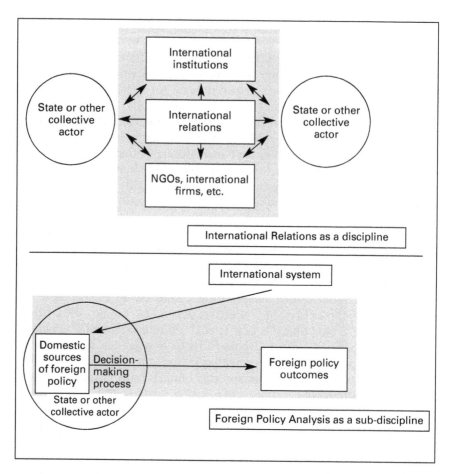

at the workings of the international system itself, including questions such as why international institutions are created and what impact they have upon world politics, and why global problems such as climate change are so difficult to tackle. The basic point is that most definitions of IR scholarship deal with almost all political phenomena that cannot be contained within the domestic political system of a single state. The broader scope of the phenomena analyzed within IR scholarship is illustrated in the figure by the gray shaded area in the top section of the figure.

In contrast, the sub-discipline of FPA has a narrower focus on explaining the determinants of the foreign policies of a single state (or other collective actor) viewed either as general trends (e.g. US foreign policy toward Latin America) or as specific actions (e.g. the US decision to go to war against Iraq in 2003). As can be seen in the bottom section of Figure 1.1, FPA investigates questions related to the impact of the international system upon foreign policy, the impact of domestic determinants like public opinion and institutions, and how different decision-making processes matter for foreign policy trends or specific actions.

The definition of the analysis of foreign policy used in this book is based upon the scope of the research question to be analyzed, with FPA being viewed as a sub-discipline of IR due to its narrower scope. Embedding FPA within the broader study of IR means that many of the theoretical tools of IR can be used to study foreign policy. For instance, Walt's (1988) balance-of-threat theory is very useful in understanding broad trends in state foreign policy, expecting that states will 'balance' against the state or group of states that they perceive to be the greatest threat – making it a relevant theoretical tool if we are attempting to explain Pakistani foreign policies toward India (see Chapters 2 and 6).

In contrast to this understanding of the study of foreign policy as a sub-discipline embedded in IR, there are scholars who argue that FPA should be understood as a distinct academic discipline. Hudson (2007), for instance, argues that FPA is more multilevel and multifactorial in its approach than IR scholarship. Inspired by the decision-making framework put forward by Snyder *et al.* (2002), Hudson contends that at the core of FPA are theories that analyze the impact of situational and cognitive factors upon foreign policy decision-making units. Whereas IR theories are 'actor-neutral', Hudson contends that FPA is an 'actor-centered' approach that is distinct from IR. In an excellent review of the history of FPA theorization she chronicles the subfield, focusing upon the common interest in decision-making and cognition. I will return to these theories in Chapters 4 and 5.

However, while this definition highlights some of the more original contributions of FPA scholars to the study of foreign policy (and IR more generally), the argument unnecessarily puts the study of foreign policy into an analytical cubbyhole focused exclusively on studying decision-making – a point made by many IR scholars (e.g. Elman 1996: 17).

The pragmatic approach argued for in this book is that there is no reason to restrict the theoretical tools available for analyzing foreign policy and, as will be seen in the chapters of this book, that many IR theories provide useful tools for analyzing specific aspects of foreign policy. Therefore the study of foreign policy should be delineated from IR by its narrower *analytical* focus of what is to be explained, and not by *theoretical* approaches. Foreign policy as understood here can be understood as a subset of the broader set of research questions tackled by IR theory.

The argument in this book is that the study of foreign policy does not require a *unique* FPA theoretical toolbox, and, while there are many distinct FPA theories on specific questions such as perceptions or crisis decision-making, IR theories can also be used productively to explain aspects of the foreign policy behavior of states or other collective actors.

On a final note, theories of public policy more generally are not introduced in this book. The reason for this is that the making of foreign policy is governed by different rules and dynamics than 'normal' public policy. While public policies have domestic groups as referent objects, foreign policies are directed at foreign collective actors (usually states), creating quite different policy-making dynamics. For example, most foreign policy issues are not very salient for voters in contrast to core domestic policy areas, making governments less responsive to public opinion. Further, in foreign policy-making, executive authorities are relatively strong *vis-à-vis* legislatures in comparison to domestic policy-making; in some constitutions foreign policy is the exclusive prerogative of the executive (see Chapter 3). Another common distinction relates to the large amount of budgeting, planning and long time horizons of many domestic policies in relation to the fluid and immediate nature of foreign policy-making, where policy-makers are forced to deal with crises and unpredictable negotiations with other governments. However, these distinctions should not be overplayed, and, as will be seen in the theories of bureaucratic and organizational politics, there has been considerable fruitful cross-fertilization between theorization on foreign and public policy more generally.

What is theory?

Theories provide simplified explanations of complex real world phenomena. In the words of King *et al.* (1994: 19), theories are reasoned and precise speculations about the answer to a research question. Elman (1996: 12) helpfully suggests that 'a theory of foreign policy makes determinate predictions for dependent variable(s) that measure the behavior of individual states'. Even historians admit that explanations of events do not manifest themselves, but that theories are necessary in order to focus our inquiry upon factors that potentially explain phenomena (Roberts 1996). Basically, without theories we will have no idea about where we should start an investigation of what explains a specific foreign policy phenomenon.

If we want to explain why US decision-makers chose to go to war against Iraq in 2003 and believe that we can develop an explanation by letting 'the facts' speak for themselves, we would encounter enormous practical difficulties due to the amount of information that we would need to collect and process; and even if this information could be collected, it would have to be processed by the analyst – a process in which working hypotheses (theories) would have to be created anyway. First, at the practical level, the analyst would have to analyze all of the threats and opportunities to US interests in the Middle East in the papers transmitted from embassies and intelligence agencies to decision-makers in Washington DC. The analyst would also have to collect all of the intelligence that the US actually possessed about Iraqi capabilities. Information would also need to be gathered on the diplomatic situation, including the interests of allies and rivals in the region and US relations with these actors in different fora (bilateral activity and within multilateral institutions like the UN). Further, in order to make sense of the information about the context of the US decision, the analyst would also have to undertake thorough examinations of the backgrounds and decision-making styles of all of the relevant US decision-makers within the US administration and Congress.

These reams of pages of 'facts' do not speak by themselves. The information would have to be processed by the analyst to construct an explanation of the outcome. To make sense of the facts, the analyst would have to develop working hypotheses about what motivated the US decision-makers that could be tested against the empirical material. These working hypotheses could be in the form of different motives, such as: Did concerns about the stability of oil supplies motivate the decision? Or was it concern about weapons of mass destruction? To test these (and other) hypotheses, the analyst would have to develop explicit hypotheses about what we should expect to see in the empirical record if hypothesis A was correct, and what we would not expect to see.

A more straightforward way of proceeding would have been to develop working hypotheses prior to collecting all of the empirical data, which would enable the analyst to cut to the chase, focusing effort upon investigating whether the expected observable implications of working hypothesis A, B or C were present or absent. Here theories play a crucial role.

Theories are tools for focusing our analytical attention upon the most important explanatory factors (variables) of a given phenomenon (e.g. a foreign policy action) (see Chapter 10). It is important to stress that a theory is not a definition of a single theoretical concept (e.g. democracy or power), but instead involves some form of explanation or understanding of what caused an empirical phenomenon (denoted by 'Y'). A theory is a 'reasoned and precise speculation about the answer to a research question ... Theories usually imply several more specific descriptive or causal hypotheses' (King *et al.* 1994: 19) (see Box 1.1). Theories deal with linkages between concepts such as democracy and

---

Box 1.1 Competing theories explaining the relationship between democracy and peace

If we are interested in investigating the relationship between democracy viewed as the explanatory factor (X) and instances of war/peace as what is to be explained (Y), liberal and realist theories offer competing answers as to whether democracy causes peace. A liberal answer is that the liberal norms that democracies should not go to war with each other, coupled with free debate within democratic societies, creates strong constraints upon the ability of such societies to go to war with each other (Owen 1994). In contrast, a realist answer would be that democracy does not cause peace, and in fact the causal relationship should be seen as running in the opposite direction (Layne 1994). The argument is that democracies can only develop in 'nice neighborhoods'; that is regions where there are not severe conflicts of interest. Peace between states due to a lack of severe conflicts (X) results in a domestic environment where democracy is able to survive and develop (Y).

---

war. A typical research question could be: Why do democracies not go to war against each other?

Variables are used to describe concepts that vary. For instance, democracy understood as a variable can either be present or not. In numerical terms, this would mean democracy is a variable that can be either 1 (present) or 0 (absent). Another way of defining this variable would be to use the term 'political regime', which could vary between 'democracy' and 'autocracy'.

However, if we are interested in explaining an outcome in a specific case, such as why the US invaded Iraq in 2003, the outcome is *not* a variable. Unless one believes in the existence of parallel universes or time travel, the only outcome in the case was that the US invaded Iraq. There is no variation in the outcome, meaning that it is not a variable per se. This does not mean that we cannot write a research paper that attempts to explain what factors motivated the US invasion. It merely means that in this type of single case study, one should not think in terms of variables; instead the term outcome should be used (see Chapter 10).

Theories describe relationships between factors that potentially cause outcomes. The term 'independent variable' (denoted by 'X' and also termed 'explanatory variable') is used to refer to the theoretical causes of another variable (outcome). Outcomes that vary are termed 'dependent variables' (Ys). A dependent variable is, in other words, the phenomenon we want to explain. For instance, a common dependent variable in FPA is whether or not states adopt more cooperative or conflictual foreign policies toward other states.

Table 1.1 *Two different families of theories: explanatory theories and analytical models*

Theories as ...	Explanatory tools to study generalizable phenomena	Analytical models to understand cases
Priority	Theory-centric	Case-centric
Types of theories	Parsimonious causal theories $(X \rightarrow Y)$ with clear hypotheses	Ideal-types, typological theories, complex models and eclectic theoretical combinations
Understanding of reality	Empirical world can be 'split' into manageable parts Theories can 'travel' across cases when we take into consideration contexts in which they operate	Empirical world is very complex and context-specific, making theorization across cases difficult
Aim of research	Measure size of causal effects of explanatory variables by *testing* hypotheses	Pragmatic and heuristic use of theories to account for particular outcomes (sufficient explanations)
Ontological position	Neopositivist and critical realism	Analyticism and interpretative traditions

Theories are tools to help us to understand, explain and predict phenomena. There are however a variety of different types of theories and ways in which they can be utilized. One basic difference is how theories are used – either as *explanatory tools* that can be *tested* empirically, or whether we use them in a more pragmatic manner as *analytical tools* to *understand* cases. Table 1.1 illustrates this difference. The table does not depict a third way in which theories can be utilized – a position that can be termed critical theorization or reflectivism (Jackson 2011). Here scholars reject the notion of a world that exists apart from the social situation of the research, where what we know is seen as inseparable from where we are situated when we produce the knowledge. Given that that way of using theories is primarily found within constructivist thought, the distinctive nature of this tradition is expounded in the section below on social constructivism (pp. 22–4).

The use of theories as explanatory tools is how most methodological texts describe working with theories. Taken to the extreme, this is the natural-science ideal of a purely experimental research design as it has been practiced in political science/IR, where we attempt to measure the causal effect of an explanatory variable while holding everything else constant. This use of theory is more prevalent in quantitative, large-*n* studies than in qualitative case studies. At its core, the ambition here is theory-centric, aiming to build or test generalizable causal explanations of phenomena, such as the impact of public opinion (X) upon foreign policy positions of a state (Y). Theory-centric research is more interested in building broader explanations of phenomena. For example, does democracy produce more peaceful foreign policies?

When using theories as explanatory tools, the most ambitious types of theories posit clear law-like hypotheses about *how* X causes outcome Y that are expected to function across time and space. Owen's (1994) article on democratic peace is a good example of how a causal mechanism can be theorized in a manner that is close to a law-like generalization independent of time and space. Owen illustrates the hypothesized causal mechanism linking X with Y, where there are two overlapping causal paths that produce the democratic peace (Y). Both start with liberal ideas as the independent variable (X). Liberal ideologies held by elites prescribe that wars against other democracies are morally abhorrent. Elites holding these views exploit the dependence of democratically elected leaders upon maintaining popularity by using the free debate in the media to pressure governments from going to war with other democratic states, creating a strong constraint upon the democratic government.

Research in the explanatory tradition is undertaken by focusing on a narrow aspect of reality, measuring the causal effect of X, controlling for other potential factors. Theories are used to make *inferences* about *causal relationships* between independent variables (Xs) and dependent variables (Ys). Inference involves using 'facts' about what we know in order to learn about relationships we do not know. For example, we can measure whether states are democratic or not (X) and instances of war (Y), but we cannot directly observe whether democracy actually causes peace. Theories about the causal mechanisms linking X and Y enable us to infer from our observations of X and Y to conclude that X is a probable cause of Y (see Chapter 10). At the level of philosophy of science, the explanatory use of theory reflects both neopositivist and critical realist approaches to science (Jackson 2011).

In contrast, using theories as analytical tools reflects a philosophy of science position where theories are seen as helpful oversimplifications that can be used to understand a very complex empirical reality (Jackson 2011). The use of theories as analytical tools is most predominant in *case-centric research*, where the ambition is to account for why a particular outcome happened in a case or set of cases (Gerring 2006; Humphreys 2010). For instance, why did the Bush administration intervene militarily in Afghanistan in 2001?

Theories as analytical tools involves a much more pragmatic and instrumental application of theories, including the use of deliberate oversimplifications (ideal-types), along with eclectic combinations of theories to account for particular outcomes. Research is more case-centric. The goal is to produce sufficient explanations of particular outcomes that account for the most important aspects of the case. But while explanatory theories aim at testing clear hypotheses, attempting to increase or decrease our confidence in the validity of a causal theory, theories are not really seen as 'testable' when they are used as analytical tools, and the goal should instead be seen as using them as heuristic tools to *understand* why a particularly puzzling outcome occurred. At the level of the philosophy of science, this tradition reflects what Jackson refers to as 'analyticism', but also includes interpretative approaches building on Weber's ideas about *Verstehen* (understanding) as the goal of social science.

We can identify several different types of theorization in the analytical tool approach. *Ideal-types* can be used in what is described as singular causal analysis (Jackson 2011: 114). Here the research traces and maps how particular configurations of ideal-typical factors come together to generate historically specific outcomes in particular cases. Good ideal-types are instrumental tools for ordering and understanding the facts of the world.

A *typological theory* is a 'contingent generalization about combinations of variables that constitute theoretical types ... [and] specify pathways through which particular types relate to specified outcomes' (George and Bennett 2005: 235). Typological theories do not specify how X causes Y – that is they do not conjecture about causal mechanisms that link X with Y. Instead the focus is upon 'pathways' whereby X produces a given outcome Y. Schweller's (1994) typological theory on balancing versus bandwagoning behavior is illustrative here. In the article Schweller categorizes states as either status quo or revisionist, and then links these categories with expected behavior (balancing, bandwagoning or aggression). However, what differentiates typological theory from a causal theory is that Schweller does not develop the theoretical basis for what links X (state type) and the dependent variable Y (state behavior).

Another way that theories are used is in *eclectic combinations*, where parts of different theories are seen as Lego bricks that can be mixed and matched in order to account for an outcome (Sil and Katzenstein 2010). Neoclassical realism is perhaps the best example of this type of 'Lego-theorization', where elements from structural realism are coupled with intervening variables drawn from both liberal and constructivist theorization (see Chapter 3), along with smatterings of cognitive theories (see Chapter 4).

More generally, theories are here used pragmatically, informing our analysis by providing a set of questions that we ask when analyzing empirical reality, especially in case-centric analysis. Here theory is used in a heuristic fashion as a framework for analysis, focusing our attention on key factors that can explain a particular event or set of events (see Chapter 10). For example, if we want to investigate the possible emergence of the EU as a global actor we could focus our analysis upon the set of analytical questions that would be raised using neorealism (see Chapter 9). Waltz has argued that, in a world of states, we should expect that the EU will sooner or later gain state-like qualities and will attempt to translate its economic power into military might (Waltz 2000). Waltz's structural realist theory can therefore be used to structure our analysis, giving us a set of questions that we can critically examine, such as: Do we see state-like qualities in EU foreign policy-making? Or do we see a strong push within the EU toward increasing the EU's military capabilities?

One final distinction is necessary as regards theories. Theories can be at the level of highly general and abstract, explaining many different phenomena, such as structural realism that attempts to provide a general theory of the big and important phenomena in IR. Theories can also be at the mid-range level, where they attempt to explain specific aspects of more restricted phenomena, such as the impact of bureaucracy upon foreign policy decision-making. Theories can also be even more specific, attempting to explain particular outcomes in a single case. For example, we can develop a theory for why the Cold War ended in a peaceful fashion, but this would arguably only be able to explain one case due to the uniqueness of the peaceful power transition in 1989–91. Some social scientists would argue that this type of $n = 1$ theory is not social science, defining social science as the quest for generalizations about causes of important phenomena within a more-or-less broad population of cases. Yet saying that theorization on particular important historical cases is not social science would exclude much of the most important FPA/IR work from the past two decades.

A theoretical toolbox for the study of foreign policy

This book does not review theory for its own sake. Instead, it intends to empower students in their choice of theoretical tools when analyzing foreign policy-related research questions, offering them a variety of theoretical tools to describe, understand and explain research questions relating to foreign policy. All of the chapters will present theories in a manner that enables them to be utilized more-or-less 'off the shelf' by students for analyzing state foreign policy.

The toolbox is structured around three distinct analytical questions relating to analyzing foreign policy:

1. What do states want?
2. How do states makes decisions in foreign policy?
3. What do states do?

Figure 1.2 *The theoretical toolbox for analyzing foreign policy-making*

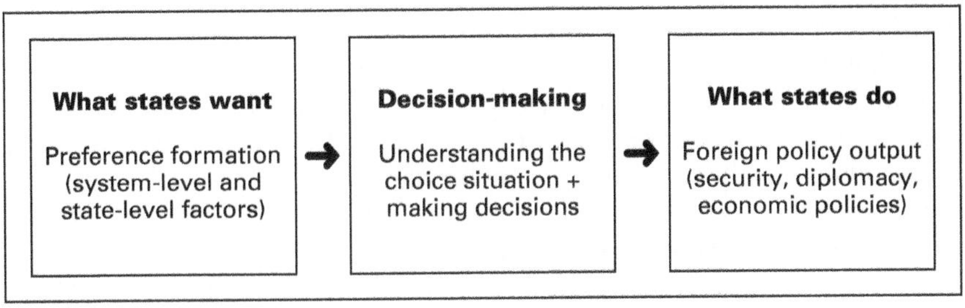

What states want	**Decision-making**	**What states do**
Preference formation (system-level and state-level factors)	Understanding the choice situation + making decisions	Foreign policy output (security, diplomacy, economic policies)

Together, these three analytical questions capture the most important research debates about foreign policy (see Figure 1.2). The rest of the book is structured around providing introductions to the debates about these three analytical questions.

In Part I, Chapters 2 and 3 introduce theories relevant to studying what states want. These chapters focus upon whether the key explanatory factors are at the level of the international system, and therefore external to states, or whether they are also found at the state level. Chapter 2 introduces theories that posit that pressures from the international system determine what states want. Chapter 3 opens up the black-box of the state, investigating how societal factors (such as public opinion) and governmental factors (such as political battles within government) can affect national preferences.

While there are numerous exceptions, the general rule of thumb is that system-level theories are strongest when explaining broad trends and developments in state foreign-policy goals, such as explaining the more assertive foreign policies of China in the last two decades as it has risen toward regional great-power status. Additionally, to explain long-term patterns in the foreign policies of states facing severe external security threats (for example Israel), we probably do not need to gather much information about the personality and beliefs of individual leaders; instead we would get the most analytical 'bang for the buck' with system-level theories that explain the impact of external systemic constraints upon state foreign policy.

State-level theories are strongest when explaining why states choose policies that *diverge* from what we would expect, simply based upon system-level factors such as the state's placement in the international system and its relative power. State-level theories are also relevant when analyzing individual foreign policy decisions or in explaining the impact of a particular group (such as interest groups) upon foreign policy-making.

In Part II I investigate decision-making, where states choose what policies to adopt based upon these national preferences. Here there are a range of theories relating to the decision-making process. For heuristic reasons the review of decision-making is split into two distinct phases: understanding the choice situation (Chapter 4) and making decisions (Chapter 5). The two chapters focus on the debate between what has been termed the Rational Actor Model (RAM), where decision-makers have a set of clearly ranked goals that they want to achieve and are able to use the available information to determine which choice will maximize the achievement of their goals with the lowest possible amount of risk. Contrasting this are a number of different theories relating to the two phases.

In Chapter 4 I review theories relating to how decision-makers understand choice situations. First is a theory about how the belief systems of decision-makers matter. The second concerns a set of theories which deal with how the subjective perceptions of decision-makers can systematically diverge from an 'objective' depiction of the choice situation they face.

Chapter 5 reviews competing theories of foreign policy decision-making, ranging from Poliheuristic theory in which the RAM plays an integral role to theories such as bureaucratic politics, where governmental decisions are the product of the 'pushing and hauling' between foreign policy actors, with the outcome far from what we would predict using a RAM.

Theories of the decision-making process are relevant when explaining both broad trends and individual decisions. For instance, a thorough analysis of the main lines of Soviet foreign policy in the 1930s and 1940s would be hard-pressed to ignore the cognitive theories at the decision-maker level that would enable us to understand Stalin's world view and the impact of this belief system upon Soviet foreign policy. However, theories of decision-making are usually most appropriate when analyzing individual decisions. For instance, analysis of the decisions by the Johnson administration to escalate the Vietnam War would benefit from analysis at the decision-making level, especially theories that explain deficient decision-making in small groups.

In Part III, in Chapters 6 to 8, I investigate the output of foreign policy-making and discuss specific types of policy that range from security and war, to diplomacy and economic policies (trade policies, sanctions and aid). Are all types of foreign policy issues the same? Security foreign policies deal with what traditionally is defined as security studies, where states attempt to counter external threats to their core values. Diplomacy refers to the range of *non-violent* foreign policy actions, including the use of declarations, meetings and negotiations with other foreign policy actors. Without diplomacy, interstate relations would be almost impossible. Economic foreign policies include a range of different policy instruments, from trade policies (decreasing or increasing tariffs or non-tariff barriers), to economic aid (often military), to various forms of economic sanctions (trade, financial and monetary), to foreign development aid.

In Chapter 9 I conclude the discussion of theories by investigating whether globalization and regional integration are resulting in fundamental transformations in the nature of foreign policy-making. Are we witnessing fundamental shifts in the nature of foreign policy due to globalization and the rise of new types of foreign policy actors in world politics today? Is the state-centric analysis of foreign policy outdated? Do we need new theoretical tools that will enable us to analyze foreign policy in a less state-centric world? In this chapter I find that while globalization has had some measurable effects, the death of the state has been strongly exaggerated.

The concluding Chapter 10 introduces the research methods available for the study of foreign policy.

Using theories

All of the chapters will present theories in a manner that enables them to be utilized by students to analyze particular research problems; in other words theories seen as tools to understand and explain foreign policy phenomena. Several considerations are important when choosing what theories are applicable in a specific research question (see Chapter 10). First there is a natural trade-off between parsimony and richer explanations. An example of a parsimonious framework is Waltz's (1979) structural realism, which attempts to explain a few 'big and important' things using only two overall explanatory variables: state capabilities and placement in the international system. However, the trade-off of parsimony is that the theory often provides an unconvincing explanation of particular situations, such as why Germany and Japan have refused to adopt 'normal' regional great-power foreign policies despite possessing the economic resources that would enable them to do so.

More complex frameworks, where multiple factors at different levels are included, will usually offer a richer explanation of a given phenomenon, especially when we are attempting to explain a specific outcome such as why Russia chose to go to war against Georgia in August 2008. Here we move toward the analytical use of theories. The downside is that while we become smarter about the causes of a particular event, we are left in the dark regarding whether the explanation for the given outcome (a specific war) can travel to explain other instances of the phenomenon (the causes of war in general).

There are three considerations that one must take when choosing which theory or set of theories is appropriate to explain a specific research question. First: Are the basic assumptions of the theory fulfilled in the given case? If one is analyzing foreign-policy-crisis decision-making in a situation where there is overwhelming evidence that leaders were so stressed that their decision-making abilities were weakened, one should not choose a RAM theory that assumes that decision-makers are fully rational.

Second: What level of analysis is appropriate to utilize when analyzing the specific research question? If one is interested in analyzing broad trends in Chinese foreign policy since World War II, it is potentially less relevant to select theories of the impact of belief systems of individual leaders, given that leaders have changed repeatedly during the period. Instead, theories at the systemic or state-level should be chosen. However, as discussed above, if we want to explain Chinese foreign policy in the 1950s and 1960s, an understanding of the belief system of Chairman Mao Zedong would be very relevant.

Third: The theory must provide a logical explanation of the phenomena that one is interested in analyzing – in other words, provide an explanation of what caused the dependent variable Y. Basically, one should choose a theory that is expected to provide a good explanation of the phenomena to be investigated. Each chapter of the book will clearly flag what a particular theory is best suited to explaining (and what it cannot explain), along with what the key explanatory factors are.

The assumptions and core arguments of the theoretical tools

While this book deals with foreign policy, the argument has been made above that IR theories provide good tools for analyzing foreign policy alongside more traditional FPA. Given that the three schools of IR are used throughout this book (realism, liberalism and social constructivism), the following provides a brief introduction to the three schools, coupled with a short introduction to what traditionally has been seen as the core of FPA – decision-making theories. For each of the theories, I present the common core of assumptions and key arguments, illustrating the positions of theories within each school on questions regarding:

- What are the *core assumptions* that bind the schools together?
- Which *level of analysis* are the key explanatory factors theorized to be at?
- What are the key *explanatory factors* in each theory?
- Is the theory primarily *structural* or is it open to *agency* by actors?
- Does the theory deal primarily with *material factors*, or are *ideational factors* also included?
- What type of theory is it (explanatory, analytical/understanding or reflectivist)?

The level of analysis should be distinguished from what is trying to be explained, which is the *unit* of analysis. When studying foreign policy, the units of analysis are broad trends of behavior and/or the particular actions taken by a state or other collective actor directed toward other collective actors within the international system. However, to explain why state A undertakes a particular action (the unit of analysis) we can use explanatory factors at different levels of analysis: the system, state and individual levels. As will be seen throughout this book, theories of foreign policy operate at different levels of analysis.

Turning to the question of agency and structure, Marx (1959: 320) famously argued that 'men make their own history, but they do not make it just as they please; they do not make it under circumstances chosen by themselves, but under circumstances directly encountered, given, and transmitted from the past'. Structural factors make up the environment within which actors operate, creating constraints and opportunities for actors. Structures can be either material (e.g. military threats from other states) or social (e.g. norms regarding the non-use of atomic weapons). Yet the behavior of actors is not simply a mechanistic reaction to the constraints/opportunities of their structural environment. In analyzing foreign policy, actors can be either individual leaders or collectives, such as a bureaucratic organization or even a state. As we are dealing with intelligent, intentional actors that have the ability to learn from past events and respond creatively to a given context, actors can actively attempt to change a given context in order to make it more amiable to the achievement of their own goals. This is defined as 'agency'.

Finally, note the use of the term 'school' instead of 'theory'. 'School' is used as it captures the fact that 'realism' or 'liberalism' is a large body of work that has many different specific theories, where the only common denominators are the basic assumptions about how the world works. For example, realist theories share the assumptions of an anarchical, self-help system and power politics. Specific variants of realism such as neoclassical realism (see Chapter 3), in contrast, offer more specific explanations of phenomena, often in the form 'X is hypothesized to cause Y'.

Realism: the dog-eat-dog world of power politics

There are two modern variants of realist theory: neoclassical and structural realism (also termed neo-realism). The core argument of realist theory is that international politics is 'a recurring struggle for wealth and power among independent actors in a state of anarchy' (Gilpin 1981: 7). Common to realism are two core assumptions: (1) the anarchical nature of the international system and (2) the struggle to survive and maintain state autonomy. These assumptions are the scope conditions for when realism is applicable as a theory. In the utopian (for realists) scenario where states were able to form a viable international government, structural realism would no longer be applicable.

First, realists argue that the international system is *anarchical*. Most realists do not define the state of anarchy faced by states as a pure state of nature, defined as a brutish and chaotic Hobbesian war of all against all (Milner 1991; Donnelly 2000). Instead, most realists adopt a moderate conceptualization of anarchy, defining it as the 'absence of government' in the international system. Anarchy is the opposite of hierarchical relations between states. 'Hierarchy' means that one state dominates the affairs of another state to the extent that one can speak of a form of imperial control.

In anarchy there is no higher authority that can impose order and resolve conflicts. States are therefore forced to fend for themselves. As states cannot trust each other, they arm themselves militarily to protect their vital national interests. Disputes between states that involve vital interests are not resolved by appeals to non-existent higher authorities but by the threat of and/or use of military power by states. Structural realists admit that international institutions such as the International Court of Justice or the United Nations do play a slight role in international affairs, but when push comes to shove they are unable to force great powers to change their behavior as they lack any form of independent enforcement mechanisms. Other international institutions such as alliances (e.g. NATO) are viewed as the vehicles of great powers. According to Kenneth Waltz (2000: 20–1), NATO after the Cold War has been a tool of the US to dominate the foreign and defense policies of European states.

Second, the uncertainties of anarchy create pressures upon states to act selfishly and not to trust others in order to survive and preserve their autonomy. If a state does not conform to the pressures of the anarchic system, Waltz argues that the system will 'punish' the state, and the state may even disappear from existence.

Given that the costs of losing in power politics are so high, states worry about how well they do compared to others. When states face the possibility of cooperating for mutual gain, each state fears that others will use any disproportionate gains from cooperation to exert influence or even destroy them. States are therefore more concerned with how much they will gain *relative* to others (relative gains) than with how much they will gain themselves (absolute gains).

To illustrate this difference, imagine two possible agreements between China and the US. Agreement 1 is a limited opening of markets that would increase US GDP by 1 per cent and Chinese GDP by 1.1 per cent. Agreement 2 involves a more expansive opening of markets, which would increase US GDP by 5 per cent and Chinese GDP by 10 per cent. If the US was solely concerned with its absolute gains it would opt for Agreement 2, as the absolute gains are greater than in the miserly Agreement 1. However, if the US was concerned that China would use its disproportional gains in ways that threatened US security (for example purchasing weapons) then the US would choose Agreement 1. In relative terms, US gains in Agreement 1 are 91 per cent of Chinese gains, whereas in Agreement 2 the US would only gain 50 per cent as much as China. A realist would argue that the US would choose Agreement 1, as they would fear that the disproportionate gains in Agreement 2 would allow China to purchase more weapons that could be used to threaten US interests. Realists argue that the obsession of states with relative gains makes meaningful cooperation impossible except when states are pulled together into an alliance in order to balance against a strong common threat. Yet when the common threat disappears, so goes the alliance. The core argument of realists is that in order to understand state foreign policy we need to look at the structural imperatives created by the relative power of the state and its placement in the international system.

What differentiates the two variants is the *level of analysis* and the key *explanatory factors* for explaining foreign policy. *Structural realists* argue that if we want to understand the big and important things that determine the foreign policy of a state we can restrict our attention to the *system level*, examining the relative position of a state in the international system (Waltz 1979). In competing for survival in the anarchical system, states discover what behaviors are conducive to survival, with the result that they come to look the same and want similar things. Given that the stakes in foreign policy are very high (the very survival of the state), a rational state leader will choose policies that maximize the ability of the state to survive and preserve its autonomy irrespective of the ideology or personality of the leader (Legro and Moravcsik 1999). States similarly placed in the international system will behave similarly regardless of domestic differences (Waltz 1996). For structural realists, whether a state is democratic or autocratic is superfluous. Irrespective of regime type, governments have to do what is necessary in order to survive in the anarchic international system. Given the pressures of survival, states come to resemble each other. They all have militaries to protect their interests, and foreign ministries and embassies for diplomatic relations with other countries. An oft-used analogy in structural realism is that states can be thought of as identical billiard balls: the only difference between them is their size, which is determined by their level of material capabilities (power). Capabilities for structural realists include latent factors such as population, level of political cohesion of the state and economic capacity that can be translated over time into military capabilities and more explicit measures of military power (Waltz, 1979). One widely used composite index of capabilities that is inspired by realist theorization is the Correlates of War measures of power (www.correlatesofwar.org/).

Despite the father of structural realism, Kenneth Waltz, denying that it could be utilized to examine state foreign policy, most structural realists believe that the theory can and should be utilized to explain state foreign policy by using it as the basis for a rational action model (e.g. Waltz 1979: 71; Walt 1988; Elman 1996; Allison and Zelikow 1999; Mearsheimer 2001, 2009; Yetiv 2004; Wivel 2005). As will be seen in Chapter 2, when structural realism is used as an explanatory tool it can be used to make predictions about what we should expect to see in both individual cases and broader trends.

In contrast, *neoclassical realists* contend that this is an excessive simplification, and to study foreign policy we also need to investigate how systemic pressures are translated through *intervening state-level variables* (Mastanduno *et al.* 1989; Snyder 1991; Zakaria 1992; Rose 1998). For instance, neoclassical realists recognize that there are differences between a Democratic Clinton and a Republican George W. Bush administration running US foreign policy (Monten 2005).

The two theories also differ on the question of agency/structure, with structural realism being predominately a structural theory. The pressures of surviving in anarchy are so strong that independent agency by states is only possible for them at their own peril. Additionally, the focus of structural realists is on longer-term trends and patterns of behavior, creating a focus upon how structure constrains state foreign policy behavior. Neoclassical realism opens the possibility of some scope for agency, with for example a factor such as the level of autonomy of leaders setting the bounds within which agency by individual leaders is possible. Neoclassical realists tend to be more interested in analyzing individual decisions, such as why the UK did not attempt to deter Hitler's Germany until it was too late (e.g. Schweller 2004). When analyzing an individual case, while the structure sets boundaries for choice, leaders will almost always have a degree of freedom that enables agency.

Finally, both theories agree that foreign policy is dominated by *material factors*, in particular the relative power of other states and the geographic placement of a state in the international system.

Liberalism: cooperation and conflict amongst self-interested rational actors

The core of liberal thought is not as easy to identify as that of realism. Many liberal thinkers and IR textbooks state that the core idea binding liberal theories together as a school of thought is the philosophical idea of *progress* toward a world of greater liberty and happiness (e.g. Smith *et al.* 2008; Jackson and Sørensen 2010). Liberalism is often depicted as an optimistic alternative to the realist cyclical vision of a world in which the 'same damn things' happen over and over again. The notion of 'progress', while an important element of liberal theory, should not be exaggerated, and many core liberal theories predict *both* conflict and cooperation depending upon the underlying distribution of state preferences (Keohane 1988; Moravcsik 1997). What is crucial in liberalism is the idea that self-interest can, depending on the circumstances, result in cooperation between states.

Liberals do not agree about the *core assumptions* underlying the school of thought. Here the primary divide is between what can be termed 'weak' and 'strong' liberal theories. *Weak liberal* theories share many of the same assumptions about the nature of international politics that realism holds, but theorize that system-level factors such as interdependence or institutions can mitigate the worst effects of anarchy, enabling cooperation for mutual gain. *Strong liberal* theories believe that international politics can be *transformed* from a conflictual anarchy into a more mature world of cooperation and civility through increased interdependence, democracy and institutionalization. For example, weak liberals like Robert Keohane and Andrew Moravcsik argue that international institutions are the tools of states, whereas strong liberals such as Ernst Haas and Leon Lindberg contend that once formed institutions take on a life of their own, resulting in an integrative process not fully controlled by states, with the result that states become integrated into a new form of political community that exists above the state.

Liberal scholarship is, like realism, split regarding the *level of analysis* – between theorists who focus upon system-level factors and those who also include state-level factors. Moravcsik (1997) has argued that the core of the liberal approach is the focus on societal actors such as voters, interest groups and firms that are engaged in a competitive struggle to influence state foreign policy. Yet this definition of liberalism excludes many key liberal theories that operate exclusively at the system level, such as Keohane's neoliberal institutionalism (see Chapter 2).

However, liberals do agree that three *explanatory factors* are most worthy of attention, although they disagree about which one is most important. The core concern of modern liberal thinkers is how these three distinct explanatory factors *can* affect rational, self-interested actors in ways that can result in more cooperative foreign policies than we would expect following realism. Liberal theories can therefore be divided into three variants according to the explanatory factor they view as most important for changing international politics from past patterns of power politics to a more peaceful and stable international

Figure 1.3   *The Kantian triangle: three explanatory factors of change in foreign policy*

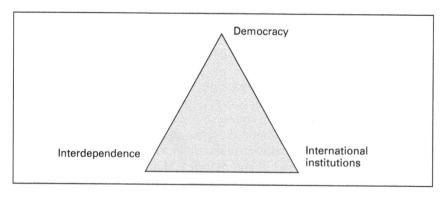

system, two of which are at the system level. Inspired by Immanuel Kant's (2006) ideas in *Towards Perpetual Peace*, the three factors are the importance of patterns of *interdependence, international institutions* and *democracy*. Together, these three factors form a 'Kantian triangle' that is the core of the liberal research agenda (Figure 1.3) (Russett and Oneal 2001).

Regarding the distinction between theories that focus on *agency or structure*, most liberal theories arguably have a focus on structure. For example, in the theories on the impact of public opinion that are reviewed in Chapter 3, public opinion can be seen as a structural factor, in that it can constrain the choices of leaders.

Finally, most liberal scholars agree that *material factors* are most important, with little role played by ideational ones. State foreign policy preferences are for example seen by many liberals as a product of the rational, self-interested preferences of societal actors as they have been aggregated through the domestic political system (Moravcsik 1997).

Social constructivism: a constructed international system

At the center of constructivism is the idea that human beings are inherently social creatures and that behavior is motivated by both material factors and immaterial ideas and norms that prescribe what acceptable behavior is and is not (see pp. 57–8). In contrast to the other schools of IR thought, there are much deeper divisions within constructivism – divides so deep that many scholars describe two different schools: a constructivist and a post-structuralist set of theories. Given the common focus on processes of construction and reconstruction of actor interests and identities, I will contend that there are enough similarities for the theories to be treated as a big tent of constructivist thought. Unlike other IR schools, the core divide splitting social constructivist scholars deals with the very nature of scientific knowledge and social reality itself. The controversy is best seen in how theories are understood.

Mainstream constructivism can be understood as theories that assert that empirical reality can be studied, but where they disagree is about how theories should be used. For scholars such as Wendt (Chapter 2), there is an objective reality that can be studied using theories as explanatory tools (the critical realist position), whereas other mainstream scholars contend that social reality is more complex, making the use of theories as analytical tools more appropriate (interpretivism). For instance, the interpretative position is that social phenomena are intended, meaning that what becomes interesting is to understand the meaning of actions and interactions from the actors' own points of view (Eckstein 1975: 81). Instead of formulating causal hypotheses that are tested empirically, interpretivists suggest we should learn a great deal about a culture prior to formulating research questions, attempting to understand the social contexts of action (King *et al.* 1994: 37). This enables us to search for the meaning of social action in relation to the set of concepts and practices in which it is embedded. Ted Hopf's theory of discourses is positioned at the other end of the explanatory/interpretive continuum (Chapter 3).

Against these mainstream constructivist theories is a post-structuralist position, where it is argued that social reality is not independent of the observer. Most post-structuralist constructivists subscribe to what is termed the 'linguistic turn', where the idea is that language is not a neutral medium that can be studied objectively (Onuf 1989; Kratochwil 1989; Kubálková 2001). Post-structuralists have a more relativistic approach, contending that there is no single 'objective' reality. Instead, humans perceive the social world through language and our senses, which are not neutral mediums. Language has the quality of representing reality, but at the same time using language involves 'speech acts' within discourses, where agents using language help to constitute the rules that underlie all social action. Therefore, there is no objective world out there; instead post-structuralist constructivists use techniques such as the deconstruction of concepts to investigate the way in which the meanings of, for example, threats to national security are socially constructed within discourses (Campbell 1992; Kubálková 2001; Hansen 2006). In the words of Campbell (1992: 2), 'it does not deny that there are "real" dangers in the world ... But not all risks are equal, and not all risks are interpreted as dangers ... Those events or factors that we identify as dangerous come to be ascribed as such only through an interpretation of their various dimensions of dangerousness. Moreover, that process of interpretation does not depend on the incidence of "objective" factors for its veracity.' In other dimensions of constructivist theorization, theories operate at different *levels of analysis*, ranging from Wendt's systemic theory (Chapter 2), to Hopf and Campbell's state-level theory (Chapter 3), to theories on the impact of differing logics of action for individual decision-makers (Chapter 5).

The core argument of constructivist theories builds upon the idea that intersubjective understandings held collectively by people are the most important object of inquiry. Intersubjectivity can be defined as the 'knowledge [that] persists beyond the lives of individual social actors, embedded in social routines and practices as they are reproduced by interpreters who participate in their production and workings' (Adler 1997: 321). Irrespective of their being either individual persons or states acting as collectives, social constructivists believe that 'social relations *make* or *construct* people *ourselves* into the kinds of being that we are. Conversely, we *make* the world what it is, by doing what we do with each other and saying what we say to each other' (Onuf 1998: 59).

Regarding the *agency–structure* distinction, many constructivist theories attempt to bridge the gap, drawing on sociological theories that utilize a role for both agency and structure. For example, Giddens (1984) points out that social institutions such as law are originally created by actors based upon functional, instrumental interests, but then subsequently form a 'frame' for future actor interaction, prescribing what types of future actions are acceptable. Social institutions are created and recreated by agent action in a dialectic process of 'structuration'. Looking at law as a social institution, a law when originally created naturally reflects the instrumental interests of actors, but over time becomes internalized by actors as a normative prescription of acceptable behavior (logic of appropriateness), making behavioral claims upon actors that cannot always be reduced to the instrumental interests of actors. Importantly, actors still maintain a degree of agency, as they act based both upon 'frames', or institutionalized social practices, and their 'rational', instrumental interests (Giddens 1976, 1984; Sewell 1992). Unfortunately, in practice most constructivist theories do not fulfill this promise, and end up providing theories of the impact of structural factors, relegating agency to the sidelines (Wight 2006).

Finally, as has been made clear above, constructivists open up the possibility of ideational factors to matter, but there are significant disagreements as to how much they matter, with scholars from the post-structuralist camp opening up little room for material factors in their work, whereas Wendt and others include material factors in their theorizing.

Decision-making theories

There is a range of different theories relating to decision-making which have traditionally been seen by FPA scholars as the core of scholarship on foreign policy (Snyder *et al.* 2002; Hudson 2007). These theories range from the simple RAM, to cognitive theories of individual perception and misperception, to small group decision-making.

What these theories have in common is the focus upon decision-making and in particular how the different phases of the decision-making process impact upon the foreign policy actions chosen by states. They do not share common assumptions nor agree about the proper level of analysis, with some focusing on larger collective actors such as bureaucratic organizations (the Bureaucratic Politics Model, see Chapter 5), while a large majority focus on individuals (cognitive theories, RAM, see Chapter 4) and small groups (e.g. social-psychological theories, see Chapter 5).

The baseline model used by most FPA scholars is the RAM, which theorizes that decision-makers are able to choose a foreign policy that maximizes gains with a minimum of cost (see Chapter 4). Here the actual decision-making process is a more-or-less seamless transmission belt between what states want and what they do (see Figure 1.3). However, several generations of FPA scholars have contended that the RAM is not an accurate representation of real-world foreign policy decision-making. Instead, they have suggested a range of theories that explain why foreign policy decisions do not always reflect what states want.

At the individual level are cognitive theories that relate to how the human mind perceives its environment by collecting and processing information, which is the first phase of any decision-making process (Chapter 4). The basic insight of cognitive approaches has been expressed by Steinbruner (2002: 13), who writes that 'the mind of man, for all its marvels, is a limited instrument'. Humans have to perceive the world subjectively before they can act. Given the limitations of human cognition, the 'objective' external environment is not always accurately reflected in the 'subjective' perception of the external environment. This is illustrated in Figure 1.4.

How then do cognitive factors matter? Cognitive theories deal with a range of factors that are believed to be systematic, meaning that they reflect recognizable and predictable patterns. For example, theories of misperceptions deal with common tendencies for the human mind to use historical analogies to make sense of new situations by comparing them to previous events.

There is also a range of theories that focus upon how the decision-making process can matter. For example, one prominent theory is the social-psychological theory of Groupthink, which suggests that in small

Figure 1.4   *Cognition and the perception of the external environment*

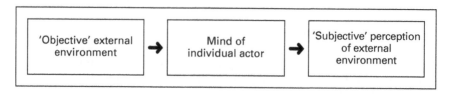

group settings the need to belong results in self-censorship and premature consensus amongst decision-makers, resulting in faulty decision-
making processes that tend to produce poor outcomes.

Most FPA theories agree that agency is important. Hudson (2007: 8)
argues that FPA theories offer a 'more robust concept of agency' than
IR theory. She contends that while IR theory provides much more
insight into structure than agency, FPA theory opens for contingency
and choice, making the theory more agent-oriented and actor-specific.
However, as with IR theories, much of FPA theorization has in reality
dealt with delineating the bounds or constraints upon agency imposed
by structural factors. However, FPA theory, in common with most
other social theorization, has been unable to theorize when 'actors are
capable of distancing themselves ... from the schemas, habits, and traditions that constrain social identities and institutions'. Strong agency
is when actors 'attempt to reconfigure received schemas by generating
alternative possible responses to the problematic situations they confront' (Emirbayer and Mische 1998: 984). In conclusion, while FPA
theories have opened up more for the possibility of agency than IR
theory, existing theories are only able to identify agency when they see
it, but are unable to predict when we should expect strong agency to be
possible.

Finally, on the material versus ideas dimension, there is a large
divergence, with some theories such as bureaucratic politics focusing
on material factors (e.g. the self-interests of bureaucrats in maximizing
the power and prestige of their ministry) (Chapter 5), while others
focus more on ideational factors such as the 'operational codes' that
form the belief systems of leaders that motivate them to take specific
decisions (Chapter 4).

A varied toolbox

Table 1.2. illustrates the positions of theories from the four schools on
the six dimensions.

Table 1.2 *The theoretical toolbox*

	Realism	Liberalism	Constructivism	FPA theories
Core set of assumptions	Anarchy Self-help system	*Weak liberalism* Anarchy Institutions can constrain behavior *Strong liberalism* Away from anarchy	Social world 'constructed'	No shared assumptions
Basic argument	Power politics	Interest-based politics (weak liberalism) Shifts away from anarchy possible due to three Kantian factors (strong liberalism)	Identity-based politics Identities and interests are constructed and reconstructed through social interaction	Decision-making matters
Level of analysis	*Systems level* Structural realism *State level* Neoclassical realism	*Systems level* Neoliberal institutionalism, interdependence liberalism *State level* Most weak and strong liberal theories	*Systems level* Wendt's theory *State level* Theories on norms, construction of state interests and identities (Hopf, Wæver)	*State level* Bureaucratic politics, small group theories such as Groupthink *Individual level* Operational code, cognitive approaches
What explanatory variables are focused on	Distribution of power. Domestic structures (neoclassical realism)	Interdependence International institutions Democratic regimes	Different cultures of anarchy (Wendt) National identity (Hopf). Threats (Wæver)	State interests (RAM). Bureaucratic self-interests (bureaucratic politics) Belief systems (operational codes)
Structure versus agency	Structure	Structure	Structure, although most theories contend they also look at agency	Agency (although in weak form)
Material or ideational factors	Material	Material	Focus on ideational factors	Different positions

Part I
What States Want

Chapter 2

System-Level Factors

The first question to ask when analyzing the foreign policy of a state is: What does the state want? That is, what are the national preferences of the state? This chapter and the next introduce theoretical debates about the sources of national foreign policy preference formation, divided into theories that suggest that the primary determinants of state foreign policy goals are system-level factors *external* to the state, whereas in Chapter 3 I discuss theories that suggest that state-level factors also matter to varying degrees. Figure 2.1 illustrates the three-stage framework of analysis for foreign policy, highlighting the research questions relating to what states want.

In this chapter I investigate system-level factors external to the state. States do not exist in a vacuum. Instead, they are subject to the pushes and pulls of their international environment. A state bordering a belligerent great power faces a very different foreign policy environment than one bordered by a number of neutral small states. I will examine theories relating to how system-level factors affect the foreign policy goals of states. The focus is upon how the 'foreign policies of nations are affected in important ways by the placement of countries in the international-political system' (Waltz 1990: 6–7).

My review will draw on theories from three different schools of IR that operate at the system level. Structural realists agree that national preferences are based upon the need to survive in the competitive anarchical international system, but beyond this there is considerable disagreement among structural realists about whether state goals are

Figure 2.1 *The three-stage framework for foreign policy*

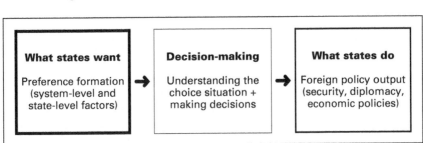

What states want	**Decision-making**	**What states do**
Preference formation (system-level and state-level factors) →	Understanding the choice situation + making decisions →	Foreign policy output (security, diplomacy, economic policies)

mainly defensive or whether the anarchical system pushes states to adopt the more offensive foreign policy goals of maximizing state power in the system. System-level liberal theories are split into those that analyze the impact of the level of interdependence upon what states want and those that investigate the effects that institution-rich environments have upon state goals. The theories have the same anarchic starting point of realism, but contend that international institutions or patterns of interdependence can change the dog-eat-dog nature of international politics, opening up the possibility that states can focus on more cooperative foreign policy goals.

In contrast to both realism and liberalism, where interests are primarily material, constructivist theorists have a broader conception of national preferences, arguing that the ideas embedded in different 'cultures' of the international system can impact on what states want (interests) and, even more fundamentally, on the very foreign policy *identity* of the state ('who' the state believes it is). At the most extreme, identities fully constitute how a state conceives of its interests and its role in the world, with little (or no) impact from material factors.

Theories should be usable analytical tools, focusing our attention on what questions we should be asking when we are analyzing foreign policy. System-level theories drawn from IR scholarship can therefore at first glance seem abstract, especially if you delve into the details of IR debates such as the nature of relative versus absolute gains. However, if used pragmatically as analytical tools, all of the theories in this chapter can be useful tools to analyze what states want.

However, many system-level theories operate at such a high level of abstraction that they offer few tools for analyzing particular episodes or issues. For instance, while a system-level theory might provide a good explanation for the broad French foreign policy orientation after the Cold War, the same theory would be hard pressed to provide analytical leverage on more specific questions such as French trade policy goals or why the Sarkozy government was so determined to intervene militarily in Libya in the spring of 2011. In the words of Keohane (1984: 29), system-level theory (or what he terms 'systemic analysis') 'will not yield determinate predictions about states' pursuit of wealth and power. Even if it did, these predictions would be subject to inaccuracy insofar as great variations in state behavior resulted from variations in their internal characteristics. Nevertheless, systemic theory can help us understand how the constraints under which governments act in the world political economy affect their behavior'.

There are several different ways in which system-level theories can be used when analyzing state foreign policy goals. At the simplest, a specific theory such as Walt's balance-of-threat theory can be used as a heuristic tool to understand broad trends in a given state's foreign policy goals, directing our attention toward factors such as the overall capabilities of other states in the region (or beyond), geographic proximity, the offensive capabilities of rivals, and historical perceptions of states in the region. System-level theories can therefore be used to explain the *broad trends* in state goals that are due to a state's placement in the international system. This can also be understood as how the international environment affects the general foreign policy orientation of a given state – what can be thought of as the grand strategy of a state.

System-level theories can also be used as an analytical 'baseline', comparing what we would expect to see if a system-level theory is correct or if a factor from either the state level or the individual level has an effect. For example, based on offensive structural realism, we would expect to see A, whereas, if a state-level factor such as public opinion impacts upon what states want, we would expect to see B. If we find evidence suggesting B and not A, then we can conclude that public opinion did have a measurable impact in the case (or cases). This way of using system-level theories is a more explanatory one.

System-level theories can also be used in composite, multilevel or multistep theoretical models when theories are used as analytical tools. Here system-level theories can form the *context* within which foreign policy choices are made, supplemented with factors at the domestic or decision-maker level. According to Zakaria (1992: 198), 'a good account of a nation's foreign policy should include systemic, domestic, and other influences, specifying what aspects of the policy can be explained by what factors'. This combination can have the form of a composite, multilevel model where all factors are present, or a multistep model, where for example system-level factors act as a 'first cut' that determines the range of policy options available, but where the actual choice between these options is then analyzed using theories at the level of decision-makers. Composite theories enable us to explain why two states facing similar strategic situations choose different foreign policies. For instance, during the Cold War France and Germany, despite having relatively similar resources and facing similar system-level threats and opportunities, chose very different foreign policy orientations: France under President de Gaulle chose to withdraw France from the military command of NATO, and Germany forged a close alliance with the US.

Creating more complex, multilevel models raises the dilemma of whether we should prioritize parsimonious theories that explain foreign policy with one or only a few explanatory variables, or whether we should aim for more complex models that give us greater explanatory leverage. In a central book on methodology, King *et al.* (1994: 104–5) suggest that 'to maximize leverage, we should attempt to formulate theories that explain as much as possible with as little as possible. Sometimes this formulation is achieved via parsimony, but sometimes not. We can conceive of examples by which a slightly more complicated theory will explain vastly more of the world. In such a situation, we would surely use the nonparsimonious theory, since it maximizes leverage more than the parsimonious theory'. As will be seen in the later chapters of this book, many theories of foreign policy are multilevel. For instance, neoclassical realists combine the predictions of structural realists at the system level with factors at the domestic level such as core national beliefs (see pp. 63–70). However, one useful suggestion for when to 'go beyond' a simple system-level explanation is: 'only when behavior and outcomes deviate from these structural-systemic theories' expectations should unit-level [state-level] variables associated with neoclassical realism be added to these theories to explain why' (Schweller 2003: 346). The next challenge is then to determine whether all of the factors from different levels have the same explanatory weight, or whether one level is more important than others (e.g. system-level factors trump state-level factors). We will return to these issues in Chapter 10.

Finally, system-level theories can be used in a competitive theory test, comparing the predictions of two or more theories against what we observe in the broad foreign policy orientation of a given state. This is again a more explanatory use of theories. For example, Walt's structural realism leads us to expect to see A, whereas, if high levels of interdependence have an effect, we should expect to see C instead. We would then collect empirical material that would allow us to test whether A or C was present.

It is important to note that different system-level theories arguably have comparative advantages in explaining different types of foreign policy phenomena. Structural realism is arguably best at explaining security foreign policies, especially those of great powers, whereas liberal theories are better at explaining non-security related issues, such as trade, although realists would contend that all important foreign policy issues at the end of the day are related to security. In contrast, Wendt's constructivist theory can be used to question the very nature of the culture of anarchy in which a given state or states find themselves, suggesting that the very identity of states is a product of what culture of anarchy dominates in the environment of a state.

Structural realism: the survival of egoistic states in an anarchic world

The core argument of structural realist theorists is that the anarchical and conflictual international system pushes states to adopt survival as the most basic foreign policy goal. The national interests of any state are determined solely by the placement of a state in the international system, especially its proximity to great powers. Waltz makes the distinction between national interests and intentions, using the term 'intention' to reflect domestically derived preferences due to short-term political or economic advantages that often ignore the pressures of the international system. In contrast, he uses the term 'national interests' to refer to state goals relating to power and security that are formed on the basis of these systemic pressures. He argues that as it is the pressures of the anarchical system that determine what states can and cannot achieve in the long term, foreign policy 'results achieved seldom correspond to the intentions of actors' (Waltz 1979: 29). An unpopular leader can decide to go to war in order to benefit from a 'rally round the flag' effect, but wars that are chosen due to short-term domestic factors often end unhappily.

There is not one structural realist theory; instead there are a range of particular theories that make different predictions about what foreign policy goals we should expect states to follow. That said, all structural realist theories start from the assumption that the international system is anarchic, creating a form of Darwinian 'survival of the fittest' environment for states. States are forced to fend for themselves to ensure survival, meaning that international politics is a 'self-help' system. The uncertainties of anarchy create pressures upon states to act selfishly and not to trust others in order to survive and preserve their autonomy. In this environment, strategic national interests are the sole motivations for state foreign policy; concerns of justice and morality play an insignificant role in comparison. States are inherently egoistic, and all foreign policy is 'self-regarding' (Waltz 1979: 91). Waltz (1979: 134) has stated that 'to say that a country acts in its national interest means that, having examined its security requirement, it tries to meet them'. Given that all other states are potential threats, concerns about *relative gains* dominate.

The key to understanding what particular states want is to understand the distribution of power in the international system, focusing upon the great powers. In other words, state goals are determined by the distribution of power in the system and the state's placement in this system relative to the great powers.

Figure 2.2 illustrates the two most common forms of the distribution of capabilities in the international system: bipolarity and multipolarity. A *bipolar system* consists of two great powers; the prototypical example being the Cold War. The international system during the Cold War consisted of two superpowers (the US and the Soviet Union), separated only by the power vacuum of exhausted and defeated countries in Europe. According to Waltz (1979: 352–3), the Cold War was inevitable as the two superpowers 'faced each other like two fighters in a short and narrow lane'.

Figure 2.2   *Bipolarity and multipolarity in the international system*

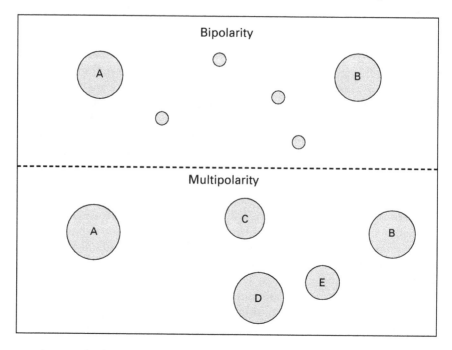

The top half of Figure 2.2 illustrates a bipolar system that is dominated by two great powers (A and B) with equal power capabilities.
Smaller states are inconsequential in this type of system unless they are
able to aggregate their power capabilities within an alliance in order to
balance against the strongest state. In this situation, Waltz would argue
that the goals of the two great powers are dominated by their interests
in maintaining a stable balance of power with the other, whereas
smaller state goals would be dominated by the need to ally with the
weaker of the two powers in order to avoid being dominated by one
great power.

A *multipolar system* has historically been the most common form of
international system; a classic example was the Concert of Europe
system of the 19th century where five powers (the UK, France, Prussia,
Austria-Hungary and Russia) dominated the continent. Multipolarity is
illustrated in the bottom half of Figure 2.2. Here there are five great
powers (A, B, C, D, E), but no state is predominant. Multipolarity is
more unstable, with states constantly switching alliances to balance
against perceived imbalances, and where the power of specific alliances
is less predictable. In multipolarity, state goals are also dominated by
the placement of the given state in the international system, although
the more unpredictable environment can make it more difficult for a
state to choose an appropriate strategy to maximize its interests.

Another way to illustrate polarity is to depict the relative share of power resources that each great power has relative to the total possessed by great powers. Three indicators of this are used in Figure 2.3: a measure of latent power (economic wealth as measured by the gross domestic product of the state (GDP)), the level of military expenditure, and the number of soldiers.

The top half of the figure shows a multipolar distribution of power in 1880, where the US was the first among equals in latent power (26 per cent of GDP), while France, Russia and the United Kingdom were the strongest military powers measured according to military budget. Here we would expect each state to obsess about their relative power and position to others, pushing them to adopt internal (growth-oriented) and external (alliances, wars, etc.) balancing powers.

The situation was dramatically different after the end of World War II, where there were only two great powers (the US and the Soviet Union). The US was vastly superior in economic resources (over 50 per cent of the total GDP of the powers), but the Soviet Union was the equal of the US in military power terms. In this distribution of power, the foreign policy goals of both the US and the Soviet Union were focused upon balancing against the other, whereas smaller states such as Germany and Japan had the goal of surviving through balancing with the US against the Soviet Union.

If a state does not conform to the pressures of the anarchic system created by the distribution of capabilities in the system, Waltz argues that the system will 'punish' the state, and the state may even disappear from existence. States that have found themselves on the wrong side of systemic pressures have disappeared from existence in the past; for example both the Austrian–Hungarian and Ottoman Empires ceased to exist as states after World War I, and states such as Denmark have lost large parts of their former territory by following ill-advised policies.

Structural realists agree that the desire to survive is the primary motive of all states. Beyond that, structural realist theories differ on the question of whether survival is the sole motive of states or whether they also have other interests, and, if so, what these are. Unfortunately, many of these theories are quite ambiguous on this point, making it difficult to use them in practice to understand the foreign policy goals of states. The most prominent example of this ambiguity is found in Waltz's theorization in his now classic 1979 book *Theory of International Politics*. At one point Waltz argues that states 'are unitary actors with a single motive – the wish to survive' (Waltz 1979: 54), whereas, in the same work, he argues that 'at a minimum, [states] seek their own preservation and, at a maximum, drive for universal domination' (Waltz 1979: 118). This ambiguity results in relatively indeterminate predictions about what goals we should expect states will have (Donnelly 2000).

38

Figure 2.3 *Multipolar and bipolar distributions of power*

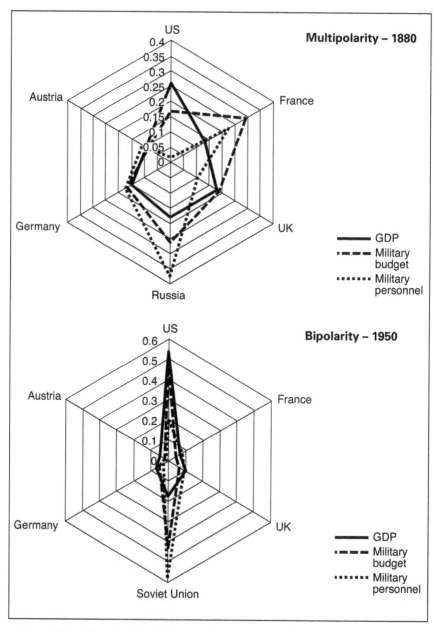

Note: Military figures for Germany are for West Germany in 1955.
Sources: GDP figures from Kennedy (1987); military budget and personnel are from the COW dataset in Singer *et al.* (1972).

To understand the debate within structural realist theorization on what interests states have, it is useful to differentiate structural realism into defensive and offensive variants. The core dispute relates to whether the condition of anarchy causes states to adopt predominately defensive or offensive foreign policy goals and policies based upon how much power states are expected to want. Defensive realists have a *relatively* benign view of the competitive pressures and the degree of mistrust created by anarchy, resulting in state goals that are status quo-oriented, whereas offensive realists contend that anarchy creates strong competitive pressures that thrust states toward aggressive and expansive goals involving maximizing state power. The defining example of defensive realist theory is the Cold War and the relative stable balance of power between the Soviet Union and the US. In contrast, offensive realism is heavily inspired by events such as Napoleon's bid for European hegemony or Hitler's aggressive attempts to dominate Europe that resulted in World War II.

Defensive structural realism

According to defensive structural realist theorists such as Waltz and Walt, states are most concerned with maintaining what they already have, resulting in goals oriented to the status quo (Waltz 1979: 161–93). In the words of Waltz (1979: 126), 'the first concern of states is ... to maintain their position in the system'.

The reasoning behind this is that the worst effects of the anarchical dog-eat-dog world are mitigated by the relative ease with which states can create stable and effective balances of power. Effective balancing is relatively swift and easy to achieve due to the ease of forming alliances. Further, the so-called offense–defense balance in warfare has historically been tilted toward defense, with an effective defense costing far fewer resources than an offensive military force that can effectively threaten other states. Counterbalancing against expansion by great powers is even easier in the nuclear age, as it is relatively inexpensive to build a credible nuclear deterrent that prevents aggression (Waltz 1993). Great powers are therefore relatively assured that they will not be attacked by other powers. These factors make offensive strategies of expansion and aggression – that aim to upset the balance of power – difficult and often even counter-productive (Waltz 1979: 126–7). Foreign policy is therefore dominated by moderate, defensive goals oriented to the status quo, with states interested in achieving what can be termed the 'appropriate' amount of power necessary to ensure survival and protect state autonomy from the domination of others (Waltz 1979: 204). Note that the term 'appropriate' is a very ambiguous one in Waltz's theory, and he has unfortunately never clearly defined how we can empirically evaluate this prediction. In a

Table 2.1 *Waltz's defensive structural realism*

Core motivation of states	To maintain their relative position in the international system
Type of theory	Can be used both as an explanatory theory, but it can also be understood as an analytical tool, where balancing is an ideal-typical behavior that is an intentional oversimplification of reality (Jackson 2011)
What do we need to measure to know the foreign policy goals of a particular state?	The strength of a state and the distribution of power in the international system, focusing primarily on the great powers, measured using size of population and territory, resource endowment, economic capabilities, military strength, political stability and competence (Waltz 1993: 50)
Example	France's foreign policy goals in the 1990s *What do we need to know about France?* Its relative capabilities and regional/global rivals *What should we expect to see?* • Based on Waltz's theory, we should expect that the core French goal is to maintain its position in the international system relative to other states • France in the 1970s and 1980s enjoyed a position of parity with Germany in the European balance-of-power • In 1980, the population was 54 million in France and 61 million in Germany; GNP was $633 billion in France and $838 billion in Germany; military expenditure was $26.4 billion in France and $26.7 billion in Germany • German reunification increased German capabilities (population and economic capabilities) • We should therefore expect that the dominating French national interest post-reunification (1990s) would be to maintain a position of parity despite the shift in relative power

Sources: Kennedy (1987: 563); Singer *et al.* (1972) (COW dataset, National Material Capabilities (v 4.0)).

similar manner, Grieco (1990: 303) contends that states are 'interested in achieving and maintaining relative capabilities sufficient to remain secure and independent in the self-help context of international anarchy'. What does Grieco mean by 'sufficient', and how do we know it when we see it empirically?

This ambiguity does not mean that defensive structural realism cannot be used to study the foreign policy goals of states. Indeed, if used in a more pragmatic fashion as a heuristic tool to focus our attention on what questions we should ask in a given case, Waltz's theory can be adapted to the study of foreign policy. An example of how this can be done is given in Table 2.1.

Table 2.2   *Walt's defensive structural realism*

Core motivation of states	To protect themselves from threats
Type of theory	Explanatory theory
What do we need to measure to know the foreign policy goals of a particular state?	The 'threats' faced by a given state, defined as a combination of the relative power of states (as in Waltz's theory), geographic proximity, offensive capability and historical perceptions of other states
Example	Pakistani foreign policy goals (2010) *What do we need to know about Pakistan?* • Relative power of states in the region and globally, including power of Russia, China, India and the US, measured using capabilities (population, economic wealth, size of armed forces, resource endowment) • Geographic proximity of powers, in particular the proximity of China and India, along with size of US forces based in Afghanistan • Offensive capabilities of China, India and the US • Historical perceptions, in particular the historical animosity between Pakistan and India Capabilities of India and Pakistan: relevant data includes: population for Pakistan is 180 million and for India is 1,200 million; GDP for Pakistan is $175 billion and for India is $1,430 billion; military budget for Pakistan is $5.2 billion and for India is $38.4 billion; armed forces for Pakistan is 0.55 million and for India is 1.1 million *What should we expect to see?* Based upon historical animosity with India, we should expect that the dominating goal of Pakistani foreign policy will be to protect against a perceived threat from India

Source: Data from *The Economist*, 19 May 2011, p. 62.

Other defensive realists such as Stephen Walt have developed more determinate theories that are arguably better adapted to analyzing the strategic foreign policy goals of states. Walt's 'balance-of-threat' theory predicts that states are motivated by a desire to protect themselves against the state that they view as the greatest threat in their environment. The core argument, hypotheses and an example are given in Table 2.2.

Threats are defined by Walt as a combination of aggregate power, geographic proximity, offensive capability and the perceived aggressiveness (Walt 1985, 1988). Aggregate power is defined as the same composition of factors described by Waltz. Walt draws on geopolitical theories when he argues that states that are geographically closer are seen as greater threats, other things being equal, than those separated by vast distances or geographic barriers such as oceans or great mountain ranges. Here one should also distinguish between the regional and global level, with regional security concerns dominating global ones in most circumstances. Further, states that have strong offensive capabilities such as the highly mobile blitzkrieg tank force of Hitler's Germany are perceived to be greater threats than states possessing primarily defensive militaries such as Switzerland. Finally, Walt contends that states also take into account the actions of other states – that is whether they are primarily cordial or conflictual – and historical patterns of animosity and friendship. This part of his theory involves studying the perceptions of elites in country A toward the other country. It is important to note that we cannot reason backwards from behavior (alliance formation) to postulate that the country did not view the ally as a threat as this would create a faulty tautological argument. Instead, we need to investigate factors such as the historical perceptions that a state holds about its neighboring states or the offensive capabilities of other states in a manner that is divorced from state behavior in order to measure the threats that a given state believes it faces from its environment.

Offensive structural realism: maximizing state power

Offensive structural realist theories contend that states are not necessarily just security-seeking actors with status quo oriented preferences. If states merely seek survival, there would be no aggression in the world, termed by Schweller (1996: 91) as 'a world of all cops and no robbers'. Instead, offensive realists contend that the extremely conflictual nature of the anarchical system pushes states to want more, resulting in revisionistic preferences aiming at maximizing state power. States are not inherently bad or aggressive, but the system can pressure them to act in such a manner.

Offensive realists believe that the consequences of anarchy are more severe than Waltz and other defensive realists theorize, resulting in a world that is seen as a dangerous and insecure place (Mearsheimer 2001). In the extreme self-help world of offensive realist theories, states are never certain whether other states will use their offensive military capabilities to attack. All other states are therefore potential enemies, and there exist many predatory states with revisionistic preferences.

Here it is impossible for states to calculate with any degree of accuracy when the 'appropriate' level of power has been achieved that can ensure state survival and autonomy. For example, any alliance entered into by a state is at best a very temporary marriage of convenience as states dare not trust their alliance partners given that their very survival is at stake. Further, given the difficulties in trusting partners, alliances are often difficult and slow to construct, meaning that they do not have the same preventive effect against aggression and expansion as they are theorized to have in defensive realism. Despite the rising threat from Hitler's aggressive foreign policies, the British–French alliance against Germany was first in place *when it was too late*, with the alliance being confirmed at the same time that German troops were pouring across Poland's borders. Balances of power are therefore not stable in the self-help world of offensive realism due to the fragility and fluidity of alliances.

Security is elusive in this very uncertain world, pushing states to want to *maximize their power* in order to survive and preserve their autonomy based upon the maxim that the strongest state is also the most secure. Beyond this, offensive realists admit that states also pursue a range of non-security related goals, including seeking greater economic prosperity, but Mearsheimer (2001: 46) admits that the theory has 'little to say about them, save for one important point: states can pursue them as long as the requisite behavior does not conflict with balance-of-power logic'.

Mearsheimer draws on the distinction between the global and regional level and the role of geography that is also used by Walt,

Table 2.3   *Mearsheimer's offensive structural realism*

Core motivation of states	Maximize state power, and if possible achieve regional hegemony
Type of theory	Analytical tool aimed at understanding great power behavior
What do we need to measure to know the foreign policy goals of a particular state?	• The distribution of power in the system, both at the regional and global level (measured using capabilities of states) • Geographical factors, in particular features that limit the ability of a state to project land forces (e.g. oceans or mountain ranges)
Example	US foreign policy goals (current) *What do we need to know?* • Relative power of the US and major regional rivals throughout the world (measured using capabilities of states) • How geographical factors limit US ability to project land forces *What should we expect to see?* The US wants to maintain regional hegemony in the Americas and prevent regional powers from attaining regional hegemony in important regions such as the Middle East, Northeast and Southeast Asia

creating a helpful tool for analyzing the foreign policy goals of particular states (Mearsheimer 2001). He thinks of the world in terms of regions, composed of one or more regional powers, along with a number of weaker states. He contends that hegemony at the global level is impossible, as no one state can dominate the whole world.

The argument behind this is that power in world affairs is primarily related to the land forces that a state possesses. The world's oceans limit the power-projection capability of armies, preventing even a superpower like the US from being able to project enough land forces to another continent like Asia to threaten China. Great powers therefore can at most aspire to regional hegemony, best illustrated by the hegemonic position of the US in North America. Great powers, in particular insular powers such as the UK or the US, also are interested in preventing the emergence of hegemons in other regions that could reduce their scope of influence. In this theory, the primary goals of US foreign policy are to maintain regional hegemony in the Americas and prevent other great powers such as China from achieving regional hegemony. (See Table 2.3.)

Using structural realism to analyze state foreign policy goals

When using the variants of structural realism to analyze what states want, it is vital that one makes absolutely clear what particular variant of structural realist theory one is using to analyze the foreign policy goals of a particular state. Furthermore, it is important to make clear what exact predictions the theory makes, if any. Unfortunately, nailing down exactly what we should expect to see for a given state can be difficult with most structural realist theories, due to the degree of ambiguity there is regarding state motivations. Many theories such as Waltz's oscillate between expecting that states are primarily motivated by concerns about survival and expecting them to seek to preserve their autonomy, improve their welfare, increase their strength or even want to achieve universal domination (Donnelly 2000: 56).

However, each of the variants of structural realism can be a useful tool to analyze state foreign policy goals if properly specified, enabling us to make determinate predictions about what we should expect to see in the empirical record, thus shaping the questions we ask. Both variants of structural realism are relatively easy to use to research foreign policy questions due to the parsimony of the theory. Both Waltz's defensive, balance-of-power theory and offensive structural realism can be primarily used to analyze the general foreign policy orientations of great powers (balancing) such as China or the US, whereas Walt's balance-of-threat variant is also applicable to smaller states.

In all of the variants of structural realism, the strength of the effect that the system-level context has on state foreign policy goals varies with the level of power of a given state and the nature of the international system. Weaker powers in a conflictual system have to pay close attention to the constraints imposed by system-level factors in order to survive and maintain their autonomy, whereas great powers (usually) face fewer structural constraints, meaning that the formation of the national preferences can be driven more by state-level factors (see Chapter 3). Having strong capabilities does not necessarily mean that the state will always get what it wants in international affairs, but only that the state is less constrained by pressures from the systemic level than weaker states and therefore has a broader range of foreign policy choices.

To take two extreme examples of the impact of structural context on what states want: if a relatively weak state faces strong external pressures from a great power, we should expect that state-level factors are analytically irrelevant as they are overwhelmed by system-level pressures. One defining example of acquiescence of a weaker power to systemic pressures was Finland after World War II. Finland wanted to remain neutral, but was forced to sign a military cooperation treaty with the Soviet Union, contrary to what we would expect based upon domestic politics (Finland remained a liberal democracy throughout the Cold War). If Finland had chosen to ignore the pressure created by its relative (lack of) strength and its unfortunate geographic placement next to one of the great powers in the Cold War by not signing the treaty with the Soviet Union, a Soviet-backed coup or even an invasion was very likely, as was seen in Eastern bloc countries like Czechoslovakia in 1948.

An opposite example is the unipolar world that many realist analysts argue exists today (Wohlforth 1999; Jervis 2009). As the US is so far ahead of any potential rivals in terms of material capabilities, the country faces few external pressures to act in specific ways, making its foreign policy goals arguably more dependent upon domestic factors such as bureaucratic politics or trends in public opinion. The unconstrained position of the US does not mean that it always gets what it wants – simply that there are few strong externally imposed constraints that pressure the country in Waltz's theory. In contrast, Mearsheimer, by explicitly theorizing state goals both at the regional and global level, is better able to analyze US interests in a unipolar global distribution of power, though one where the US faces regional powers across most of the world.

Pulling in the other direction is the relationship between capabilities and the scope of a state's interests. Weaker states (usually) have a limited scope to their national interests, often focusing upon key objectives in their immediate surroundings. Yet as a state expands its capabilities many scholars have argued that they also tend to expand the scope of their national interests (Zakaria 1992). As the scope of interests expands, so does the level of systemic pressures that push and pull upon the state in its attempt to attain national objectives. The extreme example here is the US, which has interests in most regions of the world, in particular in ensuring stability and preventing the emergence of strong regional rivals (Mearsheimer 2001).

The empirical information necessary to use Waltz's defensive and Mearsheimer's offensive structural realist theories relates to the material power capabilities of states in relation to each other and their ability to mobilize and use these capabilities. More information is necessary in Walt's balance-of-threat theory, given that we need to measure how a state perceives other powers to determine which state is seen as the greatest threat. This involves collecting information on power capabilities of potential rivals while also factoring in information on geography and offensive capabilities. Most difficult is the determination of perceptions of threat based upon historical trends. Information can be gleaned from texts on a given country's foreign policy history or other sources such as archival material that detail how the actions of potential rivals were perceived within the government of a country. In Walt's analysis of alliance choices in south-west Asia, he utilizes a combination of primary, archival sources that illustrate how rival actions were interpreted and secondary, historical texts such as *The Foreign Policy of Iran: 1500–1941* (Walt 1988: footnote 41) to reconstruct Iranian perceptions of threat from other powers.

What would we need to know if we want to use structural realism to analyze the broad trends of Chinese foreign policy goals concerning its relations with the US in the past decade. First, we need to choose whether we want to use the offensive or defensive variants. Using defensive realist theories such as balance-of-threat theory we should expect, as China's military capabilities increased to a level where they had achieved a reasonable parity in the regional balance of power with the US, assisted by the stabilizing effect of Chinese nuclear weapons, that China would fear the US less, resulting in a Chinese preference for relatively stable relations with the US (Ross 1999). To assess the proposition that as China's capabilities increased we should expect that its perception of a US threat decreased, we need valid information on its perceptions of US actions both before and after parity had been achieved. Due to the closed nature of Chinese society, hard internal information would be difficult to gain access to, making the analyst reliant upon public speeches by Chinese officials and similar open sources and secondary sources by analysts and academics.

In contrast, offensive realists would expect that 'China, like all previous potential hegemons, would be strongly inclined to become a real hegemon, and all of its rivals, including the United States, would encircle China to try to keep it from expanding' (Mearsheimer 2001: 400). Here Chinese goals would be seen as being more aggressive. To analyze this proposition we need information on the relative material capabilities of China and the US, including an evaluation of whether the increase in Chinese military spending is focused upon developing the power projection capabilities that are necessary to 'become a real hegemon'. Further, information on US relations with China's regional rivals would also be needed, including for instance alliances and agreements made by the US with countries like India and Vietnam, especially in military affairs. We should also expect to see a gradual deterioration of Chinese–US relations as China grows more powerful.

Liberalism: institutions and interdependence creates a new context for states

Given that the key value added of liberal theorization has been opening up the 'black box' of the state to investigate how domestic factors matter, it is not surprising that there are fewer liberal theories at the system level (see Chapter 3). However, there are system-level theories relating to two of the three key explanatory factors in the Kantian triangle described in Chapter 1, the first relating to the impact that interdependence can have upon state foreign policy interests, and the second focusing on the impact of international institutions on what states want.

Interdependence and state foreign policy interests

Interdependence refers to mutual dependence caused by international interactions that have consequential effects (costs or benefits) among countries or among actors in different countries (Keohane and Nye 2001: 7). The focus upon consequential effects distinguishes interdependence from mere interconnectedness. In contrast to structural realism's billiard ball model of interstate relations, interdependence liberalism views the world more as a cobweb, where complex interdependence is viewed as a system-level constraint that binds states together in patterns of mutual dependence (Burton 1972). While patterns of economic interdependence impact upon state-level factors, theories of the impact of interdependence can best be analyzed at the system level given that most interdependence theories assume that state-level actors respond in rational ways to system-level patterns of interdependence (Sterling-Folker 1997). Therefore, the key explanatory variable is the systemic level of interdependence facing a given state, whereas state-level factors are assumed away in the analysis.

Beyond the broad definition of interdependence as mutual dependence with consequential effects, there is considerable ambiguity amongst liberals about how we should understand the concept. As with any key theoretical concept, a clear and operational definition of it is necessary before it can be utilized in empirical or theoretical analysis (Adcock and Collier 2001; Goertz 2006). In this section, I will define interdependence conceptualized as cross-border exchanges, whereas in Chapter 7 I will focus on the liberal theorization of the impact of policy interdependence.

Cross-border exchanges are usually defined as economic transactions made by consumers, firms and state authorities involved in international trade, but there is a smaller number of liberal theories that adopt a more inclusive definition that also includes other forms of transactions across borders such as social exchanges and interaction, for example within social groups on the Internet.

Theorization on the importance of cross-border exchanges, or what is often referred to simply as *economic interdependence*, builds upon the idea that cross-border economic exchanges create interests amongst societal actors in either preserving or increasing exchange through freer trade or, in cases like domestic firms competing against cheap imported products, in creating interests in reducing or stopping the exchange through the imposition of trade restrictions.

These theories have two variants: weak liberals that focus on the constraining nature of high levels of trade interdependence upon foreign policy and stronger liberals for whom economic globalization and other forms of interconnectedness between societies have fundamentally transformed the nature of the state and foreign policy-making (the strong liberal theory of economic interdependence (globalization) will be reviewed in Chapter 9).

In its weak liberal variant, economic interdependence has been theorized as having two effects upon state foreign policy goals. First, one body of theorization focuses upon whether and how levels of economic interdependence create more cooperative state foreign policy interests. A related argument is that not only does trade promote more peaceful and cooperative foreign policy interests, but that it can also stimulate a demand for more institutionalized cooperation between states within regional institutions like the EU.

The idea that trade results in more peaceful foreign policies has a long history in liberal thought, stretching back at least to the writings of Kant and Montesquieu. The basic argument is that 'the greater the amount of trade, the higher the price of conflict, and the less the amount of conflict that is demanded' (Polachek 1980: 60), although many liberal scholars now accept that this relationship is conditional upon how evenly the dependence upon trade is distributed (see Chapter 8). In situations where both states are equally dependent, we should expect more pacific state foreign policy goals, whereas if one party is much more dependent upon the relationship than the other, this dependency is a source of power that can be exploited by the less dependent party (Keohane and Nye 2001). Asymmetric dependence can result in more conflictual relations and even war – a question we will return to in Chapters 6 and 8 (Moravcsik 1997).

Strong economic ties change state foreign policy interests by creating powerful, affected domestic constituencies in favor of preserving and strengthening economic ties. Societal actors such as competitive exporting firms have strong self-interests in trade and lobby governmental authorities to adopt policies that protect the trading relationship. Governments, in order to maintain the support of important societal groups, therefore have strong interests in preserving beneficial trading relationships (Rosencrance 1986; Mansfield and Pollins 2001: 841). Governments can also be dependent upon the continued willingness of foreign investors to buy government bonds in order to finance public spending. Taken as a whole, a society would incur significant exit costs if economic ties with partners were severed, making the state reluctant to engage in conflicts with the partner state (Crescenzi 2003).

This dependence upon trade results in a strong external constraint that affects what states want – a point to which we will return to in Chapter 8. In Cooper's (1968: 4) words, 'as with marriage, the benefits of close international economic relations can be enjoyed only at the expense of giving up a certain amount of national independence'.

Theories of economic interdependence usually do not open up the black box of the state; instead they assume that large trade flows between countries create a dependence upon preserving the mutually beneficial trading relationship (Sterling-Folker 1997; Russett and Oneal 2001; Mansfield and Pollins 2001: 843). Interdependence is often defined as the level of foreign trade as a ratio of GDP. Therefore theories that investigate the impact of interdependence per se are best seen as being system-level theories, whereas theories that open up the state to investigate how patterns of economic interdependence impact upon societal actors, affecting what they want, are better seen as state-level theories.

It is important to note that there are considerable disagreements amongst scholars about what constitutes trade and dependence. Many liberal peace scholars measure interdependence in a 'dyadic' fashion, meaning that they investigate the levels of trade between two states and whether higher levels of trade result in less conflictual goals and behavior and vice versa (Russett and Oneal 2001). Others contend that interdependence should be defined as the overall volume of economic activity among countries (Dorussen and Ward 2010). The higher the 'embeddedness' of a state in the 'cobweb' of interdependence, the more cooperative foreign policy goals and behavior we should expect.

Beyond potentially producing peace, other liberal scholars have investigated whether increased interdependence can produce more integration between states in the form of institutionalized cooperation through regional institutions like the EU, and in particular whether significant

Table 2.4   *Weak liberal theory of interdependence*

Core motivation of states	Survival; but when there are high levels of economic interdependence, state goals become more focused on preserving mutually beneficial economic ties
Type of theory	Explanatory theory
What do we need to measure to know the foreign policy goals of a particular state?	• The distribution of power in the system, both at the regional and global level. In particular salient threats to security of a particular state • The level of economic interdependence measured as trade as proportion of national GDP • For bilateral relations, levels of trade (imports + exports) between two states measured using bilateral level of trade with country X divided by GDP • A more inclusive analysis will include levels of bilateral investment (e.g. levels of Taiwanese direct investment in the Chinese economy)
Example	Taiwanese foreign policy goals *vis-à-vis* China *What do we need to know?* • Distribution of power in region and level of 'threat' emanating from China against Taiwan (measured using realist measures in manner similar to Walt's theory) • Levels of bilateral trade (imports + exports) and direct investment between China and Taiwan, measured as bilateral trade and investments as ratio of GDP *What should we expect to see?* As levels of commerce between the two countries increase we should expect that Taiwanese foreign policy interests *vis-à-vis* China become more cooperative, focusing upon preserving beneficial cross-border commerce

increases in cross-border trade create a demand for centralized institutions and regulations (Stone Sweet and Sandholtz 1998). Stone Sweet and Sandholtz (1998: 11) have elaborated on this, positing that 'separate national legal regimes constitute the crucial source of transaction costs for those who wish to engage in exchanges across borders'. Transaction costs are defined as all of the costs of doing business across borders, including things such as different packaging and standards for the same product in different countries, the costs of exchanging money, etc. The basic argument is that the growth of interstate commerce spurs a strong social demand for more central authority and rules that can reduce barriers to cross-border trade. This influences state goals, pushing them in a more pro-integrative direction, resulting in deeper institutionalized cooperation than governments otherwise would have agreed to. An example of how weak liberal interdependence theory can be used is seen in Table 2.4.

Turning to strong liberal theories, there are two distinct bodies of theorization based upon whether one defines interdependence as merely economic transactions or in a broader sense that also captures societal interaction and communication. As the strong liberal version of economic interdependence is reviewed in Chapter 9, here I will focus upon theories that investigate the broader impact of *increasing social exchanges* on what states want. Karl Deutsch and his colleagues in the 1950s and 1960s developed Transactionalist theory to explain the effects of increasing communication and interaction between societies

Table 2.5 *Strong liberal theory of interdependence*

Core motivation of states	When there are high levels of social exchanges, states can become socialized into a 'pluralistic security community', where the sense of community is so strong that war becomes unthinkable. Anarchy between states is replaced with a form of 'society'
Type of theory	Explanatory theory

What do we need to measure to know the foreign policy goals of a particular state?	• Levels of social exchanges between two or more countries (trade, patterns of communication (letters, internet, etc.))
	• To determine whether a pluralistic security community exists we also need to know:
	  (1) if the two societies have compatible values
	  (2) the capacity of governments to respond to one another's messages, needs and actions without resort to violence
	  (3) the mutual predictability of the relevant aspects of the societies' political, economic and social behavior

Example	Danish foreign policy identity *vis-à-vis* neighboring Scandinavian states *What do we need to know?* • Levels of exchanges across Scandinavian borders • Degree to which core Danish values are compatible with those of other Scandinavian countries • Capacity of the Danish government to respond to other Scandinavian countries' messages, needs and actions without resorting to violence • Mutual predictability of the relevant aspects of Scandinavian countries' political, economic and social behavior *What should we expect to see?* Denmark as part of a pluralistic security community with a shared Scandinavian identity that fundamentally changes the nature of Danish foreign policy interests *vis-à-vis* its Scandinavian neighbors

(Deutsch *et al.* 1957; Deutsch 1968). The term 'transactionalism' refers to the broader patterns of communication and interaction between societies and how increased intrasociety transactions could hypothetically transform the nature of interstate relations.

Deutsch theorized that as the level of communication between two societies increased, this can result in a growing sense of community between states that changes their core national interests as they relate to each other, contingent upon three factors: (1) the two societies having compatible values; (2) the capacity of governments to respond to one another's messages, needs and actions without resort to violence; and (3) the mutual predictability of the relevant aspects of one another's political, economic and social behavior (Deutsch 1968: 281). As the level of interaction increases, so does the mutual relevance of each society to the other. If the interaction is perceived of as beneficial, then the result is a further increase in interaction. When high levels of transaction occur, the result can be a qualitative transformation in the nature of the involved states' relations. The involved states become part of what Deutsch (1968) terms a 'pluralistic security community', defined as a situation where the component governments retain their legal identity but where the sense of community is so strong that it makes war unthinkable amongst its members, in effect replacing 'anarchy' between states with a form of 'society' of shared interests and even identity. (See Table 2.5.)

Box 2.1 Joking about war?

Deutsch (1968: 274) used the relationship between Scandinavian countries after World War II as an example of a pluralistic security community. A recent example of the strength of this kind of community was seen in a dispute between Denmark and Sweden in 1993 over the Barsebäk nuclear power plant (located 20 km from the Danish capital). In protest against the Swedes restarting the controversial plant after an earlier minor accident, the Danish interior minister stated that Denmark should invade Sweden to close the plant (Löfstedt 1996). While this form of verbal provocation could have resulted in a serious crisis, if not preparations for war or even worse, Sweden's defense minister countered the threat by stating that the Swedes would retaliate against any Danish attack by releasing a barrage of fermented herring (a foul-smelling (for foreigners) Swedish fish specialty). That two high-level ministers could joke about starting a war with each other illustrates the strength of the pluralistic security community between the two countries.

International institutions and state foreign policy interests

Turning back to weak liberal theories, the key explanatory variable in neoliberal institutionalism is the degree of institutionalization of the international system (Keohane 1984, 1989). International institutions are usually defined as 'explicit arrangements, negotiated among international actors, that prescribe, proscribe, and/or authorize behavior' (Koremenos *et al.* 2001: 762). Prominent examples of strong institutions that affect state behavior include trade institutions like the World Trade Organization and security institutions like NATO. The basic argument is that an institution-rich environment produces more cooperative state interests than an institution-poor environment.

How can an institution-rich international environment affect state foreign policy preferences? Perhaps surprisingly, neoliberal institutionalism has the same analytical starting point as structural realism: an anarchical system composed of state actors, with the distribution of power and wealth in the system exerting a strong influence on state behavior. States are seen as self-interested, egoistic actors. This similarity has led many liberal scholars to contend that neoliberal institutionalism is better understood as a variant of realist theory. However, what distinguishes neoliberal institutionalism from realist theorization is the idea that international relations are not just the 'same damn things happening over again': that institutions can mitigate the worst effects of anarchy.

The first step in understanding the differences between structural realism and neoliberal institutionalism is to return to the distinction between absolute and relative gains (Grieco 1988; Powell 1991) (see pp. 18–19). All variants of structural realism are pessimistic about the possibilities of cooperation between states due to state obsession with relative gains. Given the insecurity of anarchy, when faced with the possibility of cooperation, states will be solely concerned with how well they fare in relation to their competitors (*relative gains*). States fear that any disproportional gains of competing states will be used to threaten their security.

Neoliberal institutionalism contends that when states are able to use international institutions to achieve stable cooperation (see pp. 00–00), they are then able to concentrate solely upon what they get out of cooperation (*absolute gains*). Given that states are assumed to be egoistic, they focus upon their own gain irrespective of whether others benefit more from the cooperation.

How do institutions mitigate the worst consequences of anarchy, shifting state goals toward a focus on absolute gains? Neoliberal institutionalism argues that the situation facing states is one where they have common interests in cooperating with each other, but where they fear they will be cheated by, for instance, deciding to open their

Table 2.6   *The prisoner's dilemma*

		Actor B	
Actor A		*Cooperate (C)*	*Defect (D)*
Cooperate (C)		1, 1	10, 0
Defect (D)		0, 10	5, 5

markets to imports at the same time that the other state cheats by not opening its borders. Keohane uses the well-known prisoner's dilemma (PD) game to illustrate this situation (see Table 2.6).

The two actor prisoner's dilemma game is a symmetrical one in which each actor prefers mutual cooperation over mutual defection (CC > DD), but where the preferred outcome for each actor is a situation where he or she defects but the other actor cooperates (DC > CC). The classic example from which the name derives is one in which two prisoners are held in different cells for a major crime. 'Cooperation' is defined as upholding the previous agreement made with the other prisoner to *not confess* to the crime, whereas 'defecting' is *confessing*. If both prisoners cooperate with each other by not confessing their crime, the prosecutor is only able to jail them for a minor related crime where they each receive one year in jail. If one of the prisoners confess and the other does not (C, D), the prosecutor rewards the confessing prisoner with a plea bargain that lets him or her off the hook but that results in the other unrepentant prisoner being given a ten-year sentence. As they are locked in separate cells and cannot communicate with each other, both actors pursue their preferred option of confessing in the hope that the other prisoner is unrepentant and does not confess. However, when each prisoner confesses (D, D) they each receive five-year sentences – reduced from ten years due to their repentance – but a much worse outcome than would have been achieved with mutual cooperation (C, C). Therefore, due to the lack of communication that prevents coordination and the fact that the game is a 'one-shot' affair where each party has an incentive to cheat (defect), the outcome of a PD game will be mutual defection that results in a suboptimal outcome (D, D) in comparison to the situation if they cooperated with each other (C, C).

Keohane argues that states face PD-like dilemmas in many situations in international politics, where they often have shared interests in cooperation but where there are also incentives for them to cheat (defect). Two states that have shared interests in opening their domestic markets to free trade with each other also have incentives to cheat by not fully opening their markets when the other does. Yet if both states defect there will be no free market (D, D).

Box 2.2 The European Union and credible commitments

A real world example of the impact of institutions can be seen in the European Union. The European Commission monitors compliance with EU rules regarding the opening of the markets of member states to each other and sanctions by bringing cases against the infringing state to the European Court of Justice, which can decide to fine states for non-compliance. Monitoring and sanctioning in the EU makes it less attractive to cheat, as the risks of being detected are higher and the costs of sanctions makes it less profitable to cheat. This does not mean that governments never break EU rules, but for the most part they do comply, enabling member states to pursue state goals aimed at absolute gains in their economic relations with each other.

International institutions are instruments that can help states overcome this problem, enabling them to focus on absolute gains to achieve mutually beneficial cooperation. Institutions can facilitate cooperation by altering the incentives for action, making CC outcomes possible in PD-like situations. First, institutions enable states to make *credible commitments*, as they can both monitor compliance and sanction defection. In terms of the above example, an institution would enable both prisoners to agree to cooperate in the knowledge that cheating by the other (defection) would be detected and sanctioned. These problems become even greater when there are multiple parties to an agreement, making monitoring and sanctioning by an institution even more important (Axelrod and Keohane 1986).

The second way in which institutions enable states to achieve cooperation is that they lengthen the 'shadow of the future' (Axelrod and Keohane 1986). In a one-shot PD game as depicted above, the dominant strategy of both actors is defection. However, if the actors are in what is termed an 'iterated' game within an institution, it is no longer as attractive to defect. When future gains from repeated rounds of cooperation are far greater than the one-off benefits of defection, states that have institutionalized their cooperation will choose a cooperative strategy as a rational long-term one even though they forgo higher short-term benefits of defection (Axelrod 1984).

Finally, institutions provide forums for communication between actors, enabling them to detect whether they actually have common interests in cooperation, as in a PD game. If the two prisoners in the PD game are able to communicate with each other, this transforms the game, enabling them to agree upon a mutually beneficial cooperative strategy (C, C) in order to avoid the otherwise inevitable outcome

Table 2.7   *Neoliberal institutionalist theory*

Core motivation of states	To survive, but, in an institution-rich environment where survival is assured through institutions, state goals become more focused on absolute gains
Type of theory	Explanatory theory
What do we need to measure to know the foreign policy goals of a particular state?	• The distribution of power in the system, both at the regional and global level • The strength of international institutions in an issue-area and geographically
Example	German foreign policy goals in trade policy *What do we need to know?*
	• The strength of institutions that Germany is a member of in trade policy (regional and global) • The degree to which major international competitors are also members of the same trade-related international institutions
	What should we expect to see?
	• Germany has cooperative goals related to absolute gains in trade with states that are also members of the same trade-related institutions (such as the EU) • Germany has goals related to relative gains in trade with competitors that are not members of institutions

(D, D). Keohane (1984: 245) treats information produced by institutions as an institutional variable, arguing that 'international systems containing institutions that generate a great deal of high-quality information and make it available on a reasonably even basis to the major actors are likely to experience more cooperation than systems that do not contain such institutions, even if fundamental state interests and the distribution of power are the same in each system'. An example of how neoliberal institutionalism, or what is a weak liberal theory of institutions, is shown in Table 2.7.

Using systems-level liberalism to analyze state foreign policy goals

In liberal theorization there are therefore two different system-level variables that impact on what states want: levels of interdependence between states and the importance of international institutions. Both variables can influence state foreign policy goals by pushing them in a more cooperative direction in comparison to what we would expect following structural realism. Both of the variants of system-level liberalism use theories in a more explanatory fashion.

Interdependence theories can be split into weak and strong liberal variants. Weak liberal interdependence theory argues that high levels of economic interdependence create strong domestic interests in preserving beneficial trade relations, resulting in more cooperative foreign policy goals. Strong liberal interdependence theories such as Deutsch's transactionalism contend that high levels of interdependence can transform the very identity of states, resulting in the creation of pluralistic security communities in which states no longer think of neighboring states as rivals.

Regarding institutions, only the weak liberal variants work primarily at the system level. Here neoliberal institutionalism theorizes that what states want is impacted on by the level of institutionalization in the environment of states. We should first expect that if security-related institutions exist that reassure states about their security needs, then states will be able to concentrate on other goals, such as trade, in contrast to what we would expect using structural realist theories. Further, in issues such as trade, states fear they will be cheated by other states, but when there is the possibility that institutions can ensure stable cooperation state goals will be focused more on absolute gains, enabling cooperation to develop. We should therefore expect that in issue-areas where there is a high level of institutionalization, states will have more cooperative foreign policy goals that focus upon achieving absolute gains, and vice versa.

Constructivism: different cultures of anarchy, national interests and identity

In Chapter 1 we saw that despite the great variety of constructivist theories that exist, they all agree that one cannot understand what happens in the social world without taking into account idea-based factors. As with liberalism, there are few system-level constructivist theories. The following reviews the most influential system-level theory: Wendt's (1999) mainstream constructivist theory about how different cultures of anarchy affect the goals of states. Wendt's point is that there are three different cultures (outlined below) that can exist as shared ideas embedded in the collective identities of states. Constructivism at the system level details how international systems can be transformed from a Hobbesian realm of power politics to a Kantian world of friendship and pacific relations through processes of social interaction. State foreign policy goals are therefore not only determined by the material distribution of power in the system, but also by ideational factors regarding the culture of anarchy that dominates a given international system as a whole, or a region of the system, at a given time.

The key argument of constructivist theories like Wendt's is that while material factors are important, ideas also matter. State interests are not only the product of the distribution of power resources in the international system, but also reflect collective identities that can *change* through processes of social interaction between states (Wendt 1999). International relations are not necessarily the 'same damn things happening over and over again'.

As 'state interests *are* constructions of the international system' (Wendt 1999: 234), to understand what states want we need to analyze what culture of anarchy exists at a given time and in a given region. Wendt's theory views foreign policy as not solely driven by objective material factors such as patterns of trade or relative power. Instead, foreign policy goals also reflect immaterial, shared, collective beliefs such as ideas about the nature of the anarchical system that are embedded as a collective cultural consciousness of an international system. It must be noted that, like Waltz's theory, Wendt's theory is not designed to be a theory of foreign policy, but, when used in a heuristic fashion, it can supply insights about what states want depending upon which type of culture of anarchy they are embedded in.

According to Wendt, the assumption of anarchy that structural realists uncritically take as the unchangeable foundations of international politics is in fact a social creation that can change through social practices between states. In other words, 'anarchy is what states make of it' (Wendt 1992).

Wendt (1999: 313) defines a culture of anarchy as 'the deep structure of an international system', which 'is formed by the shared understandings governing organized violence, which are a key element of its political culture'. Wendt contends that there are three distinct cultures of anarchy: a Hobbesian, a Lockean and a Kantian culture. The three different cultures are differentiated by how other states are perceived: either as enemies (Hobbesian), rivals (Lockean) or friends (Kantian). How these cultures impact upon what states want depends upon the degree to which they are internalized. Wendt discusses three degrees of internationalization, ranging from the first degree, where a culture is forced upon a state, to the second degree, where states accept the culture because they perceive it is in their own self-interest, to the third degree, where the culture becomes so ingrained that states perceive it to be legitimate and part of their identity.

The Hobbesian culture is the 'world' we know from structural realist theorization (especially offensive structural realism). States view each other as enemies, and there is a strong degree of mistrust that pervades the system. States think in terms of relative gains and orient themselves toward the worst-case scenario. The system is a form of 'war of all against all', with endemic warfare, balancing and intense competition. Goals for states embedded in a Hobbesian culture match what we expect to see in structural realist theories.

Whether the Hobbesian culture forms the context in which states form their interests, or whether it forms their very identity, depends upon the degree to which a given state internalizes the culture. In the first degree, 'nice' states can be forced to follow Hobbesian culture to survive, although Wendt argues that we have only seen a first degree Hobbesian culture in a few isolated time periods, such as during the 'state of nature' power politics that dominated Europe during the rise of Hitler and World War II. The second degree is far more common, where states believe that the Hobbesian culture is in their own self-interest. One indicator that shows that the Hobbesian culture is internalized to this degree is when we see realpolitik justifications given by state leaders. The third degree is when power politics comes to be seen as an end in itself. 'Identity is here an effect of culture in the way that speech is an effect of language: in each case it is the structure of the latter, the grammar, that makes the former possible ... To say that a state has fully internalized a Hobbesian culture in this constitutive sense, therefore, is not to say that it has been affected in billiard ball fashion by something external to it, but that it is carrying the culture around in its "head", defining who it is, what it wants, and how it thinks' (Wendt 1999: 274).

A Lockean culture as conceptualized by Wendt is a more benign anarchical system, where states see each other as rivals, but where state sovereignty within the Westphalian system is an institutionalized practice shared by states. Norms regarding the respect for state sovereignty result in a situation where state foreign policies are more restrained than they are in a Hobbesian 'war of all against all' system. States also tend to take a longer term view of international affairs, seeing it less as a Darwinian survival of the fittest system but instead as a more mature anarchical 'society'. Even war itself becomes more limited, as territorial conquest becomes a form of behavior that is morally unacceptable in the 'civilized' international community. Survival is no longer an immediate concern given the norms embedded in the Lockean culture, enabling states to concentrate on secondary goals like economic growth and focus upon absolute gains.

State foreign policy goals vary depending upon the degree of internalization of the Lockean culture. In the first degree, states comply with the culture due to coercion. For example, Iraq in the first Gulf War (1991) was expelled from Kuwait by the Allied coalition. Following this, Iraq respected Kuwaiti sovereignty. Here we would expect that this did not reflect a new-found Iraqi identity that respected sovereignty; instead we would expect that underlying Iraqi foreign policy goals were unchanged, whereas the foreign policy options available to the country were limited due to the external constraints posed by the threat of renewed US-led military actions against it. In comparison, in regions where the Lockean culture is deeply embedded, respect for the norm of sovereignty becomes a part of the very identity of states, becoming a 'voice in our heads telling us that we *want* to follow them' (Wendt 1999: 288).

Finally, in a Kantian culture of anarchy, relations amongst states have been fundamentally transformed. States no longer see each other as rivals, but as friends. Disputes are no longer settled through war or even the threat of war, and if one of the states in the Kantian community is threatened then all of the states will fight as a team. Wendt draws heavily on strong liberal theorization, in particular on Deutsch's ideas of 'pluralistic security communities' and ideas of shared knowledge of the other's peaceful intentions and behavior. As mentioned in Chapter 1, the three Kantian factors in strong liberal theorization are democracy, institutions and interdependence.

An example of a 'first degree' of internalization could be that the spread of nuclear weapons rules out war between nuclear powers. A nuclear war between major powers threatens the existence of states (and potentially life as we know it), creating such a large existential threat that it coerces nuclear powers to adopt a limited version of the Kantian culture. In the second degree, friendship with other states is a strategy; whereas in the third degree states identify with each other, seeing each other's security as being part of their own (Wendt 1999: 305).

How are systemic cultures reproduced and sometimes transformed? This is a weak point of social constructivist theory in general, given that most constructivists choose to expend their analytical energy demonstrating *that* ideas matter in world politics, relegating the question of *how* cultures are constructed and reconstructed through processes of social interaction to the margins. Most social constructivist theories such as Wendt's operate with an assumption of a mutual constitution of agents and structures through actions, often drawing upon dualist sociological theorists such as Anthony Giddens (1984) (see p. 24). Language is a classic example. When we speak we follow the rules of existing language (structure), but through our use of language we both reproduce it but also subtly change the structure through the creation of new practices (for example as slang becomes acceptable language). In the same manner, in Wendt's theory states reproduce an existing culture of anarchy through their foreign policy actions, but can also, depending on four different factors, construct a new culture of anarchy that becomes embedded in the collective identities of states.

Here Wendt's theory is similar to strong liberal theorization on the transformation of the nature of international politics through four factors, including: (1) interdependence, (2) ideas relating to the perception of a common fate amongst states, (3) homogeneity and (4) self-restraint by states. Wendt theorizes that self-restraint, where states

Table 2.8   *Wendt's social constructivism*

Core motivation of states	Varies depending upon the culture of anarchy: • Hobbesian: survival • Lockean: maximizing economic gains relative to rivals • Kantian: maximizing absolute gains
Type of theory	Explanatory theory, especially given Wendt's interest in making his theory 'testable' and his focus on empirical indicators. The theory tends however more toward a critical realist position than a strongly empiricist neopositivist position (Jackson 2011)
What do we need to measure to know the foreign policy goals of a particular state?	• The 'culture of anarchy' present in a given region at a given time • The degree to which a given culture is internalized (first, second or third degrees)
Example	Chinese foreign policy goals *vis-à-vis* the US *What do we need to know?* • The culture of anarchy present in Asia • The degree to which China has internalized the culture *What should we expect to see?* As China increasingly participates in the international community, Chinese leaders will become socialized into a more cooperative 'culture' of anarchy (perhaps even a Kantian culture if Chinese economic development results in the democratization of the country), viewing its relations with the US and other countries less as a zero-sum game and more as a cooperative, positive-sum game (Friedberg 2005)

trust other states enough to focus upon absolute gains, must be present before any transformation can take place through the other three factors. For example, high levels of interdependence coupled with the self-restraint by states can undermine egoistic identities, resulting in a process of social interaction between states that can lead to a new collective identity, from, for example, a Lockean to a Kantian culture of anarchy (Wendt 1999: 343).

Wendt's theory is unfortunately somewhat short on practical applicability, despite postulating that it is an explanatory theory. In differentiating empirically the three cultures he draws heavily on existing realist and liberal theories, for instance identifying a Kantian culture of anarchy using indicators of the three factors drawn from strong liberal theorization. Table 2.8 illustrates the core argument of Wendt's theory and how we can measure which 'culture of anarchy' is present at a given time. The table also illustrates how we can use the theory to investigate what we should expect China's foreign policy goals *vis-à-vis* the US to be.

Chapter 3

Domestic Factors

The international system creates a set of constraints in which state foreign policy preferences are formed. Austria and Switzerland occupy relatively similar geographical placements in Europe, both straddling the Alps that separate Central from Southern Europe. Both countries are comparable on most parameters, including size of population, economy and military expenditures. During the Cold War both countries were neutral. Yet since 1989 the paths of the two countries have diverged significantly. Switzerland chose to remain aloof from ever closer economic, political and security cooperation within the EU, whereas Austria joined the EU in 1995. System-level theories are unable to account for these differences in foreign policy interests and behavior between these two similarly placed, comparable countries.

This chapter opens up the 'black box' of the state to describe how factors related to societal inputs – such as public opinion and interest groups, governmental actors such as bureaucratic institutions, and societal identities – matter for what states want in foreign affairs. While moving beyond simple, system-level models increases the number of factors in a theoretical model, thereby reducing the parsimony of the theory and complicating any ensuing empirical analysis, many analysts are willing to pay this price in order to gain greater explanatory traction in analyzing and explaining foreign policy goals.

As in Chapter 2, the exposition of different theories is split into the three main schools of IR theorization. Within each school, we can differentiate between theories that focus upon domestic societal factors, such as public opinion or interest groups, and government-oriented theories that concentrate upon what governmental actors (bureaucracies, high-level political authorities) want (Rosenau 1967). Note that the terms 'state' and 'domestic' are used interchangeably in the following.

Within the realist school, neoclassical realism takes as its starting point the insights of structural realism about the workings of the anarchical international system, but expands the analysis to understand how these systemic pressures are translated through the domestic process of elite debates about the 'national interest'. In contrast to structural realism, neoclassical realism is (often) able to explain why two states with similar placements in the system can have different sets of preferences.

The traditional strength of the liberal school has been the study of state-level factors. Indeed, some IR scholars have defined liberalism as *the* study of state-level factors (e.g. Moravcsik 1997). Inspired by pluralistic models of politics (Dahl 1961, 1971), liberal theories at the state level investigate the competitive domestic struggle between different societal groups (business organizations, trade unions, political parties, ethnic groups, etc.) and competing groups within government (e.g. executive–legislative relations) over defining the state's foreign policy goals. In contrast to the 'top-down', elite focus of neoclassical realist theories, liberal theories at the state level are very much 'bottom-up' approaches, with foreign policy goals of the state reflecting societal demands as they have been aggregated by the political system.

With this home turf advantage it is perhaps surprising at first glance that there is no single liberal theory of the preference formation process. Instead, there are numerous mid-range theories that describe the theorized impact of particular factors, such as public opinion or the intragovernmental battles between decision-makers, and how these factors result in foreign policy goals that do not necessarily reflect what we would expect solely based upon the placement of the state in the international system.

Constructivism at the state level explains the construction and transformation of national interests and identities. Whereas the main split in liberal theorization is between weak and strong liberal theories regarding whether the very nature of international politics can be transformed, in constructivist theorization the fundamental split regards the very nature of reality and how it can be studied (see Chapter 1). The section on constructivism reviews (i) Hopf's interpretivist theory about the discourses that form national interests and identities, and (ii) two post-structuralist theories of identity formation: Campbell's theory of the politics of identity and Wæver's securitization theory.

Neoclassical realism: anarchy with a domestic face

As realist theorization became increasingly dominated by system-level variants in the 1980s, state-level realism became a neglected backwater, found predominately amongst more empirically oriented scholars and practitioners (e.g. Kissinger 1994). State-level realism was reborn as 'neoclassical realism' in the 1990s in a series of books and articles written by scholars who were dissatisfied with the poor explanatory power of structural realism that was a product of the exclusive focus on system-level factors, and in particular the inability to explain major historical events such as the end of the Cold War.

Neoclassical realists contend that structural realists have valued theoretical parsimony over explanatory power, with theoretical elegance
blinding structural realists from noticing that real world politics did
not function as their models predicted (Schroeder 1994; Vasquez 1998;
Legro and Moravcsik 1999). Neoclassical realists use theories as
heuristic tools and in a very pragmatic fashion. The goal of accounting
for puzzling outcomes results in what can be thought of as Lego-like
theoretical models that put together parts from different theoretical
toolkits. For example, Schweller combines a structural realist explanatory variable (placement and relative power of the state) with what can
be thought of as a liberal state-level intervening variable (autonomy of
leaders). Other neoclassical scholars combine structural realism with
constructivist-inspired intervening variables, opening up a strong role
for identities and ideas. An ability to account for outcomes is prioritized over parsimony and theoretical consistency.

Neoclassical realists posit that if we want to understand actual
foreign policies we also need to investigate how state-level factors
affect the process whereby system-level factors are translated into
foreign policies. Neoclassical realists for example investigate how elite
debates affect how the national interest is defined in a given state at a
particular time, along with theorization on the ability of leaders to
follow their own conception of the national interest depending upon
the level of autonomy they enjoy in the national system. It must be
noted that many neoclassical realists draw on research on the beliefs
and perceptions of leaders, but these cognitive factors are not distinctly
neoclassical. I will return to this work in Chapters 4 and 5.

What distinguishes neoclassical realist theories from earlier classical
realism was that the latter did not clearly distinguish between attrib-
utes at the individual level (human nature) and the state and system
levels. In contrast, neoclassical realism is marked by its focus upon
state-level factors as crucial intervening variables between systemic
forces and foreign policy goals, investigating how and under what conditions state-level factors matter. This is illustrated in Figure 3.1.

Neoclassical realism builds upon the same basic theoretical tenets as
structural realism, including the anarchical system and the competitive
nature of interstate relations. As with structural realism, the scope and
ambition of a state's foreign policy goals are determined by its placement in the international system and its relative material power
resources. Further, when the relative material power resources of a
state increase, so do the magnitude and ambition of the interests of the
state (Rose 1998).

Yet neoclassical realists contend that we cannot assume that
domestic elites will always adopt a conception of the national interest
that accurately reflects system-level constraints and opportunities.
Domestic political processes are a crucial intervening variable between

Figure 3.1   *Neoclassical realism and system and state-level factors*

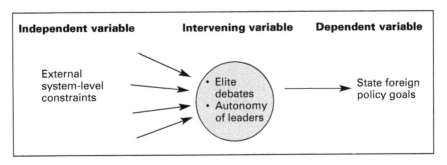

systemic pressures and the foreign policy preferences of a given state. Neoclassical realist theories are very much 'top-down' approaches, focusing upon elite debates with a state and the autonomy of leaders.

Despite being a central concept in the realist school as a whole, the national interest is unfortunately very vague in most theories. Most realists assume that the 'national interest' is to ensure survival and the broader security of the state. Morgenthau (1951: 972) defined the national interests as the desire 'to protect physical, political, and cultural identity against encroachments by other nations'. As we saw in Chapter 2, structural realists have quite ambiguous ideas about what the national interest is. Waltz (1979: 134) stated that 'to say that a country acts in its national interest means that, having examined its security requirement, it tries to meet them'. This conception of national interest as the pursuit of security is quite broad and it raises the question of what exactly is 'security' beyond the mere survival of the state. Does it mean the absence of *any* threat to the state?

To deal with this ambiguity, some neoclassical realists have suggested that it is necessary to go a step deeper by investigating national identity, defined as how a given state understands its national interests and role in the world. In structural realism these two concepts are synonymous, as a given state's national identity corresponds to the national interests that follow from the state's placement in the international system and relative power. However, neoclassical realists contend that national identity is broader and more complex, and point out that two states with similar levels of power and placement can have very different national identities. For instance, whereas France during the Cold War had an ambitious conception of French national interests, seeing itself as independent of both the US and the Soviet bloc, West Germany had, in light of its defeats in World Wars I and II, a very restrained understanding of its own national interests.

Many neoclassical realists have investigated the peculiar nature of US national identity; for example Monten (2005: 119) writes that the US national foreign political identity is centered on the idea of 'exceptionalism' that 'has been organized around a particular conception of the national purpose, expressed in foreign policy as the belief that Americans are "a chosen people", an elect nation guided by a "special providence" to demonstrate the viability and spread of the democratic institutions and values that inform the American experiment'. He argues that there is a pendulum-like shift between two different sides of exceptionalism in the US foreign policy identity: (1) an 'exemplarist' ideology that sees any attempt by the US to pursue a more vigorous foreign policy as doomed to fail, despite good intentions, as other states will not trust its motives and the use of force will corrupt it internally; and (2) a 'vindicationalist' ideology that holds that as it has the power to do good in the world, it is also obliged to use this power to promote liberty and democracy abroad. Monten contends that in periods when the US has strong relative power we should expect that the vindicationalist ideology will be more likely to be dominant, but we should also expect oscillations between these two different national identities due to subtle but significant ideational shifts due to debates amongst elites within domestic political processes. This is a far cry from structural realist arguments that contend that US identity and interests are mere reflections of the US placement in the international system at a given time. Here ideas and identities are posited to matter in a way that echoes constructivist theorization.

A coherent combination of foreign policy interests and identity can be helpfully defined as a foreign policy *doctrine*. Together with ideas of appropriate strategies they can be thought of as coherent overall foreign policy *grand strategies*. In the US context, doctrines are often named after the president in whose administration the doctrine was expressly formulated. For example, the Monroe Doctrine as formulated by President Monroe in 1823 stated that any manipulation by European powers in the affairs of independent states in the Western hemisphere would be viewed as an unwanted intrusion into the US sphere of interests. The Truman Doctrine linked US national interests with the protection of free peoples throughout the world that were resisting Soviet pressures, resulting in the overarching US grand strategy of containment of the Soviet Union during the Cold War. Yet doctrines and grand strategies are readily apparent in other countries. President de Gaulle in France developed an understanding of French interests that saw the country as an independent great power despite possessing low power relative to the Soviet Union and the US – an understanding of French interests and identity that arguably did not match the imperatives of their structural environment. The strategy to attain and/or maintain great power status was to adopt relatively independent foreign and security policies, resulting in the development of independent French nuclear forces and the withdrawal of France from NATO (Martin 2011).

The next question is: What are the sources of national identity, and what processes result in different national identities being formed or adopted? Unfortunately, neoclassical realist theories do not provide practical analytical tools that can be used to investigate processes of identity formation and change. In response to this, several neoclassical realists have recently explored whether constructivist theories of identity formation can be incorporated into neoclassical realist theories.

For example, Sterling-Folker (2009) has combined realist ideas about anarchy and security with constructivist theories of group identity, noting that humans are social beings that naturally form groups, and that groups construct their identity by differentiating themselves from other groups. She contends that the processes whereby groups form their identity in competition with other groups both within and outside of the state are best analyzed using constructivist theories of identity construction, where images of the Self (i.e. identity) are formed and reconstructed in relation to other groups (the Other). She analyzes how domestic elites form and strengthen their own identities (Self) by differentiating themselves from the Other (usually foreign countries).

Turning to the autonomy of leaders, many neoclassical realists have looked at how domestic political factors influence the ability of leaders to pursue what they perceive to be the national interest. When there are weak domestic constraints, leaders can pursue their own conception of the national interest, whereas when they are restrictive they are forced to accommodate the understandings of the national interest of the constraining domestic actors (Dueck 2009). Ripsman (2009) suggests that, while leaders are interested in securing the state in an anarchic international system, they are also motivated by the desire to stay in office, resulting in domestic political conditions influencing national goals. Domestic actors matter when they are able 'to provide a sufficient payoff to policy-makers if they construct policies in the desired direction, or to impose sufficient penalties if they do not' (Ripsman 2009: 181). Ripsman suggests a series of hypotheses for when domestic actors will have more influence upon state goals. First, they should have more influence when a state faces a low-threat international environment than when the very survival of the state is at stake. Second, when a government is vulnerable, for example when it expects an electoral defeat or coup, domestic actors can be used to shore up support to avoid the defeat. Third, when the executive has a low level of autonomy, for example in a political system where the president only has weak foreign policy powers, domestic actors matter more.

Box 3.1 Identity and the China–Taiwan conflict

Sterling-Folker applies her analytical framework to the China–Taiwan conflict, attempting to show how both external systemic pressures and domestic identity politics drive Chinese, Taiwanese and US foreign policy interests toward each other. The conflict started in 1949 when the nationalist KMT government fled China to Taiwan after it lost in the Chinese civil war. In Taiwan the KMT party declared itself the legitimate government of all of China, and was backed by the US in this claim until the easing of US–Chinese tensions in the early 1970s. This easing of relations resulted in China taking a seat in the UN Security Council, relegating Taiwan to a semi-sovereign status without representation in international organizations, and where only a handful of states in the world officially recognized Taiwan as an independent country. China has maintained since 1949 that Taiwan is a mere rebellious province that should be reintegrated into China, potentially by military force. In Taiwan, the ruling KMT party in the 1980s and 1990s officially supported independence but accepted the status quo.

Sterling-Folker argues that liberals are wrong in thinking that the dramatic increase in economic interdependence in the 1990s and 2000s between the two countries will result in an easing of tensions. She argues that at the system level there is a natural tension between Chinese interests in expanding their power in the region and US interests in balancing against this expansion by supporting Taiwan. Domestically, in both China and Taiwan, groups had strong interests in using the conflict with the other as a means of forging stronger national identities that could be exploited for domestic political gain. For instance, in Taiwan the DPP party won elections in 2000 and 2004 based partly upon its pro-independence stance *vis-à-vis* China, using negative views of the 'Other' for domestic political gains. The nationalistic tactics resulted in more aggressive, pro-independence Taiwanese foreign policy goals *vis-à-vis* China (see also Clark 2007).

Yet recent events in Taiwan have also shown that analysts of foreign policy preferences should not read too much into events over the short term as Sterling-Folker has. The elections in 2008 brought the more conciliatory KMT party back to power, shifting the Taiwanese foreign policy goal away from independence; and recent developments have included a major trade agreement in 2010 that has cemented the thawing of relations.

While producing models with stronger explanatory power, neoclassical work that focuses on how domestic politics matter becomes increasingly indistinguishable from liberal theorization, raising the question of why the analyst should not just use weak liberal theories on the impact of domestic factors instead, given that these analytical tools are much more developed both empirically and theoretically.

Conclusions: using neoclassical realism to analyze state foreign policy goals

Neoclassical realism explains deviations in state foreign policy goals from what we should expect simply based upon system-level constraints. As such, it is a very useful tool to introduce some empirical 'realism' into realist scholarship. Yet as an analytical tool it is more difficult to use: precisely because it prioritizes empirical accuracy over theoretical parsimony. Neoclassical realism in this respect is often closer to historical scholarship than theory-driven political science. Many of the theoretical concepts such as national identity are quite 'fluffy', meaning that there are no precise definitions of key terms that can be empirically measured.

Analysts that use neoclassical realism use system-level constraints as their starting point. They then engage in what can be termed 'thick description', using theoretical terms to structure their analysis. Glenn (2009) has suggested that neoclassical realism is most applicable in two situations. First, when threats are clear and policy responses are self-evident, but where the state adopts an interpretation of the national

Table 3.1   *Neoclassical realism*

Core motivation of states	To maintain their relative position in the international system and follow policy in line with the foreign policy interests of the state
Type of theory	Analytical tool to understand foreign policy behavior
What do we need to measure to know the foreign policy goals of a particular state?	• Strength of a state and the distribution of power in the international system, focusing primarily on the great powers • What is the dominant conception of national identity amongst elites at a given time?
Example (Monten 2005)	US foreign policy goals since the end of the Cold War. *What do we need to know about the US?* • Its relative capabilities *vis-à-vis* other great powers • Which core 'idea' of the US national identity is dominant amongst elites at a given time *What should we expect to see?* • In periods where US relative power is very strong, we should expect the US foreign policy goals will tend toward vindicationalism • However, when relative power is unchanged, oscillation should still occur due to the negative consequences of each of the two sides of the exceptionalistic idea (exemplarism or vindicationalism)

interest that deviates strongly from what we should expect. One example here was France under President de Gaulle. Second, when threats and opportunities are obvious, but the environment provides little information about what the most appropriate way to respond would be.

Table 3.1 illustrates the core argument in neoclassical realism about what states want, along with suggestions for what information is needed to measure the foreign policy goals of a given state. The table also illustrates how neoclassical realism analyzes cases, using an article by Monten (2005) that investigates the interplay between system-level factors and domestic elite debates in determining what the US wants in foreign policy at a given time. The sources that are used by Monten to detect the prevailing ideology held by elites at a given time are both secondary accounts of US foreign policy and speeches and other primary sources. It is again important to underline that theory is used here as a heuristic tool to understand why US goals toward promoting democracy shift over time.

Liberalism: opening up the black box

Liberal theories at the state level are inspired by pluralistic models of democracy, in which policy is seen to be the product of the competitive struggle for influence between different societal groups both within and outside of government. The following review examines both weak and strong liberal theories about the importance of a range of societal and governmental explanatory factors that can impact upon what states want in foreign affairs.

Weak liberal theories

There is not one single weak liberal theory that attempts to explain how state-level factors impact on what states want. Instead, there are mid-range theories that attempt to explain the impact of particular factors such as public opinion, interest groups or the bureaucracy. All of the theories share a 'bottom-up' method of analysis in which state preferences are theorized to reflect competing societal demands as they have been aggregated by a given political system (Moravcsik 1997). Factors such as public opinion and interest groups can be understood as *societal* inputs into the political system: pressures which are then mediated by the jostling of political and bureaucratic actors within *government* to produce national foreign policy preferences. This is illustrated in Figure 3.2. Factors within the dotted line are state and government-related factors, whereas those preceding these are termed societal factors and include the media, interest groups and public

Figure 3.2 *Societal and governmental factors in defining national preferences*

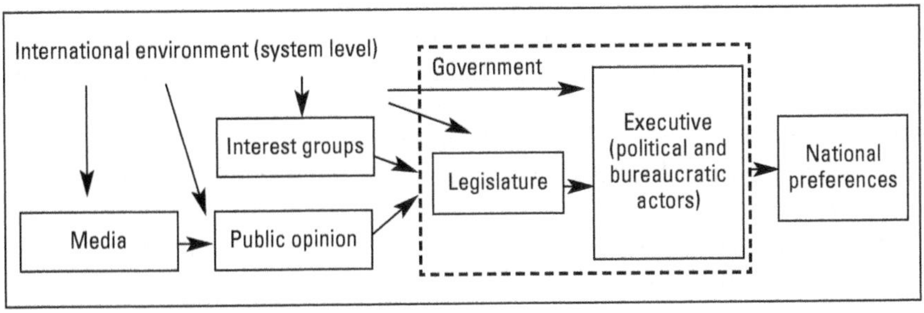

opinion. The basic idea of the figure is that national preferences are the result of the aggregation of societal demands through a country's political system.

Weak liberal theories can be thought of as tools that are more applicable when analyzing particular issues and particular cases. For example, there has been considerable scholarship on the impact of the pro-Israeli lobby in the US on the preferences of the US in the Middle East (Mearsheimer and Walt 2007; Rosenson *et al.* 2009). Using theories about the different ways that interest groups can affect national interests, these studies empirically investigate whether, when and how the pro-Israeli lobby succeeds in influencing US national interests. Instead of the more overreaching analyses of US foreign policy goals that realist theories make, weak liberal theories are usually more circumscribed, partial theories that explain bounded phenomena such as US interests in the Middle East. On the other hand, by lowering the level of abstraction, weak liberal theories are usually able to account for more of the most important aspects of a particular case or set of cases.

Public opinion

What impact do citizens have upon the foreign policy goals of their country? Numerous empirical studies have documented the relationship between public opinion and national preferences, but there has been less explicit theorization on how public opinion matters. This was especially the case in the first generation of scholarship on public opinion and foreign policy in the 1950s until the 1970s, which dealt with the question of *whether* average voters hold informed views of foreign policy issues. In a series of path-breaking studies in the US, Almond and Lippmann both found little evidence that suggested informed opinion, instead suggesting that the American public held capricious and unstructured attitudes toward foreign policy issues and were prone to 'mood swings' (Almond, 1950; Lippmann, 1955). These conclusions came to be termed the Almond–Lippmann thesis. The thesis implied that the US government should not listen to public opinion, as the uninformed mood swings would result in foreign policies that do not reflect the national interest, however defined. These findings neatly dovetailed into the then popular classical realist theorization, where figures such as Morgenthau and Carr believed that state leaders would best follow the national interest by ignoring public opinion.

Public opposition in the US and abroad to the Vietnam War in the late 1960s suggested that a scholarly re-examination of the Almond–Lippmann thesis was warranted. Scholars found that public opinion in the US was more structured and stable than previously thought, and that it responded rationally to changes in the international environment. It is important to note that most scholars did not contend that the average citizen possessed sophisticated views toward foreign events; instead citizens often use relatively simple pieces of information such as the number of casualties in a conflict as a simple heuristic device to develop a reasonably informed attitude toward the war as an issue, enabling them to make a simple calculation of whether a war is worth the blood and treasure being expended. More recently, scholars have extended this work to other democratic systems, finding that public opinion in countries such as France, Germany and Italy is also relatively well-informed and reasoned on the most salient foreign policy issues.

After finding that public opinion was structured and relatively well-informed, the next natural question was *to what degree* public opinion actually influenced how political leaders defined the national interest. In an early theoretical study, Rosenau (1961) suggested that public opinion could be seen as a 'slumbering giant', in that if foreign policies diverged too far from the boundaries set by public opinion, leaders would incur substantial political costs, a hypothesis that was validated by events during the Vietnam War.

Further empirical work provided some evidence that US foreign policy changed in the same direction that public opinion had previously changed (Page and Shapiro 1983; Bartels 1991). The responsiveness of elected officials to public opinion in foreign policy issues is, however, still an understudied area, with the primary reason for this neglect being the daunting methodological challenge of measuring responsiveness. To measure the impact of public opinion requires at the very least a detailed time-series of opinion polls on specific foreign policy issues in order to track fluctuations in public opinion over time and whether they occurred before changes in the goals articulated by leaders. Stronger research designs would for example track public opinion within individual electoral districts and relate them to voting records of the elected representatives of the district, controlling for other potential explanatory factors (for one example, see Bartels 1991).

While many studies have found that public opinion does have an impact on national preferences, some scholars contend that it is in fact elite driven, with elite sources such as the media and politicians influencing the content of public attitudes toward salient foreign policy issues and not vice versa. Recent theorization on the role of 'elite cues' in forming public attitudes has drawn on cognitive psychological theories of perception (see Chapter 4) and public opinion studies of the motivated processing of information (Taber and Lodge 2006) to suggest that public attitudes are affected most strongly by what can be termed 'surprising events'. Cues are statements of opinion by leaders that are aimed at influencing public opinion. In relation to normal elite cues – where leaders and their spokespeople push the official line – a surprising event occurs when there is internal party disagreement on salient foreign policy issues that becomes public (Baum and Groeling 2009; Gelpi 2010). Voters are, other things being equal, more prone to listen to politicians that refuse to toe the party line or civil servants who speak out against official administration policy, and these minority voices tend to be more widely reported in the media. For example, the negative comments about the US strategy in Afghanistan by the general in charge of the US-led war, Stanley McChrystal, in the summer of 2010 made front-page news – ultimately also leading to his dismissal by President Obama. We expect that voters would pay much more attention to this type of elite cue – and potentially use it to update their beliefs about the war in Afghanistan – than to statements by President Obama or other members of his administration. However, the empirical support for the theory is patchy and tentative, at best.

Turning back to the more general theoretical discussion of *how* public opinion is aggregated into national preferences, there are two mechanisms that have been investigated in the US context for how public opinion can theoretically matter: one is the direct electoral channel and the second is the more indirect one through the popularity of the president and the ensuing political capital in Congress that high approval ratings give the president.

The election of representatives is a direct channel whereby public opinion can be aggregated into national preferences. Early research found that there was not a strong relationship between foreign policy and voting behavior in the US, yet in recent years these findings have been challenged. Aldrich *et al.* (1989), however, found that public opinion on foreign affairs mattered for voter choice when: (1) voters actually held attitudes toward the foreign policy, (2) citizens accessed those attitudes for use when evaluating and choosing between candidates, and (3) when parties and candidates presented citizens with different foreign policy choices. The scholarly consensus today is that public opinion does impact on US foreign policy goals, but at the same time it is necessary for voters to be both aware of the issues and able to discern differences between candidates in foreign policy issues.

A more indirect way in which public opinion gets aggregated is through the popularity of the president. A widely held thesis is that the power of the US president in foreign affairs is based on his 'power to persuade' Congress to adopt his policy agenda (Neustadt 1969). The US Constitution does not endow the president with strong formal powers; instead an effective president's powers are directly related to

Table 3.2   *Investigating the impact of public opinion and interest groups*

Focus of theory	• Whether interest groups can influence the formation of national preferences • Which factors are effective when interest groups can gain influence
Type of theory	Explanatory theory
Methods that can be used to study question	• Quantitative (e.g. measuring correlations between positions held by politicians and their party membership (partisanship), ethnic/religious identity of politicians and the composition of the districts they represent, and ideological factors) • Qualitative (e.g. in-depth case studies using process tracing methods in an attempt to discover whether the actions of an interest group affected the final national preference formulated)

Example (Rosenson *et al.* 2009)	Is support for Israel due to elite-driven factors or due to societal demands (public opinion, interest groups)?
	What do we need to know?
	
	• Dependent variable = level of support for Israel by each senator (103–107th Congress)
	• Independent variables that can explain why senators support Israel (individual characteristics of senators' and societal demands)
	• Characteristics of individual senator:
	  1. Religion of the senator;
	  2. Ideological position of the senator (measured using an index of ideology)
	• Societal demands:
	  1. Public opinion (measured using ethnic composition of electoral districts)
	  2. Interest groups (measured using level of pro-Israeli campaign donations of each senator)
	• Method: investigate correlation between independent and dependent variables using statistical methods

his abilities as a leader and negotiator *vis-à-vis* Congress. In the presidential–Congressional relationship, a key asset of the president is a high approval rating (Sobel 2001). For example, a popular president can campaign on behalf of individual legislators, helping them secure re-election. In return the legislator will help pass the president's policy agenda in Congress. In contrast, being linked with the policies of an unpopular president can be the electoral kiss of death for a member of Congress seeking re-election. Unpopular foreign policies, such as costly and protracted wars or free trade policies that adversely impact on key domestic constituencies, can result in a decline in a president's ability to push his domestic agenda. Therefore the prospect of unpopular foreign policy actions is a significant constraint upon the president, making him more prone to listen to public opinion when defining the national interest.

Taken together, scholars have found that public opinion in the US matters most for foreign policy preferences when the issues involved are very salient for voters, and in particular when the issue involves the use of military force (Knecht and Weatherford 2006). Further, public opinion matters most in crisis situations, whereas it matters less in more routine, non-crisis issues such as foreign trade or aid. (See Table 3.2.)

The impact of the media: framing effects

Citizens are usually unable to gain direct information about foreign policies, making them dependent upon the media as a source of information. The media has been theorized to be a variable that can impact upon public opinion, shaping how citizens view the constraints imposed by the external environment, but also to be an important intervening variable between public opinion and decision-making, influencing which foreign crises reach the top of the political agenda after the advent of 24/7 news coverage of international events. Here I focus on the framing effects that media coverage can have upon public opinion.

Framing effects have especially been investigated as regards terrorism news in the media and its impact upon the public's foreign policy attitudes. As with the study of the impact of public opinion, this literature is primarily empirically descriptive, attempting to uncover whether framing effects are empirically important as opposed to uncovering theoretical causal mechanisms that explain how it matters.

The findings of several studies suggest that threatening information and images do actually increase the public's support for hawkish foreign policies, implying that framing matters (Merolla and Zechmeister 2009; Gadarian 2010). However, these findings need to be treated with some caution for two reasons. First, it is almost impossible to detect the media effects using existing survey data. For example, researchers measure the difference in public support for hawkish foreign policies in two different groups: those with newspapers as their primary media outlet and those that use television. However, finding that the television group has more hawkish attitudes, controlled for other factors, does not automatically mean that it was television that was the cause of these more hawkish views. In order to make this causal inference, the analyst needs to make many assumptions such as that television reporting of events uses more evocative, threatening images that create a stronger threat frame than similar reporting in newspapers.

Second, the strongest findings of these studies are based upon experimental research. In this type of study, a sample population is recruited to watch news segments and their views concerning foreign policy issues are measured before and after the 'treatment'. While this permits us to isolate the media effect of threat frames, it is by no means certain that framing effects function in the same manner in the construction of public attitudes outside of the laboratory.

Interest groups

Besides public opinion, weak liberal scholars have concentrated upon how interest groups can impact upon state foreign policy goals, in particular on the impact of economic and ethnic interest groups. The role of economic interest groups such as business and labor interests will be discussed further in Chapter 8.

As with the study of public opinion, most scholarship on interest group activity has been undertaken in the US context and has concentrated upon the impact of ethnic interest groups. Given the relatively unique nature of the US as a country predominantly composed of immigrants, the findings for the US context are not necessarily relevant for most nation states (although they are potentially for other immigrant countries such as Australia and Canada). On the other hand, recent years have seen the growth of immigrant communities in many countries in Western Europe and throughout Asia, suggesting that ethnic interest groups should increasingly impact upon how the national preferences of these countries are formulated.

The term 'ethnic interest group' is used in the literature to refer to groups organized along cultural, ethnic, religious or racial lines. Prominent examples of ethnic interest groups in the US include Jewish American groups that support Israel (religious), Cuban American groups that lobby for regime change in Cuba (ethnic, cultural) and African American groups that supported sanctions against South Africa during the 1980s (racial). As with the public opinion literature, most of the work on the impact of ethnic interest groups has been primarily descriptive. Distilling the findings of the literature has revealed that

---

Box 3.2 The impact of the Israel lobby on US foreign policy

Walt and Mearsheimer in a controversial 2007 book suggest that the Israeli lobby has been able to significantly influence US foreign policy in the Middle East, diverting it from what can be termed a hard-nosed, realist interpretation of the US national interest, jeopardizing its national security in the process. According to Walt and Mearsheimer, the lobby has been successful due to direct support from Jewish senators and representatives, but more importantly due to the financial support that the American Israeli Public Affairs Committee is able to give to politicians that support pro-Israeli positions, enabling these politicians to become re-elected.

---

ethnic groups are able to influence national goals when one or more of the following factors are present:

1. Organization: they have a strong organization that is able to lobby effectively decision-makers and has sufficient financial resources for this task.
2. Electoral strength: meaning that their members vote together, they are concentrated geographically and they have high turnout rates.
3. Saliency: the message being promoted by the group is salient and resonates with the general public, in particular when they are able to appeal to politically potent symbols such as 'freedom'.
4. Target: depends upon whether the decisions are solely within the executive branch, which is less permeable to lobbying, or whether the area of foreign policy also involves Congress (Haney and Vanderbush 1999; Vanderbush 2009).

In the US political system, interest groups are better able to target members of the House of Representatives, as they represent relatively small local districts and face re-election every two years, whereas Senators have six-year terms and are elected in state-wide districts, making them less receptive.

Domestic political institutions: government and levels of executive constraints

To what degree do executives, such as presidents and prime ministers, have to take into account societal demands when defining national foreign policy preferences? In the US context, the debate has concentrated upon the ability of Congress to influence US foreign policy goals. A much smaller body of literature investigates the impact that coalition government has upon national preference formation in parliamentary systems. The basic idea is that there are varying degrees to which executives have to be responsive to societal demands and those of the legislature when defining the national foreign policy interest. In strong states, the executive dominates state–society relations, whereas in weaker states executives are constrained by societal demands and the legislature (e.g. Krasner 1978).

At the heart of this literature is the assumption that executives want to remain in office, making them dependent upon societal support to varying degrees. In autocratic systems, this can entail ensuring support from institutions such as the military or key bureaucratic actors, whereas in democratic systems an executive needs the support of a larger set of societal and governmental actors.

Taken as a whole, most theorization on the importance of executive constraints builds on neo-institutional theory within political science, where the level of executive constraint by the legislature is determined primarily by the decision-making rules and formal prerogatives of the legislature in foreign policy-making. Most important is the number of 'veto players' in foreign policy-making, with 'veto players' defined as actors that have the power to veto a given decision (Tsebelis 1995). This factor is especially crucial when executives negotiate international agreements that have to be ratified by domestic legislatures, where decision-making rules for approval determine how much the executive must listen to domestic veto players (Milner 1997). In parliamentary systems where a government enjoys a large majority, the prime minister as head of government has quite free hands to negotiate deals, whereas in minority or coalition governments the executive is forced to accommodate the interests of a parliamentary majority. Veto players are usually more influential in presidential systems such as the US, where powers are split between the president and Congress (see Box 3.3).

When legislatures are able to influence foreign policy preferences we need to expand our analysis to investigate the preferences of important veto players. These preferences can for example be based upon the narrow concerns of the voters in their constituency (see pp. 72–5). Given that members of legislatures are concerned with re-election, when foreign policy issues are salient for voters legislators can be forced to accommodate constituency demands. This is especially the case for military actions that have significant casualties, but can also be the case in economic issues that have domestic impacts. In the US context, Congressional members that represent districts that are adversely affected by international competition will tend to favor protectionist trade policies, and vice versa.

Additionally, the preferences of members of the legislature can be influenced by their own individual ideology and their individual perceptions of the 'national interest' based upon the information that they have available. Finally, party membership can matter when the opposition attempts to use foreign policy issues for partisan gains. For instance, Meernik (1995) finds that Congress is more likely to restrict the use of force when there is divided government (one party holds Congress, the other the presidency).

The degree to which legislative foreign policy preferences matter depends upon the degree to which the legislature can constrain and control the executive in foreign policy. This topic has been most closely studied in the US context. The general conclusion of much of the research is that the US president enjoys relatively strong powers *vis-à-vis* Congress in foreign policy in comparison to his weaker powers in domestic law making, leading some scholars to comment on the nature of the 'dual presidency' (strong foreign policy and weaker domestic powers, see Box 3.3). As with the study of public opinion, most of this literature is relatively descriptive, although this does not mean that this work is unimportant, as an accurate empirical description of a phenomenon is vital before we can make the next step of theorizing about the causes of it.

The strength of the presidency *vis-à-vis* Congress has varied over time, and it also varies across issue areas. During the Cold War, and especially prior to the Vietnam War, national security was seen to be the prerogative of the president. Due to the perceived severe Soviet threat there was bipartisan accord, with normal Washington politics

---

Box 3.3 Congressional foreign policy powers

According to the US Constitution, Congress has the following powers in foreign policy:

- Treaty-making powers, where two-thirds of the Senate must approve international treaties signed by the US. The president can however conclude 'executive agreements' with other countries (e.g. Lend-Lease in 1941 and SALT I in 1972) to avoid congressional approval.
- Only Congress may declare war, but the president as commander-in-chief can deploy troops in military actions without congressional approval for a limited time period, after which the War Powers Resolution mandates congressional consent. No war has been formally declared by the US since World War II, although numerous military actions have been pursued.
- Congress has the power of the purse, meaning that all funds for foreign and domestic programs must be approved by it. This includes foreign aid and military spending.

stopping at the water's edge. Although there had been serious recriminations in the aftermath of the Korean War and debates about who 'lost China' after the Communist takeover in 1949, the general picture was one of Congressional acquiescence to the president.

However, in the wake of the unpopular Vietnam War (especially the expansion of the war into Cambodia by the Nixon administration) and the foreign policy excesses of that administration (including covert support for the coup in Chile in 1973), Congress became increasingly assertive. The primary tool for reasserting Congressional control of foreign policy was to change the decision-making rules themselves. One example of this was the Hughes-Ryan amendment (1974), which required that future covert actions by the CIA were to be reported to the appropriate committees of Congress.

Former national security advisor Brzezinski noted in 1984 that

> our foreign policy became increasingly the object of contestation, of sharp cleavage, and even of some reversal of traditional political commitments. The Democratic Party, the party of internationalism, became increasingly prone to the appeal of neo-isolationism. And the Republican Party, the party of isolationism, became increasingly prone to the appeal of militant interventionism. And both parties increasingly found their center of gravity shifting to the extreme, thereby further polarizing our public opinion. (Brzezinski 1984: 15–16)

The era of bipartisanship waned even further after the overarching security threat disappeared with the collapse of the Soviet Union in 1991. Economic issues such as international trade came to the fore as external security threats to the US declined. Whereas members of both parties in Congress tend to defer to the president as commander-in-chief in security matters, international economic issues can be termed 'intermestic' issues, as they combine the international and the domestic. For example, agreeing a free trade agreement with another country can have adverse domestic consequences in certain areas when manufacturing jobs are moved overseas, resulting in domestic unemployment. This gives legislators strong incentives to put pressure on the executive to ensure that their constituents' interests are represented in US foreign policy.

Yet even in security affairs Congress became split along party lines in the 1990s. In the resolutions in Congress in 1990, authorizing military force to be used to force Iraq to withdraw from Kuwait, the measure was barely passed in the Senate (52–47), with only 10 Democrats out of 56 supporting Republican President Bush's proposed action.

The US foreign policy of the Clinton administration in the 1990s that resulted from these political struggles was an overall policy that lurched from one crisis to another. Partisan clashes make it exceedingly difficult to adopt a coherent 'grand strategy'. Although bipartisanship resurfaced briefly after 9/11 in security policies (in particular the decision to invade Iraq in 2003), partisan politics still dominates foreign policy issues, making a coherent set of US foreign policy goals difficult to formulate.

While the degree of executive constraint on the US president has varied over time due to changes in the assertiveness of Congress, it also varies depending upon the formal institutional decision-making rules that govern particular issue areas and decision types. Basically, the stronger the powers of Congress are in a given area, the more the president must accommodate the interests of Congress. For instance, in international negotiations where the final outcome is a treaty, the Senate must approve the treaty by a two-thirds majority, creating a significant constraint upon the president.

The influence of Congress is less clear in security affairs, and in particular as regards the use of military force. Meernik (1994: 122–3) notes that, 'because of his constitutional prerogatives and political incentives as well as congressional weakness in foreign policy, it is the president who exercises supreme control over the nation's military actions'. While Congress does have the power to declare war and provide funds for the military, the president as commander-in-chief can deploy military forces for extended time periods without declaring war, as happened in both Korea and Vietnam. In response to Vietnam, Congress adopted the War Powers Resolution of 1973, which mandates that Congress should be consulted 'in every possible instance' prior to military action, and must authorize the action within 60 or 90 days or the forces must be withdrawn. Further, Congress can refuse to allocate funds for military operations, although this can be politically difficult as politicians run the risk of being accused of not 'supporting the troops.'

There is unfortunately a lack of comparative literature on how foreign policy-making differs across political systems. There was an ambitious research agenda in the 1960s and 1970s that attempted to examine foreign policies in a comparative fashion, for example by using adaptation theories (e.g. Rosenau 1974). The agenda lost momentum both within an FPA field that was becoming dominated by theories at the level of the decision-maker and within IR that turned toward theorization at the system level, making comparisons of factors at the state level less relevant.

This said, there have been several attempts to develop more comparative theories that explain when we should expect societal preferences to matter. Thomas Risse in an influential article in 1991 (under the name Risse-Kappen) argues that the strong versus weak state distinction that has been used in realist theorization is too simplistic. Building upon the work of Peter Gourevitch and Peter Katzenstein, he contends that there are three different factors that determine whether foreign policy-makers have to follow public opinion in defining national preferences. The first factor that Risse discusses is the degree of centralization of the political system. Is executive power to conduct foreign policy concentrated in a few hands, or are there numerous veto points in the political system as regards foreign policy? As we saw above, in US foreign policy powers are split between Congress and the president, and, as we will discuss below, also within the executive between, for instance, the Pentagon and the State Department. At the other extreme is the French foreign policy apparatus, where power is concentrated with the president.

The second factor is the degree of polarization and mobilization of domestic society, ranging from very homogeneous to heterogeneous systems. In systems such as that in the US, where public opinion is split and societal actors are able to mobilize support for their demands, foreign policies are more influenced by public opinion.

Finally, what is the nature of coalition building? Are there policy networks that link government with society, or is the system a state-dominated one? In state-dominated systems, political elites dominate foreign policy-making, whereas in systems with homogeneous societies and high degrees of social mobilization that are coupled with weak state structures, public opinion potentially plays a major role. One example of this type of coalition building is found in the US, where the openness of the system allows societal interests numerous access points. In contrast to this is France, where the foreign policy network is dominated by the executive (in particular the president).

Taken together, these three factors determine the degree to which a given state is constrained by public opinion. In strong states such as France, executives do not need to take into account public opinion, whereas in open and decentralized systems such as the US, public opinion matters. In a comparative analysis of France, Germany, Japan and the US, Risse contends that differences in domestic structure account for the variations in the impact of public opinion on national preferences across the four political systems.

Another example of a comparative theory of the importance of societal demands is Alons's (2007) theory of when system-level and domestic state-level factors matter for the process of preference formation. The first factor is the degree to which power is centralized in the state. This includes whether the state is a unitary or a federal one, where the lower levels are potentially veto players that limit the power of the executive. The second factor deals with the strength of executive–legislative relations. These relations are balanced when there is a coalition government or a single-party majority, whereas they are

Table 3.3   *Internal institutional indicators and the degree of constraint on a government*

	High degree of centralization		Low degree of centralization	
	Executive–legislative balance	*Legislative-dominated*	*Executive–legislative balance*	*Legislative-dominated*
Pluralism	Low constraint	Low–medium constraint	Low–medium constraint	Medium constraint
Corporatism	Low–medium constraint	Medium constraint	Medium constraint	High constraint

Source: Adapted from Alons (2007: 217).

legislature-dominated when there is a minority government. Finally, the method of interest mediation affects the governance capacity of the state. When the relationship with societal actors is highly institutionalized (a corporatist relationship), we should expect that the preferences of domestic actors need to be taken more into account.

Taken together, three factors determine the degree to which societal demands need to be listened to in the formation of national preferences. In societies where there is a high degree of centralization, executive–legislative balance and non-institutionalized interest group relations (pluralism), a government has the ability to ignore societal foreign policy demands, whereas when the opposite is the case the government is highly constrained by societal demands. This is illustrated in Table 3.3.

Strong liberalism at the state-level: the transformation of state interests and identities

Strong liberal theories are distinguished from weak liberal variants by the idea that fundamental *transformations* in the nature of relations between and within states can take place. The following will describe neo-functionalism: a strong liberal theory about how participation in institutions by states can fundamentally transform the foreign policy interests and identities of societal and state actors.

Neo-functionalism and the impact of international institutions on state foreign policy goals

Neo-functionalism is a theory that explains how the participation of governmental and non-governmental elites in international institutions can transform state interests from being purely centered on national interests toward a more cooperative understanding of interests.

Neo-functionalism was developed in the study of European integration within the EU, but this should not be understood as meaning that it is only relevant in the European context. Many scholars have used elements of the theory to study the importance of institutional participation in other parts of the world, in particular as regards regional integration (Mattli 1999). Regional integration schemes are now found in most regions of the world, with examples including North America (the North American Free Trade Agreement), South America (Mercosur, the Andean Community), Africa (the African Union) and Asia (ASEAN). On the other hand, most scholars agree that the explanatory factors that promote interest and identity transformations in the EU context are not sufficiently strong in other regional integrative schemes for them to matter, resulting in a lack of integrative dynamics and little regional integration outside of Europe.

Weak liberals theorize that institutions can mitigate the worst effects of anarchy by enabling governments to engage in credible commitments (see Chapter 2). In contrast, the strong liberal theory of neo-functionalism posits that when states decide to create institutions, this can start a process that results in the transformation of the very nature of interstate relations due to shifts in the interests and identities of states, moving them in a more pro-cooperative direction. Here foreign policy is defined as the policies governments adopt in their negotiations with other governments within an institution on the question of whether more powers should be transferred to the institution or not. Neo-functionalism is based upon the pluralist model of politics, where interest groups (primarily business and trade associations) and political parties struggle for control over governmental policy-making.

Groups both within and outside of government are motivated by self-interest when they argue for or against more integration. It is important to note that they do *not* have altruistic motivations such as promoting the common good. According to Haas (1964: 35), there 'is no common good other than that perceived through the interest-tinted lenses worn by international actors'.

To analyze how the self-interests of actors can be transformed by participating in a strong institution, neo-functionalism uses the theoretical concept of 'spill-over', which can have three different faces (Haas 1964). The first face of spill-over is what is termed *functional* spill-over. Building upon the idea that modern economies are strongly interdependent both within and across national borders, functional spill-over is defined as 'a situation in which a given action, related to a specific goal, creates a situation in which the original goal can be assured only by taking further actions, which in turn create a further condition and a need for more action and so forth' (Lindberg 1963:

10). For instance, achieving the goals of an effective common market within the EU, where goods and services can freely move across borders, implied that further integrative steps would be needed such as the creation of a single currency for the common market given the high transaction costs involved with currency exchanges. Functional spill-over creates a dynamic where elite interests become more pro-integrative as they become aware that in order to achieve A they need to take the next step (B), and so on.

The second face of spill-over is *political*, which describes the process where interest groups and political parties become more positive toward integration as they become involved in the process. Business groups, while perhaps reticent at first, become supporters of integration after they have made investment decisions that are based upon the existence of the common market. As they become aware of the opportunities that a larger market creates, they gradually shift their interests in a more pro-integrative direction. Political parties who oppose integration also change their views over time once they perceive that the institution, like it or not, will continue to exist and therefore they should try to make the best of it. Once they start to participate in the institution's political process, these parties discover that the best strategy is not just to sit on the sidelines in protest, but to try to push the institution in the direction that they favor. In the 1990s, Nordic green and left parties who earlier had been vehement opponents of EU integration discovered that the best strategy was to participate actively in an attempt to push the EU in a greener and more social direction, often resulting in more integration. What is key to note is that this shift in group interests is based upon egoistic calculations of 'what is in it for me?', but the result is a trans-formation of the interests of societal groups in a more pro-integrative direction through their participation in the activities of the institution.

Finally, strong institutions like the EU possess supranational author-ities that are independent of governments. In the EU this role is played by the EU Commission, which is an independent bureaucracy 'above the state' (supranational). A strong supranational authority can exploit its powers to engage in *cultivated* spill-over, which refers to the activi-ties of a strong institution to promote further integration beyond what states originally intended. In traditional intergovernmental organiza-tions decisions are taken unanimously. This results in decisions tending to congregate around the lowest common denominator, i.e. what the most reluctant government wants, unless there is a hegemon in the institution that has enough 'muscle' to push reluctant governments. With a strong supranational institution mediating between states, the institution can exploit its position in an attempt to convince govern-ments to 'upgrade' the common interest (Haas 1961). The result is more pro-cooperative outcomes than governments left to themselves would have agreed upon. For instance, in negotiations within the EU in the mid-1980s about further integrative steps, the EU Commission exploited the knowledge and authority that it possessed from managing the common market to link subtly a range of proposals together that upgraded the common interest, resulting in a treaty that significantly expanded the level of EU integration beyond what governments intended (Budden 2002; Beach 2005).

Taken together, the three faces of spill-over describe a process that, once started, results in a gradual transformation of the self-interests of governments and societal groups (business groups and political parties) in a more pro-cooperation direction. The result of integration is that 'political actors in several distinct national settings are persuaded to shift their loyalties, expectations and political activities toward a new center, whose institutions possess or demand jurisdiction over pre-existing national states. The end result of a process of political integration is a new political community, superimposed over the pre-existing ones' (Haas 1958: 16).

However, one key problem with neo-functional theorization is that the theory predicts a more-or-less continual transformation toward an ever closer union that is not reflected in the empirical record. The theory was hard pressed to explain 'stops' in the integration process, such as the stagnation caused by the 1970s oil crises, a problem that led the original founders of the theory to turn their attention to other international phenomena at that time. On the other hand, important revisions of the theory were made that attempted to account for these stops. Lindberg (1966) suggested that when integration encroached on core areas of governmental competence, the political stakes of integration were increased significantly, making it less likely that the process would continue. Schmitter (1971) built on this, suggesting that when the political stakes were sufficiently high, a countervailing 'politicization' of the process would occur that could even result in 'spill-back' toward less integration.

Yet while it is important to acknowledge that there are limits to how far spill-over processes can go, the original insights are still relevant for the study of foreign policy preference formation in situations where states participate in institutional projects such as the EU that possess strong supranational institutions. In particular, spill-over processes can explain the gradual transformation of interests amongst governments and societal groups that results in a change of their foreign policies toward supporting more integration than they originally had intended.

Conclusion: using state-level liberal theories to study foreign policy

There is no single state-level liberal theory of national preference formation. Instead, there are a number of mid-range theories that explain narrower phenomena than system-level theories or neoclassical realism, such as the hypothesized impact of public opinion upon foreign policy preferences.

This mid-range focus on explaining aspects of national preference formation is especially the case for weak state-level liberal theories. There are both societal factors, such as interest groups and public opinion, and governmental factors, such as executive–legislative relations, that can influence the formation of national preferences.

Research on how and when public opinion matter is usually based upon analysis of mass surveys. If you want to engage in this form of research, a good grounding in statistics is usually necessary. In contrast, most work on the impact of interest groups is primarily based upon in-depth case studies of the impact (or lack thereof) of a particular interest group. This choice of in-depth analysis is taken due to the difficulty of measuring the 'influence' of interest groups in a quantitative, large-n study. One way that one can measure influence in such a study would be by asking all of the members of Congress whether they supported a measure due to pressure from, for example, the Israeli or Cuban lobby. However, it is not very likely that we would be measuring the true motivations of these politicians, given the sensitive nature of the question. Another way is by measuring the positions taken by politicians on an issue in debates, such as support for Taiwan, and using this as a proxy measure for their preferences.

Neo-functionalist theory explains how participation by a state in strong international institutions such as the EU transforms the interests of societal and governmental actors in a more pro-integrative direction. Neo-functionalist analysis has been examined using both (a) in-depth case studies of either the transformation of the interests of particular actors (such as political parties) or the role and impact of the EU Commission in driving integration forward, and (b) more limited quantitative statistical analysis of how increasing trade results in a push toward more integration.

Social constructivism at the state-level: interest and identity construction

Social constructivists study the importance of ideas, norms and culture for foreign policy and international relations. At the state level, realist and liberal theory treats national interest as exogenously determined givens that exist prior to social interaction (Price and Reus-Smit 1998: 267). In contrast, social constructivist theories examine the processes whereby collectively held (intersubjective) ideas and understandings of the foreign policy interests of the state are constructed and reconstructed through processes of social interaction, meaning that they can be termed 'endogenous' to processes of social interaction within and between states.

Here I introduce mainstream constructivist theories of how actor interests and identities are constructed using Hopf's theory of discursive formations and national identity as an example. This is followed by an elaboration of the post-structuralist theories of *securitization*, which postulates that threats to security are constructed and reconstructed through speech acts.

Mainstream constructivism: discourses of identity

How are the interests and identities of states constructed? One prominent example of a social constructivist theory of identity is Hopf's theory of discourses of national identity. Hopf (2002: 3–4) maintains that 'society is assumed to consist of a social cognitive structure within which operate many discursive formations. Identities are constituted by these formations. Individuals can hold many identities; they participate in a variety of discursive formations. Their daily social practices constitute both themselves and Others, and the identities and discursive formations that constitute the cognitive structure in which they live'. Identities that are shaped within discursive formations allow individuals to make sense of the outside world, playing a role similar to the heuristic shortcuts postulated in the cognitive theories of foreign policy discussed in the next chapter.

Discursive formations are the product of processes of domestic identity construction, influenced by external events. Looking at Russia, Hopf (2005: 238) argues that 'while Russian identity has deep daily roots, its great power identity is in a daily construction project with the external world, especially with the US and Europe. Interaction with the US and Europe produces, reinforces, and counteracts the discourses of Russian identity at home'.

Hopf distances his theory from constructivist theories that suggest that norm-following behavior is based upon a logic of appropriate action (see p. 24). He contends that this logic assumes that individuals take conscious, deliberate decisions to follow a norm. In contrast, he argues for a logic of 'habitual' action, where most actions are relatively unmotivated and unexamined in everyday life (Hopf 2002). Identities make certain things unthinkable. For example, in his analysis of Russian identity in 1999, he finds that within the prevailing discourses the idea that Russia could be anything but a great power (at least regionally) is simply unthinkable.

In Hopf's constructivist theory, different discourses of national identity compete for dominance within the national political system. Once dominance is achieved at a given time, the discourse of identity forms that basis for the formulation of national interests upon which foreign

Table 3.4 *Three discursive formations in Russian identity, 1999*

	New Western Russian	*Liberal Essentialist*	*New Soviet Russian*
Russian nation Nuclear weapons	Irrelevant category Russian security guaranteed	Russian uniqueness Russian security enhanced, great power status assured	Slavic fraternity Enables great power behavior *vis-à-vis* US
Centering Russia	Become the West	Become the real Russia	Restore as much of the USSR as feasible
International institutions	Route to great power status	Route to great power status and security	Poor substitute for military power
Bipolar balance of power?	No external binary; Russia is part of a unipolar coalition	No bipolarity; Russia is a part of an irreducibly multipolar world	Bipolarities at home and abroad; bipolar competition prevails
The West	West = US + Europe	West = Europe	US controls West

Source: Based on Hopf (2002: 220).

policy decisions are made. In an analysis of the adoption by Russia of moderate interventionist foreign policies toward neighboring states in the 1990s, Hopf (2005) argues that the shift toward more intervention was due to a change in the prevailing discourse of Russian identity toward a 'centrist' one that was wedged between a non-interventionist 'liberal' discourse and a strongly interventionist 'conservative' discourse.

Theorization on the process whereby one discourse wins over the other is unfortunately less developed in the theory. In many respects, this is a natural consequence of Hopf's decision to develop a theory that functions more as an interpretive tool for understanding different foreign policy identities of states instead of a causal theory that puts forward clear hypotheses about what factors determine which discourse becomes dominant at a given time (see Chapter 10).

Table 3.4 illustrates how Hopf depicts the three prominent discourses that he found in his reconstruction of Russian identity in 1999. The New Western Russian discourse identified with the US and Europe as a cordial external Other. This discourse promotes alliances with the West. In contrast, the New Soviet Russian discourse held a much more conflictual view of the US, based upon the role that the US as an Other played in the Soviet past. Here a form of new Cold War with the US is seen as inevitable. The Liberal Essentialist discourse does not want a return to the Soviet past, but instead identifies with Europe (not the US) as it finds that 'authentic' Russian qualities are most evident in Europe. Depending upon which one is dominant, these discourses result in very different Russian foreign policies, ranging from a 'return to the West' to a strongly conflictual relationship with the US.

The descriptions of the three discursive formations can then inform our understanding of Russian foreign policy identity by analyzing at a given time which discourse was dominant in the domestic political system. Understanding which identity is dominant also enables us to understand why particular foreign policy actions were chosen at a given time in contrast to possible alternatives.

Post-structuralism: the politics of identity and securitization theory

Post-structuralism involves adopting a relativistic view of the world in which there is no single 'objective' truth or reality. Humans need to perceive the social world through language, and post-structuralists contend that language is not a neutral medium. For example, threats are not just 'objective' threats; they have to be perceived and described through speech acts as threats for them to matter. Drezner gives a very good example of this understanding of social reality in his entertaining book that applies IR theory to a (hopefully) hypothetical case – a zombie apocalypse:

For constructivists, material factors such as economic wealth and military power are important – but even more important are how social structures filter and interpret the meaning of those material capabilities. For example, zombies are hardly the only actors in the social world to crave human flesh. Cannibals, sharks, and very hungry bears will also target *Homo sapiens* if there is sufficient opportunity and willingness. Nevertheless, zombies are perceived to be a much greater threat to humankind. Why?' (Drezner 2011: 68)

David Campbell's theory on the politics of identity starts with the post-structuralist idea that states do not have an objective, independent existence. He utilizes the term 'performative' to mean that discourses constitute the objects of which they speak. He writes that 'foreign policy *shifts* from a concern of relations *between* states that take place *across* ahistorical, frozen, and pregiven boundaries, *to* a concern with *the establishment of the boundaries* that constitute, at one and the same time, the "state" and "the international system". Conceptualized in this way, foreign policy comes to be seen as a political practice that makes "foreign" certain events and actors ... In other words, foreign policy is "a specific sort of *boundary-producing political performance*"' (Campbell 1992: 61–2).

From space we can see no borders. Instead, borders should be understood as social constructions (performances) that play a role in defining the 'Self' by distancing it from the 'Other'. Drawing on Benedict Anderson's (1990) book *Imagined Communities*, Campbell argues that the US is the imagined community par excellence. Anderson posited that there is no such thing as an objective 'English' or 'German' identity; instead they are fictional national myths that were created in the 19th century. Campbell contends that the US also does not have an objective existence per se, although there are naturally material manifestations such as national symbols and infrastructure. Yet a 'state' has no ontological status apart from its actions (Campbell 1992: 10). Instead, the national identity of the US is a social construction created through US foreign policy by defining the 'self' in terms of a demarcation from what is 'foreign'.

Of particular importance for the creation of national identity is the national discourse of danger. During the Cold War, the Soviet threat played a crucial role in producing and reproducing US national identity. Afterwards, Campbell suggested that the US would search for a new external danger that could be used to reproduce US national identity.

Securitization theory posits that threats are constructed and deconstructed through speech acts by dominant actors (usually leaders). Through speech acts 'by definition a problem is a security problem when they declare it to be'. What is of interest in analyzing speech acts is not that they refer to a real object; instead it is the 'utterance itself that is the act: by saying it something is done' that has a reality (Wæver 1997: 221).

Dominant actors through speech acts attempt to convince an audience (usually within a state) that a referent object such as 'terror' is an existential threat. A threat has been constructed when an audience believes that 'if we do not tackle this problem, everything else will be irrelevant (because we will not be here or will not be free to deal with it in our own way)' (Buzan *et al.* 1998: 24).

In securitization theory there are no obvious pre-existing and objective threats to the national interest. But 'by stating that a particular referent object is threatened in its existence, a securitizing actor claims a right to extraordinary measures to ensure the referent object's survival' (Buzan *et al.* 1998: 24). Despite the obvious point that all representations of threat in speech acts will not convince an audience, the theory unfortunately lacks a comprehensive model for why some representations resonate with an audience and others do not (McDonald 2008).

Box 3.4 Tony Blair and threat construction

In the build-up to the Iraq War, Tony Blair and his government attempted to construct a threat, arguing that the UK faced a deadly combination of global terror and tyrannical regimes possessing weapons of mass destruction (WMD). Although the mass protests against the war in March 2003 illustrate that Blair did not fully succeed in convincing his audience, he was able to convince enough members of his own party and the general electorate about a threat from Iraqi WMD to lead the UK into war in Iraq:

> So let me explain the *nature of this threat as I see it*. The threat today is not that of the 1930s. It's not big powers going to war with each other. The ravages which fundamentalist political ideology inflicted on the 20th century are memories. The Cold war is over. Europe is at peace, if not always diplomatically ...
>
> The *threat is chaos*. And there are two begetters of chaos. *Tyrannical regimes with WMD* and *extreme terrorist groups* who profess a perverted and false view of Islam ...
>
> And these two threats have different motives and different origins but they share one basic common view: they detest the freedom, democracy and tolerance that are the hallmarks of our way of life. At the moment, I accept that association between them is loose. But it is hardening. And the *possibility of the two coming together* – of terrorist groups in possession of WMD, even of a so-called dirty radiological bomb is now, in my judgement, *a real and present danger*. (Tony Blair, Speech to the House of Commons, 18 March, 2003; my italics)

How does securitization theory inform our understanding of foreign policy? First, the theory points our attention to the discursive power of leaders and their ability to 'construct' threats to national security through speech acts that have real effects upon state foreign policy.

Second, in a recent expansion of the theory, Buzan and Wæver have taken it to the global level, where they replace domestic dominant actors with great power leaders. For instance, they postulate that US leadership in the last decade has been made possible in part through the construction of a global threat (the global war on terror), enabling cooperation with regimes throughout the world to combat the common threat – regimes such as China, Russia and others with whom the US otherwise has few shared interests (Buzan 2006; Buzan and Wæver 2009). Therefore they argue that a key part to understanding the US foreign policy strategy of the past decade is to investigate the construction and strengthening of security discourses on the global war on terror.

Using state-level constructivist theory to analyze state foreign policy goals

Analysis of national identity and discourses has primarily utilized discourse analysis, where key speeches and other representations of speech acts are probed to detect prevailing discourses. Here it is important to note that if discourse analysis is not carefully structured, this type of analysis can be prone to a form of 'anything goes' where the analyst reads his or her own preconceptions and biases into an analysis of a text. However, it is also important to note that most constructivist approaches to national identity utilize interpretivist methods, where the focus is on using theories as analytical tools for interpretation and understanding instead of explaining and predicting.

For example, Hopf (2002: 25) contends that 'theorizing is a form of interpretation, and it destroys meaning ... For a work on identity, it is absolutely imperative that meanings remain what they mean and do not become what the researcher needs to test a hypothesis'. He then engages in an interpretation that aims at 'illuminating structures' in texts (Hopf 2002: 26). In his book, he identifies prominent discursive formations that underlie Russian identity in 1955 and 1999 through his reading of texts, including daily newspapers, scholarly journals, news magazines, novels and works of non-fiction. Post-structuralists utilize a range of techniques, using critical discourse analysis to uncover what they term the hidden meanings in texts, showing the role of language in relation to ideologies and constructing and restructuring power relations.

Part II
Decision-Making

Part II

Chapter 4

Understanding the Choice Situation

Decision-making is at the heart of what traditionally has been defined as the subdiscipline of FPA (see Snyder *et al.* 2002). However, as is illustrated in the heuristic framework for analysis presented in Figure 4.1, decision-making is but one step of the foreign-policy-making process. In Chapters 2 and 3 I reviewed the theoretical answers to the question of what states want in foreign affairs, while in Chapters 6 to 8 I will investigate theories of how the dynamics of policy-making in three policy areas (security, diplomacy and economic relations) are different.

In this chapter and the next I investigate theories relating to decision-making. The process of foreign policy decision-making can be divided into two analytically distinct phases: (1) the collection and processing of information about the choice situation and (2) the decision-taking stage. In reality, these phases can overlap, with information, for example, being gathered continually throughout the process and goals updated in light of new information. However, in most research the two are treated as two distinct sets of research questions.

Figure 4.2 illustrates two different sets of competing theories of the foreign policy decision-making process. Irrespective of which set of theories is being utilized, we should expect that decision-making is based upon national preferences/interests, however defined by the theory that we are using. The result is a foreign policy action (or non-action), or set of actions. The top half of Figure 4.2 illustrates what is commonly

Figure 4.1 *Foreign policy at Stage Two: decision-making*

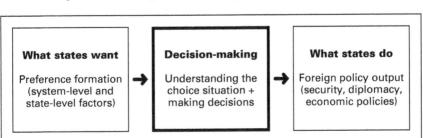

Figure 4.2   *Two different sets of theories of the foreign policy decision-making process*

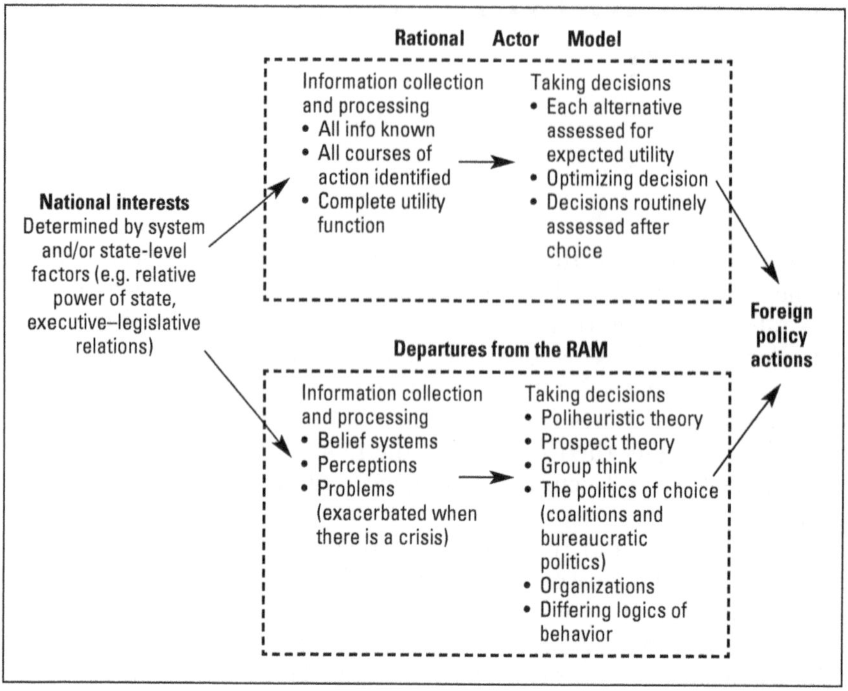

termed the Rational Actor Model (RAM) (Allison and Zelikow 1999). In the RAM, decision-makers have a set of clearly ranked goals that they want to achieve, and they are able to use the available information to determine which choice will maximize the achievement of their goals with the lowest possible amount of risk (Oneal 1988: 601; Cashman 1993: 77–8). In the first phase the RAM predicts that decision-makers:

- Identify the problem.
- Identify and rank goals (a constant and complete utility function establishes the values affected and trade-off between them).
- All relevant available information is gathered.
- All possible courses of action are identified.

In the second phase decision-makers undertake the following:

- Each alternative is assessed on the basis of the utilities and probabilities associated with all possible outcomes (*expected utility*).
- An optimizing decision is made in choosing among alternative courses of action (*utility maximization*).

- The decision is assessed routinely after it has been made, and any relevant alterations in strategy are implemented.

The result of a rational decision-making process is that a foreign policy action or set of actions is chosen that maximizes the expected achievement of goals with the lowest level of risk.

The bottom half of the figure depicts a range of alternative theories that all share in common the argument that the RAM is an unrealistic and oversimplified depiction of real world foreign policy decision-making. The list is by no means exhaustive, but reflects the most widely used theories of different factors that describe deviations or departures from the RAM of decision-making.

The first phase (understanding the choice situation) includes two different cognitive theories. First is a theory about how the belief systems of decision-makers matter. The second theory deals with how the subjective perceptions of decision-makers can systematically diverge from an 'objective' depiction of the choice situation they face. The second phase (taking decisions) details a number of competing theories of foreign policy decision-making, ranging from Poliheuristic theory, in which the RAM plays an integral role, to theories such as bureaucratic politics, where governmental decisions are the product of the 'pushing and hauling' between foreign policy actors, with the outcome far from what we would predict using a RAM.

Naturally, FPA scholars do not argue that factors associated with decision-making fully explain the foreign policy actions of states, nor that only one theoretical factor (such as the role of perceptions) is sufficient to explain fully foreign policy actions. Most of this theorization attempts instead to discover the extent to which the decision-making process matters, often suggesting thereafter that their theory can be incorporated into a broader, multifactor and multilevel model. For example, in the conceptual model Snyder *et al.* (2002) take as their starting point individual decision-makers and how they define the choices that they face. However, they theorize that the *context* of choice is determined by both the external setting (international system level) and state-level factors (such as major institutional patterns) within a state (depicted in Figure 4.2 as the 'national interest').

Theories of decision-making that depart from the RAM are arguably better able to capture the *agency* involved in foreign policy decision-making than more structural theories at the system or state levels. The question of agency versus structure as the determinant of human behavior has been one of the central debates in the history of political theory and sociology. While this is not the time and place to engage in a deeper debate, the key controversy is whether humans as agents have a degree of freedom in their actions (free will) or whether structures such as institutions or norms shape and determine their actions. Most of the theories in this book describe more structural theories, such as social constructivist theories of norms and identities.

With the benefit of hindsight, most foreign policy choices can appear to the analyst as being determined by structural factors. For example, Waltz's analysis of the start of the Cold War sees the Soviet–US rivalry as the inevitable product of a bipolar distribution of power in the international system; in other words more-or-less determined by system-level factors. On the other hand, FPA scholars that have found that the perceptions of decision-makers mattered, with the result that the form of US–Soviet conflict was *not* predetermined by structural factors. As Yergin (1977: 8) states, 'diplomacy *did* matter. There has been too much of a tendency to assume that all that happened was of a single piece, foreordained and determined. But how world leaders perceived their interests and acted on those perceptions counted for a very great deal'. Larson (1985) contends that within the constraints imposed by the international system, the US–Soviet relationship could have varied from a form of gentleman's agreement involving mutual respect for 'spheres of influence' to total war. Due to the beliefs held by key decision-makers, American officials believed the Soviets were ruthlessly aggressive and expansionistic, removing the possibility of establishing a 'limited adversary' relationship. Based upon, but not determined by, these beliefs, US decision-makers chose a confrontational foreign policy with the Soviets.

After describing the RAM, I will present two competing theories relating to the first phase of decision-making (understanding the choice context). In Chapter 5 I will present theories of the next step of the decision-making process (taking decisions).

The Rational Actor Model (RAM)

In the words of Keohane (1986: 167), 'the link between system structure and actor behavior is forged by the rationality assumption, which enables the theorist to predict that leaders will respond to the incentives and constraints imposed by their environments'. Faced with a choice situation, the RAM predicts that a rational actor will choose the foreign policy that maximizes gains with the minimum of cost. In the words of strategic theorist Thomas Shelling, 'you can sit in your armchair and try to predict how people will behave by asking how you would behave if you had your wits about you' (quoted in Allison and Zellikow 1999: 49).

Underpinning any rational actor analysis of foreign policy decisions are the theoretical assumptions adopted about the nature of the international system and the goals of states. A theory that predicts what states want is therefore a critical component of any use of the RAM, as it forms the basis for the assessment of the costs and benefits of different possible choices; the technical term for this is a 'utility function' that describes how much 'utility' a state gains from different outcomes in relation to actor goals. Most scholars use the more realistic term 'expected utility' when analyzing rational choice, as an actor cannot realistically know with 100 per cent certainty whether his or her predictions of gains will actually be realized. Predictions about what a given state would want in a given situation can be derived from either system-level theories such as structural realism (e.g. maintain the relative power position of the state) or state-level theories (e.g. a liberal theory that combines system-level constraints with the impact of societal demands such as public opinion).

The RAM builds upon the assumption that foreign policy actors are *synoptically rational* (also termed 'comprehensive rationality'); an assumption that is central in rational choice theorization. It means that we can treat actors 'as if' they are human computers able to make sense out of enormous amounts of information. Actors have a set of clearly ranked goals that they want to achieve, and they are able to use the available information to determine which choice will result in the maximization of the achievement of their goals with the lowest level of risk. Synoptic rationality does not necessarily mean that actors possess *perfect information* about the capacities of adversaries or the consequences of actions; instead it means, based upon the *available* information, that an actor is able to comprehend the situation and 'game through' the myriad of different options to choose the one that maximizes the attainment of goals.

The RAM also does not mean that just because a decision-making *process* is 'rational' that optimal *outcomes* are reached in relation to goals. However, foreign policy actions taken with the best intentions often have results that were far from what was intended. Choice situations can be where one can only choose between bad and worse options. Additionally, a rational decision-making process does not necessarily mean that the outcome will be beneficial, and a rational process can end up choosing an option that turns out to be bad policy. A case in point was the US intervention in Somalia in late 1992 that was intended to provide security for UN humanitarian assistance, but resulted in the US being dragged into a bloody internecine conflict that ended with a humiliating exit for it after 18 marines were killed in October 1993.

All of the theories about what states want that were described in Chapters 2 and 3 can be coupled with the RAM in order to explain foreign policy decision-making, with certain caveats. Here the RAM can be thought of in terms analogous to the undercarriage and wheels of a car, where the different theories can then be thought of as an engine and drive-train that can be put into the RAM to drive it.

However, these theories disagree about what the most important factors are that create the background for 'rational' choices in foreign policy. For instance, structural realists believe that anarchy and the struggle for power dominate foreign policy choices, whereas liberals direct attention toward patterns of interdependence between states and the conflicting and converging interests that result from them.

Some scholars have questioned whether structural realism is compatible with the RAM model. Waltz himself (1979: 118) contends that 'the theory requires no assumptions of rationality or of constancy of will on the part of all of the actors', suggesting that his theory is perhaps not compatible with a RAM. However, what Waltz is saying is that states face systemic pressures from competition within the anarchical system that shape state goals. While states can freely choose whichever policy they want, in order to avoid relative decline or, even worse, being wiped off the map as a state, states should respond to the pressures in a rational manner by adopting balancing policies. Therefore, we can use a Waltz-inspired analysis of state goals with a RAM. Furthermore, most other systemic realists do assume rational behavior on the part of states (e.g. Grieco 1997; Mearsheimer 2001).

At first glance it might appear to be a misnomer to couple social constructivist theories with a 'rational' actor model that sees actors as utility-maximizing human computers that are able to determine the optimum action based upon a calculation of the costs and benefits of all feasible options. Indeed, as will be discussed in Chapter 5, the RAM of action, where actors calculate costs and benefits, has been termed a 'logic of consequences' by March and Olsen (1998), and they contrast this with a social constructivist 'logic of appropriate action', where decision-making calculations are based more on habitualized norms than utility calculations.

However, if we adopt Wendt's system-level constructivist argument that there are three different 'cultures of anarchy' that can dominate international systems, it is possible to proceed 'as if' rational actors are acting within three different backdrops, with three different potential utility functions for each of the 'cultures'. One way this can be done is to do an analytical 'two-step' (Legro 1996), where the first stage of the analysis uses social constructivism to analyze why one of the three cultures of anarchy is predominant in a given region at a given time. Thereafter, the analysis can proceed 'as if' states rationally act within each of the three different possible cultures. For instance, in a part of the world where a Hobbesian 'war of all against all' culture of anarchy is dominant, the rational choices by states would echo structural realist predictions. In contrast, in more peaceful areas where a Kantian culture of democracy and interdependence exist, the rational choices of states would be based upon very different utility functions. Here rational states would engage in deep cooperation with other states, for example opening their borders to free trade as they do not fear being cheated by the other party, based upon the Kantian culture of anarchy.

The RAM model is relatively easy to use in practice. As an example, Allison and Zelikow 1999: 27) present the following set of research questions that can be used to explain why the Soviet Union placed nuclear missiles in Cuba using structural realist theories as the basis for what states want. They start with a set of assumptions: X is the action of the state, the state is a unified actor with a coherent utility function, the state acts in relation to threats and opportunities, and the state's actions maximize expected utility. Based upon these assumptions, the analyst would then ask:

1. What threats and opportunities arise for the actor (e.g. what is the balance of strategic nuclear forces in 1962)?
2. Who is the actor (e.g. the Soviet Union or its leader in 1962, Nikita Khrushchev)?
3. What is the utility function (e.g. survival, maximization of power, minimization of threat, etc.)?
4. In order to maximize the actor's objectives in the specified conditions, what is the best choice (e.g. Soviet installation of nuclear armed missiles in Cuba)?

The analyst must delineate the external constraints for state choice. What are the goals of the state in the issue? What are the system-level and state-level constraints and pressures that form the context for choice? What are the different options? And, in light of the goals, what is the expected utility of different options?

Cognitive theories: a more realistic understanding of the collection and processing of information

In contrast to most IR theorization, where decision-makers are seen as being *synoptically rational*, cognitive approaches build upon the assumption that there are natural limitations upon the cognitive abilities of human actors to perceive correctly the choice situation they face. System-level theories such as neoliberal institutionalism build upon the assumption that foreign policy actors are synoptically rational; an assumption that is central in rational choice theorization. Cognitive theorists such as Steinbruner (2002: 13) contend that 'the mind of man, for all its marvels, is a limited instrument'. Cognitive theorists argue that real world foreign policy decisions are made in very complex choice environments where actors face many challenges, of which three are most important.

First, the understanding that decision-makers have of the situation they face is often murky. Given the immense complexity of both the international and domestic political environments facing them, even with the best intelligence gathering and processing capabilities there are natural limits upon the ability of decision-makers to make sense of the choice situation facing them. Additionally, decision-makers from two different countries can perceive the same foreign policy action in very different ways based upon their perceptions of their own and their opponent's goals. For instance, while US decision-makers perceived the enlargement of NATO to include former Soviet allies in Central and Eastern Europe as a non-threatening action aimed at spreading a zone of peace and democracy in Europe, Russian decision-makers saw the action as inherently hostile, aimed at exploiting Russian weakness to create an expansion of the US zone of influence in Europe. This can be exacerbated by the tendency of the human mind to see what it wants to see based upon its goals.

Second, the goals of decision-makers are often far from the synoptically rational ideal of clearly rank-ordered preferences. Due to complexity, goals can also be quite ambiguous, and it can be very difficult to formulate a single criteria for 'success' by which to choose the alternative course of action that is expected to fulfill the criteria best. Further, goals can even conflict with each other in instances where, for instance, domestic goals conflict with the foreign policy goals of a state. During the Vietnam War, to maintain the momentum of his domestic political agenda in Congress, President Johnson needed to avoid 'failure'. This led him down an increasingly counter-productive path that involved incremental escalations of the war to stave off a defeat.

Finally, as students of decision-making processes have conclusively shown, taking a decision in the real world is not just a process where goals and actions are mechanically matched. For example, the psychological need for belonging can produce artificial consensus in small group decision-making settings, resulting in key options not being discussed and suboptimal decisions being taken (see pp. 125–32).

Cognitive theories build on the more realistic assumption that actors are only *boundedly rational*, an idea that was developed by Herbert Simon (1997). This term refers to the fact that rationality has natural 'bounds' created by cognitive limitations. Bounded rationality does not mean that actors are irrational or unintelligent. Simon argued that decision-makers should be seen as intelligent, goal-seeking individuals, but that there also exist natural cognitive limitations that prevent them from undertaking a fully synoptic, utility-maximizing search for the perfect coupling of a problem with an optimal solution.

In response, cognitive theorists adopt a thicker, more realistic conception of actor rationality that posits that ambiguity and uncertainty are two factors that define complex choice situations in which actors face a mesmerizing amount of information that needs to be transformed into operational knowledge. Further, given this complexity, actors are unable to engage in a computer-like matching of all potential courses of action with utility payoffs. Instead, actor behavior tends to be 'satisfying', not utility-maximizing, with actors seeking to minimize the costs of decision-making by choosing policies that 'satisfy' basic goals instead of maximizing utility. This means that actors will only calculate costs and benefits for a handful of the most promising options, and that these calculations will not be nearly as thorough as assumed in the RAM.

The two different sets of cognitive psychological theories are elaborated in the following, each of which builds upon the assumption of bounded rationality. The first deals with how *belief systems* and, in particular, the so-called 'operational codes' of decision-makers matter for the choices decision-makers take. The second deals with how our *perceptions* of the world can diverge from objective 'reality' in four systematic and detectable patterns. I will also introduce the theoretical debate about how decision-making during crises potentially differs from normal decision-making situations, with stress potentially producing even less rational decision-making processes.

The content of decision-maker beliefs: the 'operational codes' of leaders

The belief systems of decision-makers can impact upon how they perceive the world, thereby also affecting what choices they take. Scholarship on operational codes is in essence the study of how leaders matter. Here we are dealing with the idea that who leads can matter in certain circumstances, instead of the widespread view within IR theorization that leaders mechanically respond to the incentives and constraints of the environment. For instance, an operational code theorist would contend that in the counterfactual situation where Al Gore had been elected US president in 2000, the US reaction to an event like 9/11 would have been different due to his different belief system. While a liberal, state-level analysis would contend that any hypothesized differences would be due to factors such as which constituencies the two leaders represent (Gore = Democrat, Bush = Republican), or the partisan composition of Congress, a cognitive, operational code theorist would posit that the different belief systems of the two leaders also mattered. In particular, Bush's beliefs of a permanent state of conflict and the efficacy of force versus Gore's emphasis on the possibilities for peaceful relations and negotiation would be expected to matter for how they reacted to the 9/11 attacks.

Operational code research attempts to codify how the world views of leaders affect how they perceive and react toward the world, building upon the insight that individuals do not necessarily respond to the same stimuli in a similar manner. Belief systems are most important when there is an individual person who is acting as the predominant leader of the state in a particular issue, often when the issue is perceived to be critical to the survival and well-being of the regime (Hermann, Preston, Korany and Shaw, 2001).

Leaders are seen as possessing a more-or-less coherent set of beliefs about the nature of political life, although there is some disagreement amongst scholars on the issue of whether leaders only possess one overall belief system, or whether they can hold different systems that can exist in different circumstances and for different issues (see pp. 108–9). However, all scholars agree that relatively stable belief systems result in the decision-maker becoming less responsive to incoming information that is not compatible with the world view, even manipulating it to fit with existing images or ignoring it as the basis for decisions (Walker *et al.* 1999: 612).

Taking the work of Nathan Leites as his starting point, Alexander George systematized the theory of operational codes into a set of two core beliefs held by leaders about the nature of the world, each comprising five different elements. 'Philosophical beliefs' were theorized to help the leader define a specific choice situation, whereas 'instrumental beliefs' related to what type of action was likely for a specific leader (George, 1969). The ten elements are depicted in Box 4.1.

The picture of interstate relations as being fundamentally conflictual or harmonious is a key element of a leader's operational code (element A1, Box 4.1). If one views one's opponents as inherently hostile, this affects how one deals with them. For example, the Bush administration's characterization of Iran, Iraq and North Korea as being part of an 'axis of evil' is an illustration of how philosophical beliefs matter, in that Bush viewed these states as being thoroughly hostile, making any form of reconciliation or negotiation impossible. Even seemingly conciliatory actions from these states would be perceived as part of a hostile hidden agenda.

Elements A2 to A5 link with the instrumental beliefs and the actions that a leader is predisposed to take. If a leader views the world as relatively predictable and controllable, he or she will tend to adopt more comprehensive strategies. On the other hand, if a leader believes that there is a high degree of 'chance' in world affairs and events are unpredictable, he or she will tend to adopt more limited and flexible strategies aimed at more restricted goals.

These ten components of the operational code have been further refined into a typology of four clusters of components along two different dimensions: (1) whether conflict is permanent or temporary and (2) the sources of conflict (Walker 1995) (see Table 4.1). The first of the four clusters is a 'need for power' belief system, where the belief

---

Box 4.1   The ten elements of George's operational code

A.   *The philosophical content of an operational code*

A1.   What is the 'essential' nature of political life? Is it primarily harmonious or conflictual? What is the fundamental character of one's political opponents?

A2.   How optimistic is the actor about the prospects of realizing his or her fundamental political values and aspirations?

A3.   Is the political future predictable or unpredictable?

A4.   How much 'control' can one have over historical developments?

A5.   What is the role of 'chance' in human affairs?

B.   *The instrumental beliefs in an operational code*

B1.   What is the best approach for selecting goals or objectives for political action? Does the leader have one single objective or a set of graduated objectives? Does the leader focus upon what is desirable or merely what is feasible to achieve?

B2.   How are the goals of action pursued most effectively?

B3.   How are the risks of political action calculated, controlled and accepted?

B4.   What is the best 'timing' of action to advance one's interests?

B5.   What is the utility and role of different means for advancing one's interests (rewards, promises, support, opposition, threats and punishments)?

Source: Adapted from George (1969).

---

that conflict is permanent is married to the belief that leaders have limited control over developments. The 'need for power' belief system results in leaders favoring only limited goals with moderate means. In contrast, the 'need for affiliation' belief system cluster is the result of beliefs that conflict is temporary with the source of conflict being miscalculation and poor communication. In this belief system, control over events is possible, resulting in a leader being optimistic about the potential for negotiation and compromise on the basis of shared interests. The 'need for achievement and affiliation' belief system incorporates a pessimism about the nature of the international system (anarchy), resulting in a more wary outlook on world affairs. Finally, the 'need for power and achievement' belief system cluster couples the belief that control over events is possible (miscalculation being a major source of conflict) with a belief that opponents are rational and deterrable, resulting in a more vigorous outlook on world affairs.

Most theorists agree that the more coherent a belief system that a decision-maker possesses, the stronger impacts it has upon how they

Table 4.1 *Cognitive and motivational contents of Walker's operational code typology*

Need for power
- Conflict is permanent
- Responses to conciliation or firmness are uncertain
- Predictability is limited, as is control over developments
- Seek limited goals flexibly with moderate means
- Use military force if opponent and circumstances require it, but only as final resource

(Example: President Truman)

Need for power and achievement
- Conflict is temporary
- Miscalculation and appeasement are major causes of war
- Opponents are rational and deterrable
- Optimism warranted regarding realization of goals
- Future is predictable and control over events possible
- Seek optimum goals vigorously within comprehensive framework
- Control risk by limiting means, not ends

(Example: President Johnson)

Need for affiliation
- Conflict is temporary
- Miscalculation and miscommunication are major causes of war ('conflict spirals')
- Opponents tend to respond in kind to conciliation and firmness
- Optimism warranted, with future relatively predictable and control possible
- Establish goals within framework, emphasizing shared interests
- Pursue broadly international goals incrementally with flexible strategies that control risks of escalation
- Emphasize resources that establish climate for negotiation and compromise and avoid early use of force

(Example: President Eisenhower)

Need for achievement and affiliation
- Conflict is temporary
- Source of conflict is anarchical state system
- Opponents vary in nature, goals and responses to conciliation and firmness
- Pessimistic about goals unless state system is changed, as predictability and control over historical development is low under anarchy
- Establish optimal goals vigorously within comprehensive framework.
- Pursue shared goals, but control risks by limiting means, not ends
- Act quickly when conciliation opportunities arise and delay escalation when possible

(Example: President Kennedy)

Source: Based on Walker (1995: 701).

perceive the world and the choices that are available to them (Walker 2003: 252). The importance of belief systems varies both according to the type of decision-maker involved and the strength of the external constraints under which a leader is operating.

Steinbruner (2002) develops a theory about how the coherence of belief systems varies across different types of actors. First, he argues that lower-level bureaucrats often do not possess coherent belief systems. Instead they exhibit what he terms 'grooved thinking', where they engage in simple decision-making based upon standardized routines. Second, expert mid-level officials have 'abstract and extensive belief patterns'. This enables them to engage in 'theoretical thinking', but the possession of a strongly internally consistent and stable system of beliefs also often results in strong cognitive effects of the belief system, where they discount new information that is inconsistent with pre-existing beliefs. Finally, wedged between a weak and strong impact of belief systems are the views held by high-level officials, who exhibit 'uncommitted thinking' due to the cross-pressures faced by such generalists. He posits that they are 'beset with uncertainty and sitting at the intersection of a number of information channels, [and] will tend to at different times to adopt *different* belief patterns for the same decision problem' (Steinbruner 2002: 129).

The strength of external constraints also matters. For instance, after the Cold War, the strength of external structural constraints upon the US was reduced, increasing the importance of the belief systems possessed by leaders (Jervis 1994; Walker *et al.* 1999). Kupchan (1994) has argued that the belief systems of leaders matter most when states are highly vulnerable, defined as a situation where the state's resources are not sufficient to deal with security and domestic political constraints, or the impact of external events makes it difficult to adjust old beliefs to new realities. High vulnerability therefore creates a propensity for extremist policies (too much cooperation or competition in relation to the strategic situation) due to the strong impact of belief systems.

Another useful intervening variable between external constraints and the impact of belief systems is the degree to which a leader respects external constraints or not (Hermann, Preston, Korany and Shaw, 2001; Dyson 2007). Dyson uses this distinction to explain why Tony Blair led the UK into the 2003 Iraq War despite strong domestic opposition (constraint challenging), whereas Prime Minister Harold Wilson chose not to take the UK into the Vietnam War (respected domestic constraints).

The degree to which a leader respects external constraints can be investigated by analyzing how sensitive a leader is to contextual information. If a leader is contextually responsive, their behavior will be more pragmatic and situationally driven, making factors such as public opinion or the views of the legislature more important (Hermann, Preston, Korany and Shaw, 2001). However, if the leader is goal-driven and does not respect constraints, the belief system will be more important for understanding how the leader understands the choice situation facing him or her, and what likely actions will be chosen.

Table 4.2 illustrates the core argument of the theory, alongside a set of questions that can be asked in a case study. An example of operational code research is also shown. Using operational code theory is

Table 4.2   *Operational code theory*

What is being explained?	The belief systems of decision-makers and how they affect the way they perceive the world and the choices they make
Type of theory	Explanatory theory, although in practice most applications tend to use the theory in a more interpretative/analytical fashion
Core argument	Leaders possess a coherent set of beliefs about the nature of political life and instrumental beliefs about the efficacy of different types of actions. Taken together, these beliefs form the 'operational code' of leaders and can be distinguished into four different systems: 1. Need for power 2. Need for power and achievement 3. Need for affiliation 4. Need for achievement and affiliation
Hypotheses	In order to detect the degree to which operational codes mattered, we can ask the following questions: 1. How do leaders react to political constraints in their environment: do they respect or challenge such constraints? 2. How open are leaders to incoming information: do they selectively use information or are they open to information directing their response? 3. What motivates leaders to take action: are they driven by an internal focus of attention or by responses from salient constituents? (Hermann, Preston, Korany and Shaw, 2001: 89–90) In order to evaluate the content of a leader's belief system, ask the ten questions posed by George
Example (Walker 1995)	President Woodrow Wilson's operational code Walker assesses Wilson's operational code for three decision-making episodes (the Mexican Revolution, World War I and the Versailles Treaty) by coding key speeches for power, achievement and affiliation imagery. He finds quantitative evidence that the president framed his actions with need-for-power motivational imagery that was consistent with the need for power operational code. However, in the first two cases, the code did not fully dominate the president's decision-making process 'so as to exclude totally the mediation of thought' (RAM). In contrast, in the Versailles case, the code has more than an 'intermittent' effect, producing a flawed decision-making process, resulting in intransigent behavior that led to a self-defeating outcome

however often difficult in practice, as it involves measuring the belief systems of individual leaders. Scholars have attempted to get 'inside' the heads of leaders using different types of sources. Some scholars have used archive documents that detail the internal deliberation amongst decision-makers, such as cabinet briefs and planning documents

(Kupchan 1994). Others have used public speeches, coding certain key phrases to uncover what ideal type of belief system best reflects that of a specific leader. For instance, Walker *et al.* (1999) measured the belief systems of Presidents Bush Sr. and Bill Clinton by coding key phrases that illustrated how the leader perceived the nature of the political environment and other elements of his operational codes.

Patterns of perception and misperception

The second set of theories relates to how the human mind actually perceives and makes sense of the world. Drawing on advances in cognitive psychology, FPA scholars have concentrated upon four common sources of misperceptions that can affect the level of rationality of decision-making processes (Rosati 2000). Misperception can be defined as 'a discrepancy between the psychological environment of the decision makers and the operational environment of the "real world"' (Levy 1983: 79).

First, the human mind has a tendency to *categorize and stereotype*, creating self-images and images of opponents that do not necessarily reflect objective reality. Self-images tend to be benevolent and positive, whereas those of opponents tend to be negative. Whereas they are often originally formed due to social-psychological reasons (need for self-esteem and/or to bolster the cohesiveness of a group), once they are formed they can be very resistant to change, forming a cognitive filter upon perceptions of oneself and one's opponents. Therefore, actors will reject or discount new information such as conciliatory actions that are inconsistent with the 'inherent bad faith' view of one's opponent (Holsti 1967). The prison of negative images of one's opponent can partially explain why Israeli and Palestinian leaders have been unable to negotiate a peace agreement that would resolve their conflict, as actions that were intended to be conciliatory and friendly can be perceived as non-friendly: that the action is a hostile action hidden behind a false smile.

The second factor is the tendency to *simplify causal inferences*. In the words of Jervis (1976: 319), 'people want to be able to explain as much as possible of what goes on around them. To admit that a phenomenon cannot be explained, or at least cannot be explained without adding numerous and complex exceptions to our beliefs, is both psychologically uncomfortable and intellectually unsatisfying'. Therefore, the human mind tends to see the actions of others as intentional and planned, whereas there is a tendency to overemphasize the situational causes of one's own behavior. Furthermore, actors tend to overemphasize or underemphasize their role in others' policies. 'When the other behaves in accord with the actor's desires, he will overestimate the degree to which his policies are responsible for the outcome … When

---

Box 4.2 Intentionality and the Cuban Missile crisis

An example of attributing intention when there was none can been seen during the height of the Cuban Missile Crisis, where a U-2 aircraft based in Alaska undertaking a routine mission accidentally strayed into Soviet airspace. The aircraft was luckily able to return to US airspace without incident. However, despite the mission being routine and planned before the crisis, the Soviet leadership perceived this accident to be a planned US provocation.

Source: Allison and Zelikow (1999: 240).

---

the other's behavior is undesired, the actor is likely to see it as derived from internal sources rather than as being a response to his own actions' (Jervis 1976: 343).

Third, to simplify reality decision-makers tend to use *historical analogies* to make sense of the massive amount of information they face in any choice situation, enabling them to make inferences about the nature of the problems facing them, the stakes of the problem and the dangers and prospects of alternative strategies (Khong 1992: 252). Khong describes historical analogous reasoning as: 'event A resembles event B in having characteristic X; A also has characteristic Y; therefore it is inferred that B also has characteristic Y' (Khong 1992: 7). For instance, when Saddam Hussein invaded Kuwait in 1990, President Bush reasoned by analogy that the situation was analogous to the situation prior to World War II (Yetiv 2004). In the Munich analogy, the UK Prime Minister Chamberlain accepted Hitler's annexation of parts of Czechoslovakia (conciliation is characteristic X). However, this conciliatory policy did not stop Hitler's aggression – and perhaps even emboldened him. Within a year Hitler had invaded Poland, starting World War II (further aggression is characteristic Y). Applying this analogy to Saddam Hussein's invasion of Kuwait, if the US decided to accept the invasion (conciliation – characteristic X), then the resultant action by Hussein would be expected to be the same as Hitler's, with further aggression and expansion against neighboring states like Saudi Arabia (further aggression – Y).

As historical analogies shape the content of the inferences that decision-makers take regarding the problems they confront and the efficacy of potential solutions, they become schemas that exert a causal impact upon foreign policy decisions, making certain options more attractive and others less so (Khong 1992: 252). These schemas are particularly influential during the process of the selection and rejection of particular policy options. The problem with historical analogies is that event A never completely resembles event B, and the 'lessons' of history can

---

Box 4.3   Neoclassical realism and perception theories

In the real world, systemic pressures are rarely clear – at least without the benefit of hindsight. Neoclassical realists therefore draw on cognitive arguments when they attempt to analyze how policy-makers actually understood the choice situations that they faced. A classic example of a misperception of the systemic pressures facing the US is the Kennedy/Johnson administrations' understanding of the emerging crisis in southern Vietnam in the early 1960s (Jervis 1976). Instead of recognizing that the insurgency against the US-backed Vietnamese government was both an indigenous struggle against an unpopular and increasingly brutal regime and a post-colonial movement aiming at achieving national unification, the Kennedy and Johnson administrations believed the insurgency was part of a push by the Soviet-led Communist bloc for global domination. In the case of South Vietnam, a 'rational' analysis would suggest that there were few systemic pressures pushing the US to engage in the country. The key national interests of the US in the Cold War were instead in securing existing bastions in strategically important areas such as Berlin, Japan and South Korea. Regarding South East Asia, a more rational analysis would suggest that the US should stop supporting South Vietnam, which was peripheral to US national interests, and instead bolster more reliable and stable anti-communist bastions in the region, such as Thailand.

Neoclassical realists analyze how policy-makers understand choice situations by doing historical case studies, often based upon research in governmental archives, where they attempt to reconstruct this cognitive picture using the internal information that was available to decision-makers at the time. Wohlforth (1994/95) for instance explores the perceptions of power amongst Soviet decision-makers and how they changed in the last years of the Cold War. He finds that when Soviet analysts in the early 1980s replaced 'old brute indicators' of power with more contemporary ones, such as high technology, Soviet elites were forced to reassess their relative power *vis-à-vis* the US, resulting in the decision to adopt far-reaching reforms that eventually led to the collapse of the Soviet Union.

---

be (and often are) misapplied. Excessive reliance on historical analogies results in a misperception of event B and predisposes decision-makers to choose inappropriate actions. In other words, 'the tyranny of the past upon imagination' (Jervis 1976: 217).

Finally, actors tend to ignore information and avoid situations that produce *dissonance* with existing beliefs and images. Actors have a strong *confirmation bias* in processing information, focusing on the information that corresponds with preconceived world views and that

Table 4.3 *Theories of perception and misperception*

What is being explained?	How human cognition affects how decision-makers perceive their operational environment
Type of theory	Explanatory theory
Core argument	There are four sources of misperception: 1. The tendency to categorize and stereotype 2. The tendency to simplify causal inferences 3. The tendency to use historical analogies to understand new situations 4. The tendency to ignore information and avoid situations that produce dissonance with existing beliefs and images
Hypotheses	As an example of how hypotheses can be formulated, the following set of questions could be used to test the degree to which historical analogy X affects how they define situation Y: 1. How will X define situation Y? 2. What might X say about the stakes in situation Y? 3. Does X provide an implicit prescription about what to do concerning Y? 4. What does X say about the chances of success? 5. The morality? 6. And the risks of the prescription or other alternatives to deal with Y? (Khong 1992)
Example (Khong 1992)	The use of the Munich analogy in the Vietnam Decisions of 1965 Khong uses process tracing methods to show that the Munich analogy was on the minds of central decision-makers and that it was used at important junctures of the policy process. Khong uses the congruence procedure to show that the lessons of Munich were consistent with the options chosen in Vietnam. As applied to the diagnoses of Vietnam, the Munich historical analogy suggests that: 1. The situation was defined in terms of aggression by a hostile power, who if not stopped will invade further countries like dominoes falling 2. The stakes were vital. The domino theory that is part of the Munich analogy suggest that, if not stopped, Communist aggression will result in the US loss of Asia 3. The analogy suggested that aggression should be firmly met with US intervention 4. And met with a forceful demonstration of US resolve: Hanoi would back down 5. Appeasement of the Communists was just as shameful and unwise as Chamberlain appeasing Hitler Taken together, use of the analogy makes forceful intervention by the US more likely

are consistent with prior actions taken, while ignoring inconsistent information (Jervis 1976: 117). Regarding consistency with existing beliefs, information is processed in accordance with pre-existing images, and decision-makers often see only what they expect to be there.

After action is taken, people 'seek to believe that the reasons for acting or deciding as they did were overwhelming. The person will then rearrange his beliefs so that they provide increased support for his actions. Knowledge of the advantages of rejected courses of action and costs of the chosen one will be a source of uncomfortable dissonance that he will try to reduce. To do this he will alter his earlier opinions, seeing more drawbacks and fewer advantages in the policies he rejected and more good points and fewer bad ones in the policy he adopted' (Jervis 1976: 384).

The confirmation bias and rejection of dissonance makes it not surprising that people are rarely convinced in arguments, despite new information being presented. Jervis offers the example that

> the debate about the nature of Soviet intentions went on throughout the cold war, with few people being converted and fewer being swayed by intelligence or compelling analysis. Without going so far as to say that everyone is born either a little hawk or a little dove ... on the broadest issues of the nature and intentions of other countries and the existence and characteristics of broad historical trends, people's beliefs are determined more by their general worldviews, predispositions, and ideologies than they are by the sort of specific evidence that can be pieced together by intelligence. (Jervis 2010: 170)

Table 4.3 illustrates the core argument of the theory of perceptions and misperceptions, illustrated using the historical analogies part of the theory.

Crisis decision-making: does a crisis increase the importance of operational codes and perceptions?

A crisis can be defined as an unexpected event in which there is a threat to high priority goals of the state and where there is a short time frame available for a response (Hermann 1972). Brecher (1972) contends that another criterion for a crisis should be that there is a high probability of war. In a crisis situation, high-level decision-makers become more important as the size of the decision-making group decreases to only the most central advisors, making cognitive theories potentially more relevant as individual leaders matter more.

During a crisis individual decision-makers can be prone to experience high levels of stress, with the result that 'cognitive processes become more rigid; [there is] less tolerance for uncertainty, insensitivity to alternative points of view, and reliance on operational codes and established cognitive sets ... increases' (Oneal 1988: 613). In other words, with the onset of crisis, the impact of the cognitive distortions described above increases, at least in theory.

However, empirical evidence on the impact of stress upon decision-making suggests that, while there are numerous examples of cognitive performance declining as stress increases, there are at least as many examples that suggest that the high stakes involved in major crises might actually provoke leaders to become more vigilant and expend more cognitive resources, with the result that they end up more than compensating for the adverse impacts of stress (Oneal 1988; Shafer and Crichlow 2002). For example, this was arguably the case during the Cuban Missile Crisis, where the stakes involved (potential world annihilation) and the lessons of the faulty decision-making process during the early Bay of Pigs debacle resulted in a conscious decision by President Kennedy to create as rational a decision-making process as possible.

Chapter 5

Making Choices

When decision-makers face a range of options, how are foreign policy decisions actually taken? In the RAM, the expected utility of all possible alternatives are assessed thoroughly, with the option chosen being the one that maximizes utility for the state. The RAM provides a simplified model of decision-making that underlies much of IR and FPA theorization.

However, the RAM is seldom an empirically accurate model of how foreign policy decisions are taken in the real world. States are rarely unitary actors with a single national interest that forms the basis for the assessment of utility; instead there are often conflicting goals held by various political and bureaucratic actors. The RAM also assumes that all possible alternative courses of action are assessed. While gaming through hypothetical scenarios and potential courses of action can be done by internal think tanks of foreign ministries far in advance, in the heat of battle the best laid plans become quickly outdated. In most important foreign policy choice situations there are time pressures that limit the search and assessment of possible courses of action, with the result that usually only a handful of options are even considered. And even if decision-makers have the luxury of having a plethora of potential courses of action, can we expect that they are able to rank each option for its expected utility, evaluating both the utility of each option and the probability of success? Finally, even if they were able to make the utility assessment that is assumed by the RAM, can we then expect that they make an optimizing decision when faced with time constraints and complexity? Or more realistically, do foreign policy actors choose the option that is perceived to be 'good enough', satisfying the core objectives of a policy like ensuring political survival of the regime?

In this chapter I investigate theories that depart from the RAM by adopting more 'realistic' assumptions about the choice process. These include questioning whether (1) we can assume that states do have a single national interest, (2) governments undertake a fully synoptic assessment of the utility of each option and (3) whether utility maximization realistically models how actors choose between options in the real world.

The first theories reviewed build on the RAM, whereas the theories in the later part of the chapter mark significant departures from it. The chapter starts with Poliheuristic theory, which is a two-step theory that contends that decision-makers undertake a rough first cut where they eliminate with little consideration options that do not fulfill certain key objectives. This is followed by a more synoptic, RAM-like evaluation and choice between the remaining options.

Prospect theory is a cognitive psychological theory that departs from the RAM by contending that decision-makers evaluate gains and losses differently. The idea is that decision-makers attach more weight to losses than prospective gains and will choose riskier options with lower levels of expected success when in the domain of losses than when in gains. For example, the US continued to follow an ever more risky failed policy in Vietnam in order to avoid losing long after a RAM would suggest that the US would change strategy.

I also investigate two theories that look at how foreign policy decisions are affected by politics and organizations. Formulated by Allison in his 1971 classic *Essence of Decision* as model II (organizational politics) and model III (bureaucratic/governmental politics), these two theoretical models have been extensively modified and updated by Allison and many other scholars (Allison, 1971; Rosati 1981; Bendor and Hammond 1992; Allison and Zelikow 1999; Preston and t'Hart 1999; Michaud 2002; Mitchell and Massoud 2009). Theories of bureaucratic and governmental politics are first presented, illustrating how the 'pulling and hauling' between different governmental actors can affect which foreign policy actions are chosen. Here, foreign policy actions are not the product of careful evaluation, and the option chosen does not necessarily maximize state utility as in the RAM; instead actions are political resultants, the product of battles between different executive actors (politicians and bureaucratic actors).

Model II, the organizational model, suggests in contrast that foreign policy choice is affected by what actions are possible in terms of organizational implementation. A country with a strong military with power projection capabilities but with an atrophied diplomatic corps will tend to choose militarized foreign policy actions, and vice versa.

Finally, mainstream social constructivist theories mark an even more dramatic departure from the expectations of the RAM. Social constructivists contend that in decision-making situations where there are highly embedded norms, actor decisions do not follow the RAM but instead are dominated by what is termed a 'logic of appropriate action'. Instead of the instrumental, cost–benefit rationality of the RAM, in the logic of appropriate action, actors comply with norms that correspond to their identities, choosing to comply because it 'feels right'. At an even deeper level of departure from the conscious and calculating RAM is the theory of a logic of habit, where decisions are not made consciously; instead much action taken by actors is more-or-less automatic and habitual.

Cognitive and social-psychological theories of decision-making

Poliheuristic theory

Unsatisfied with the heroic assumptions made in the RAM, Alex Mintz and a number of other FPA scholars have formulated an integrative, two-step theory that attempts to improve the RAM by modeling more realistically how actual foreign policy decisions are taken (Mintz 1993, 2004; Mintz and Geva 1997; Dacey and Carlson 2004). The theory attempts to build bridges between the RAM and cognitive approaches by describing decision-making as involving two steps: a first step where cognitive theories are used to describe the non-compensatory and non-holistic search for options, followed by a second RAM step where a utility maximizing choice is made between the remaining options. The term 'poliheuristic' is composed of the 'roots poly (many) and heuristic (shortcuts), which alludes to the cognitive mechanisms used by decision makers to simplify complex foreign policy decisions' (Mintz *et al.* 1997: 554).

The first stage of decision-making can be thought of as a screening process, where the set of possible options is reduced into a manageable number using a series of cognitive shortcuts. Whereas the RAM assumes that all possible options are carefully assessed, Poliheuristic theory suggests that politically unviable options are eliminated out of hand. The first stage can be termed a non-compensatory, non-holistic search. 'Non-compensation' means for example that economic benefits of an option cannot compensate for political losses. There is therefore no substitution or trade-off effect between different utility dimensions (political, economic, etc.) as assumed by the RAM. For example, options that would result in certain political defeat in the next election are (usually) not even seriously considered by decision-makers. The first stage is also non-holistic, with the search for options stopping when a handful of acceptable alternatives survives scrutiny on the key criteria (Mintz and Geva 1997). Here actors are assumed to engage in satisfying instead of maximizing behavior, settling for a handful of viable options.

The criteria for choosing which options survive the first cut is based upon domestic politics, where the domestic political audience costs of foreign policy actions are central. The political survival of leaders is theorized to be the key criteria, defined as expectations that a foreign policy action will result in a significant drop in popularity that would dramatically increase the prospects of electoral defeat or that would, for example, be expected to result in the collapse of a coalition government (Mintz 2004: 9).

After an acceptable number of options are found using these cognitive shortcuts, decision-making is then dominated by a careful, utility

Table 5.1   *Poliheuristic theory*

What is being explained?	How states make decisions
Type of theory	Explanatory theory
Core argument	Decision-making is a two-stage process:
	1. A non-compensatory, non-holistic search that eliminates options that are threats to the leader's political survival 2. A RAM choice between the remaining options
Hypotheses	1. During the first stage of decision-making, leaders tend to avert political loss by using the non-compensatory rule with an emphasis on the political dimension 2. During the second stage, leaders tend to make the final choice among the remaining options by using the utility-maximizing principle along a more diverse set of dimensions (political, military, economic, diplomatic) (James and Zhang 2005: 35)
Example	Chinese foreign policy decision-making during crises
(James and Zang, 2005)	In a comparative analysis of Chinese foreign policy decision-making in crises, James and Zhang test the two hypotheses of Poliheuristic theory
	Data Coding using the dataset of the International Crisis Behavior project for nine crises involving China (Korean Wars I, II, III; Taiwan Strait I, II, IV; China/India Border II; Ussuri River; the Sino–Vietnam War)
	Findings Decision-makers used the political dimension to eliminate options that have strong unwanted domestic political costs early in the decision-making process (Hypothesis 1 found support)
	In contrast, the results were mixed for Hypothesis 2, with some cases such as the Korean War II (1950–51) and the Taiwan Strait crisis II (1958) and IV (1995–96) exhibiting behavior where options were chosen based upon a two-stage assessment, where the second stage involved considering all four dimensions, whereas other cases did not exhibit two-stage behavior, with political considerations dominating throughout the decision-making process

maximizing decision, where the option that is chosen maximizes the utility benefits to the leader while minimizing risks. This is based upon an assessment of the utility of options along four dimensions: political, military, economic and diplomatic (Mintz 1993, 2004). The political dimension is defined as considerations about the domestic political consequences that particular outcomes are expected to have for political leaders. The military dimension involves implications related to the strength and weakness of the military, for example for the condition of military equipment and personnel. The economic dimension relates to expected effects of policies on the national economy. The diplomatic dimension relates to the external political consequences that actions are expected to have.

There have been numerous analyses using Poliheuristic theory to investigate actual decision-making, investigating numerous types of decisions ranging from the use or non-use of force, to war termination and conflict resolution, to negotiations, to crisis decision-making (see Mintz 2004). Most uses of Poliheuristic theory have been single case studies, although there do exist a handful of comparative studies. An example of the use of Poliheuristic theory by James and Zhang (2005) is illustrated in Table 5.1. In a comparative study of Chinese foreign policy decision-making during nine crises, they find strong support for the first stage of decision-making, whereas they find mixed support for a RAM in the second stage. They found that political considerations dominated throughout the decision-making process in some of the cases. However, as James and Zhang point out, crisis decision-making can be thought of as a 'least likely' case for Poliheuristic theory, given that the high stakes involved would suggest that decision-makers would have incentives to mobilize all of the necessary resources to engage in a rational decision-making process. Therefore, finding evidence supporting a two-stage process in more than half of these least-likely cases suggests relatively strong support for Poliheuristic theory as a model of foreign policy decision-making.

Prospect theory: different evaluations of gains and losses

Prospect theory marks a stronger departure from the RAM than Poliheuristic theory. In Poliheuristic theory the RAM is still central in the second stage where decision-makers choose between the options that passed a certain threshold on the key political criteria. In contrast, Prospect theory is a psychological theory that suggests that the human mind does not function totally 'rationally', with the argument being that humans evaluate the utility of gains differently than losses (Kahneman and Tversky 1979; Jervis 1989b; Levy 1992a, 1992b).

Based on experimental studies, Kahneman and Tversky suggested that instead of the RAM's theory that actors evaluate utility based on net asset levels, the human mind evaluates gains and losses based upon deviations from a reference point, usually the status quo (Kahneman and Tversky 1979). In evaluating the utility of gains and losses, they contend that the human mind tends to give more weight to losses than comparable gains. Often it is the loss itself that is more important than the actual magnitude of the loss.

In connection with evaluating gains and losses differently, actors tend to be more risk-averse with respect to gains, whereas they are more risk-acceptant with respect to losses. An everyday example is poker players who take large risks when trying to win back their losses, whereas when they have a large pile of winnings in front of them they become more cautious. Loss aversion can result in risky behavior that is often counter-productive, making a bad situation even worse.

Once gains are made, they are accepted as a new status quo very quickly, creating what is termed an 'endowment effect'. On the other hand, losses are not accepted as quickly, and actors will often cling to the old status quo (prior to loss), as the reference point, for long periods of time, engaging in risk-acceptant behavior in an attempt to restore that old status quo.

Prospect theory models both phases of the decision-making process: first, the understanding of the choice situation phase, followed by the actual choice. The theory uses the term 'framing phase' for the first phase, involving a preliminary analysis of the situation where options are identified and the expected utility and probability of each outcome are evaluated (Levy 1992a). Levy describes a set of analytical questions that can be used to study the framing phase, where we have to identify how the actor (1) defines the reference point, (2) identifies the available options and (3) assesses the value and probability of each outcome as perceived by the actor. It is important to make clear that we should expect to see that actors evaluate gains and losses relative to the status quo quite differently if Prospect theory is correct.

The analyst then has to (4) modify these subjective probabilities by an appropriate probability weighting function and (5) show that the resulting value of the preferred prospect or option exceeds the value of alternative prospects (Levy 1992b: 296). In the choice phase, these edited options are evaluated and the option with the highest utility is chosen. The actual weighing of options does not differ significantly from the predictions of the RAM, although it again must be emphasized that actors weigh gains and losses differently and tend to be more risk-acceptant in the domain of losses, whereas they are risk-averse in the domain of gains.

Prospect theory has been applied in the realm of foreign policy decision-making by Jervis and Levy, among others. Here Prospect theory results in many patterns of predicted behavior that significantly diverge from what we would expect in the RAM. First, if we use the RAM coupled with Waltz's structural realism (see Chapter 2), we would expect that states would evaluate the utility of different options in terms of how each option is expected to affect the relative power position of the state. In contrast, Prospect theory would suggest that states would evaluate gains/losses in relation to an existing status quo and that they would prefer the status quo over change (Levy 1992b).

Where predictions significantly diverge is the type of behavior we should expect when states perceive they are in the domain of losses in contrast to gains. A state in a deteriorating situation (perceived losses in relation to the status quo) would be expected to be more risk-acceptant than would otherwise be expected in structural realist theory, whereas a state would be quite risk-averse when dealing with gains. States are expected for instance to make greater efforts to preserve territory against a threatened loss than they would have been to acquire it in the first place (Levy 1992b).

If state A makes a gain at the expense of state B, B's attempts to restore the old status quo by recovering losses will however be perceived as a potential loss by state A due to the endowment effect. Here state A would quickly accept the gains as a new status quo, whereas state B would cling to the previous status quo as a reference point. In their interaction, both states will therefore perceive that they are in the domain of losses, resulting in riskier options being chosen (Levy 1992a).

The difference between risk-acceptance and aversion can also explain why states follow failing policies much longer than we would expect in the RAM (Jervis 1992). The US continued to follow a failed policy in Vietnam much longer than the RAM would predict, refusing to accept a new status quo in the region, instead adopting increasingly risky strategies in a futile attempt to avoid losses.

While offering many predictions, most of the theory has actually been developed using psychological experiments in the laboratory, measuring how individuals react to carefully controlled and monitored situations, where clearly defined choices are presented and utility can be objectively measured as the experiment uses monetary terms. There is some doubt about whether these conditions match the highly unstructured choice situations faced by foreign policy decision-makers in the real world (Levy 1992b: 293). In many real-world situations, decision-makers do not have clearly defined options and utility cannot be measured in monetary terms but instead is highly subjective. In this type of situation, it is empirically difficult to test whether the predictions of Prospect theory are confirmed or disconfirmed.

Table 5.2 illustrates the core argument of Prospect theory and two hypotheses (sets of questions) that should be asked in any case study using the theory. An example of a case study is depicted in the table. McDermott (1992) finds that the Carter administration chose the riskiest option with the lowest probability of success because the situation was framed in terms of a domain of losses, resulting in a very risk-acceptant choice by Carter being taken that is inexplicable using the RAM.

Table 5.2   *Prospect theory*

What is being explained?	How actors evaluate utility
Type of theory	Explanatory theory
Core argument	Actors evaluate utility depending upon whether in the domain of losses or gains: 1. Actors are more risk-averse in the domain of gains, and more risk-acceptant in the domain of losses 2. Actors evaluate utility in relation to a reference point (status quo). They quickly accept gains as part of a new status quo (endowment effect), whereas losses are not accepted in the short term
Hypotheses	1. In terms of *framing*, do decision-makers perceive their options to involve losses or gains (or a mixed lottery of losses and gains)? Do they appear to dwell more on potential losses than potential gains and possibly exaggerate the dangers through psychological bolstering? Do they consider alternative frames, and why is one selected over another? 2. In terms of *probability assessment*, do any of these assessments approach certainty? If so, is there evidence that they give disproportionate weight to these outcomes? Do they take excessive risks to avoid certain losses? Are they surprisingly cautious when they have the opportunity to secure a certain gain? (Quoted from Levy 1992b: 300)
Example (McDermott 1992)	Carter administration decision-making in the Iranian Hostage Rescue Mission (1980) The puzzle is that Carter chose to use force despite his predilection for the peaceful resolution of conflict *Data* Detailed case study material investigating the two hypotheses. *Findings* The Carter administration was in the domain of losses both domestically and internationally. Domestically Carter faced a difficult re-election campaign during an economic crisis. Internationally, the taking of hostages was a severe blow to US prestige and credibility The rescue mission was the riskiest military option that was seriously considered, but one that could have (if successful) restored the former status quo. Carter took a risk-acceptant choice that backfired, whereas a more risk-averse strategy (do nothing) had a much larger chance of success. This risky choice with little probability of success is unexplainable using the RAM but can be understood using Prospect theory

Groupthink

The difference between the two cognitive psychological theories presented above and the social-psychological theory of Groupthink is that cognitive theories investigate how the human mind works in assessing and deciding between different options, whereas social psychology investigates the 'social' side of human decision-making, assessing the importance of the social-psychological needs of individuals and their impact upon decision-making.

The most widely debated and most influential social-psychological theory within FPA is the theory of Groupthink (Janis 1983). The idea of Groupthink is that the self-esteem needs of individuals within small groups can produce tendencies toward concurrence-seeking, resulting in defective decision-making processes and poor foreign policy outcomes due to premature consensus. In plain English, Groupthink results in the group becoming 'dumber' than the individual decision-maker.

At the heart of the Groupthink phenomena is the small, cohesive, decision-making group. The Groupthink phenomenon originates from the social-psychological needs of individuals within small groups. Janis pointed toward the self-esteem needs of individuals and their dependency upon being accepted by the group as key factors, both of which can vary from individual to individual. A group is termed 'cohesive' when its members place a high value upon membership in the group and their continued affiliation with it.

The dynamic within cohesive groups that can create Groupthink behavior (concurrence-seeking) is complex. If members of a group feel that they have been accepted within the group, this should in theory give them greater freedom to speak their minds freely (Janis 1983: 246). However, the key to Groupthink is that while an individual might feel free to express his or her views, the *desire* for concurrence and harmony within the group results in individuals *not* expressing their true views (Janis 1983: 247). Other scholars have updated the model based upon advances in social-psychological theory, arguing that there are three types of social rewards that come with increased group cohesiveness: friendship; the prestige of being part of an 'elite' group; and enhanced competences from being part of an in-group. All three factors pull in the direction of a desire amongst members to *maintain consensus* in order to preserve friendly relations within the group, resulting in *premature* or *artificial* consensus, where members censure themselves, leading to faulty decision-making (McCauley 1998).

Group cohesiveness is a necessary but *not* sufficient condition for Groupthink. Groupthink only occurs in cohesive groups that take collective decisions. If a prime minister or president takes an authoritative foreign policy decision by him or herself without using advisors, then Groupthink is not possible. This does not mean that the decision-making process is fully rational; merely that Groupthink cannot be the cause of any potential defects in the process.

According to Janis's (1983) original model, the conditions that should be present for Groupthink mechanism to be triggered are:

1.   The decision-makers are a cohesive group.
2.   There are structural faults in the organization (isolation, lack of impartial leadership, lack of methodical procedures, homogeneity of members' social backgrounds and ideology).
3.   The group faces a stressful situational context (low self-esteem due to recent failures and lack of morally acceptable alternatives, high stress due to external threats with little hope of a better solution).

Concurrence-seeking behavior caused by cohesiveness can be exacerbated by faulty group structure and a provocative situational context. Both sets of conditions increase the probability of the occurrence of Groupthink and can therefore also be thought of as triggering factors for it. First, the way a group is structured can increase the probability of Groupthink. For instance, if there is a highly cohesive and insulated group where a leader promotes a particular outcome (lack of impartial leadership), we should expect Groupthink to be more probable. Furthermore, Groupthink is more likely when the nature of the situation facing the group is one of high stress where the members at the same time have relatively low self-esteem due to recent policy failures.

The importance of the three conditions can be seen in a comparison of two decision-making processes involving the same decision-making group. Janis argues that the decision-making group within the Kennedy administration (1961–63) in the Bay of Pigs decision (1961) became prey to Groupthink due to structural faults, whereas during the Cuban Missile Crisis (1963) the same group had learned from its mistakes and was very vigilant in avoiding another defective decision-making process.

Together these conditions can produce a concurrence-seeking tendency (Groupthink). Groupthink has a series of symptoms that can be observed in a given decision-making process; symptoms that can be divided into three main types:

1.   Overestimation of the group (including illusions of invulnerability and a belief in an inherent morality of the group).
2.   Closed-mindedness of the group due to collective rationalizations and stereotyping of outsiders.
3.   Pressures toward consensus (self-censorship, illusions of unanimity and direct pressure on dissenters).

First are the overestimations of the group, both in terms of illusions of invulnerability and an unquestioned belief in the inherent morality of the group. In the words of Robert Kennedy, 'it seemed that, with John Kennedy leading us and with all the talent he had assembled, *nothing could stop us*' (quoted in Janis 1983: 35).

The second type of symptom involves the closed mindedness of the group, with collective efforts to discount information that might lead to a reconsideration of decisions and stereotyped views of the opponent. During the escalation of the Vietnam War in the mid-1960s, decision-makers engaged in extensive collective rationalizations of the wisdom of the growing US presence in Vietnam, including ascribing unrelated but favorable regional developments such as a change of power in Indonesia in 1965–66 to the US efforts in Vietnam (Janis 1983: 113–14).

The final type of symptom is that there are social-psychological forces that pressure the group toward unanimity, including self-censorship, illusions of unanimity and direct pressures on dissenters, especially from self-appointed 'mindguards'. In the escalation of the Vietnam War strong conformity pressures were put upon those that questioned the policy. For instance, officials that questioned the wisdom of the policy were spoken about as 'losing their effectiveness', or were slowly frozen out through the use of snide comments such as 'Well, here comes Mr. Stop-the-Bombing' (Janis 1983: 115). Meetings take place in an atmosphere of *assumed* consensus where no one speaks out in opposition.

The result of Groupthink being present is that a decision-making process by a group is significantly different from a synoptically rational decision-making process (the RAM). Indicators for a poor decision-making process include finding:

1. An incomplete survey of alternatives and objectives.
2. A failure to examine the risks of the preferred option.
3. A lack of reappraisal of options initially not chosen.
4. A lack of effective information searching.
5. A biased information processing.
6. A lack of contingency planning.

Compare these defects to the synoptically rational decision process detailed above. The result is defective decision-making, meaning that we can expect the final outcome will have a lower probability of success. This does not mean that bad outcomes, defined as a poor attainment of one's goals, are the natural product of a poor decision-making process. Bad outcomes can also be the result of poor implementation by people outside of the decision-making group or unexpected accidents (Janis 1983: 195). However, Janis contends that the two are correlated, and that poor outcomes tend to follow poor decision-making processes.

In comparison to how widely cited the phenomena of Groupthink is, there have been surprisingly few empirical studies that have employed the theory (for a review, see Turner and Pratkanis 1998). This is partially a function of the complexity of the theory itself, given that it involves numerous different triggering factors and symptoms of Groupthink. It is also a challenging task to collect reliable and valid data on the internal deliberations of elite decision-makers. For cases where classified material (such as internal meeting minutes) have not been declassified (usually archives are opened after 30 or 50 years, depending upon the country), the analyst is forced to resort to journalistic accounts or participant interviews. Journalistic accounts are often quite biased, as participants usually have the agenda of portraying events in a manner that puts their own role in the best possible light. Yet the analyst runs into many challenges even when archives have been opened. One challenge is information overload. Another is that archival material is not necessarily the whole truth. For instance, meeting minutes capture only the discussions that took place within the meeting room, while most important decisions may have been taken outside in the corridors before or after a meeting. Additionally, civil servants writing the minutes would be expected to mask over any overt signs of Groupthink in the proceedings in order to protect their bosses.

Those that have empirically studied the Groupthink phenomenon have found surprisingly little support for the entire model. While some scholars have found support for the key tenets of the model, such as the importance of group structure for the occurrence of Groupthink (Shafer and Crichlow 2002), there have not been any studies that have found support for the entire model (Turner and Pratkanis 1998; Fuller and Aldag 1998). The natural question then is whether *all* of the triggering factors are actually causally linked with Groupthink or whether it makes more sense to utilize parts of the theory by themselves.

Another line of criticism comes from scholars that have attempted to re-analyze the cases that Janis used to develop the theory using empirical material that has become accessible (for example through declassification) after Janis did his research. Kramer (1998) in a critical re-examination finds that Janis overstated the impact of small group dynamics and the political considerations behind poor decisions such as the escalation of the Vietnam War. He argues that the escalation of that war was not the product of a poor decision-making process but instead was the result of President Johnson's political calculus in which he prioritized his domestic political agenda over foreign developments. Kramer contends that Johnson expected that he would be exposed to harsh domestic criticism for 'losing Vietnam' if he had pulled the plug on US support for the South Vietnamese regime, resulting in a fall in his support in Congress.

Table 5.3   *Groupthink theory*

What is being explained?	How social dynamics can affect group decision-making
Type of theory	Explanatory theory
Core argument	The self-esteem needs of individuals within small groups can result in concurrence-seeking tendencies, producing premature/artificial consensus where there are significant divergences from the RAM
Hypotheses	1. Was the decision taken collectively by a group? 2. Was the group cohesive and did the striving by group members to maintain the group override their critical judgment and rational choices? 3. Were the antecedent conditions and the symptoms of Groupthink evident in the deliberations of the group? 4. Was the decision an avoidable error?
Example (Yetiv 2004)	Bush administration decision to invade Iraq in the first Gulf War (1990–91) Yetiv first investigates whether the antecedent conditions are present: (1) a cohesive group; (2) structural faults in the organization; (3) a provocative situational context. He finds a closely knit group fueled by norms of loyalty, and that all of the expected structural faults were present. He further finds that the group was facing a high stress environment arising from an external threat, and had recently suffered failures (e.g. reneging on the 'no new taxes' pledge) Yetiv finds that the symptoms of Groupthink were also present. For example, when the chairman of the Joint Chiefs of Staff Colin Powell questioned whether it was worth going to war to liberate Kuwait, Chief of Staff Cheney cautioned him to 'just do the military options. Don't be the Secretary of State or the Secretary of Defense or the National Security Advisor' (quoted in Yetiv 2004: 115) Finally, Yetiv finds evidence suggesting a defective decision-making process as the result of Groupthink. For example, all alternatives were not evaluated, nor did they engage in a complete survey of objectives

The loss of support would scupper his chances of pushing his domestic agenda through Congress. Therefore, the escalation can be seen as the product of a rational strategy where it was simply politically expedient for Johnson to prioritize domestic politics over foreign affairs.

Due to the lack of empirical support, some scholars have attempted to modify the theory. One important modification was introduced by t'Hart and Kroon (1997). They argue that Groupthink is most likely to occur when there is a strong leader and/or strong hierarchy in the decision- making group. In this type of situation, if the leader does not

Box 5.1   The decision-making process leading to the invasion of Iraq in 2003: a symptom of Groupthink?

Drawing on participant and journalistic accounts, Mitchell and Massoud (2009) argue that the decision-making process within the Bush administration that led to the invasion of Iraq in 2003 displays many of the characteristics of Groupthink. A key question is why there was no real planning by the Bush administration for the post-war stabilization and reconstruction of Iraq. Once US soldiers had secured their objectives in the invasion they had no real orders. The result was that unprepared US soldiers watched in horror as the jubilant scenes changed into anarchic looting and violence. The situation went from bad to worse as US administrators in Iraq took the disastrous decisions to purge the Iraqi administration of any official that had been a member of the ruling Baath Party (a requirement for many public sector jobs) and to dismantle the Iraqi army, sending hundreds of thousands of armed men (predominantly Sunni) into unemployment and poverty. Why was US planning for the post-invasion phase so poor when almost all Middle Eastern experts in both the State Department and the CIA had warned that severe civil strife and chaos was the most likely scenario? One possible explanation is that there were faulty decision-making processes due to Groupthink. The following will test this hypothesis based upon answering Janis's four questions.

(1) Was the decision taken collectively by a group? (2) Was the group cohesive and did the striving by group members to maintain the group override their critical judgment and rational choices? At first glance one can argue that the decision-makers did not really form a cohesive group, as there were two clashing groups: one skeptical and centered around Secretary of State Powell, and the other pro-invasion group centered around Secretary of Defense Rumsfeld and his assistant Secretary Wolfowitz. However, the inner core of decision-making centering on President Bush and powerful Vice President Cheney was composed of officials like Rumsfeld and National Security Advisor Rice that formed a cohesive group.

(3) Were the triggering conditions and the symptoms of Groupthink evident in the deliberations of the group? There were many structural faults in the organization, with an insulated inner circle and a high degree of secrecy. Most critical however was the lack of a tradition within the Bush administration for 'impartial' leadership. Bush's leadership style was more instinctive instead of being based upon a logical examination of options. Within the critical discussions in the National Security Council, responsibility for ensuring that there were clear methodological procedures for deliberations and taking discussions fell to the weak National Security Advisor Rice, who was ineffective in managing discussions. In these meetings between the principals there was no real debate and options were not discussed (Mitchell and Massoud 2009).

➜

→

There was also a provocative situational context, with the group working under high stress due to the 9/11 attacks and the belief that the US was at risk from another terrorist threat. The greatest fear posed the question: What would 9/11 have looked like if weapons of mass destruction had been used?

Do we see the symptoms of Groupthink in the decision-making process? There was some Type II closed-mindedness, where collective rationalizations were made to discount warnings or other information that might lead the members to reconsider their assumptions before they recommitted themselves. Warnings by experts from the State Department and CIA that the occupation of Iraq would be difficult and bloody were systematically ignored. Instead, members of the group welcomed the views from Iraqi advocates of an invasion from the exiled Iraqi National Congress that the US forces would be 'greeted with flowers' (Phillips 2005; Mitchell and Massoud 2009). There were also pressures toward unanimity, including self-censorship, as members of the group engaged in anticipatory compliance to the views of the president. Advisors believed that Bush did not like to hear bad news, and therefore did not bring him any for fear of losing his confidence, telling him instead what he wanted to hear, not what he needed to hear (Mitchell and Massoud 2009).

(4) Was the decision an avoidable error? Invading multi-ethnic Iraq was always going to be difficult. However, the combination of an incomplete survey of alternatives and objectives, along with a failure to examine risks, reassess the situation and a failure to work out contingency plans, resulted in a more chaotic situation than was necessary.

The survey of alternatives was very incomplete. The choice was made to invade by Bush, but there was no discussion of other alternatives to military action. In the meeting of the National Security Council in December 2001, where the first plans for an invasion were presented, the group did not even discuss the rationale behind the invasion or the advisability of an attack, nor was this ever discussed openly within the group. This was complemented by Bush's own decision-making style, where he did not critically examine the views presented by advisors (Mitchell and Massoud 2009: 281). There was also no serious consideration of objectives, such as what was the desired 'end state' and how to get there (Mitchell and Massoud 2009: 278).

No contingency plans for what happens if things go wrong were developed, and even more surprisingly there were not even any real postwar plans. The result of this faulty decision-making process was therefore a quite predictable policy fiasco. Iraq descended into a bloody civil war that was first stopped when Bush re-examined his course of action in 2007 after the electoral losses incurred by the Republican Party in the 2006 congressional mid-term elections, deciding to adopt General Petraeus's counter-insurgency strategy and to increase the number of troops in Iraq in the so-called 'surge'.

undertake 'impartial' leadership we can expect a strong concurrence-seeking tendency in the form of 'anticipated compliance'. This means that group members will attempt to anticipate the views that their leader has as a means to ensure their continued presence in the group or for other career reasons.

Table 5.3 illustrates the core argument of Groupthink theory, along with four questions that Janis suggests should be asked in a case study investigating it and its impact upon decision-making. The table illustrates how Groupthink theory can be used to investigate decision-making, using an example from Yetiv's (2004) book on decision-making in the first Gulf War.

The politics of choice: foreign policy decisions as the product of political battles

In this section I look at two theories that explain decision-making as the product of political battles instead of cognitive or social-psychological factors. The first is coalition theory, illustrated using Hagan *et al.*'s (2001) model of coalition decision-making; the second is a review of bureaucratic/governmental politics. Originally one theory, these two variants of the original bureaucratic politics model explain foreign policy choices as the result of political battles within government, either at the civil servant level (bureaucratic) or at the minister/politician level (governmental).

Coalitions and foreign policy decision-making

Hagan *et al.* (2001) have developed a model that predicts what types of decision outcomes we should expect in foreign policy in different political situations. Figure 5.1 illustrates their model, which is applicable to both multiparty cabinets in parliamentary democracies, split government in presidential systems (where one party controls the executive and the other controls the legislature), and authoritarian regimes where power is dispersed across separate factions, groups or institutions. The first question to be asked when using the model is whether there exist well-established rules regarding how decisions should be taken. This can take the form of constitutional rules for foreign policy decision-taking or more informal rules and norms that detail how cabinet decisions should be taken in a coalition government. In less institutionalized political systems (most often authoritarian), there do not exist clear rules for how foreign policy decisions are taken, resulting in what Hagan *et al.* term the 'anarchy model'.

The next question to ask of systems with well-established decision-making rules is whether the decision needs to be taken by unanimity or

Figure 5.1   *Summary of decision tree for coalitions in foreign policy-making*

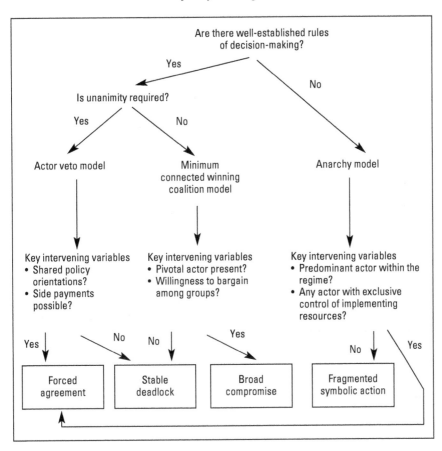

Source: Based on Hagan *et al.* (2001: 180).

by a majority vote. Under unanimity each actor (or unit) has a veto, making it very difficult to reach an agreement unless there is a shared policy orientation across all actors and/or side-payments are available that can be used to pay off dissenting actors. This is an intervening variable in the model.

In a majority voting system, we should expect that coalitions will form based upon the principle of a minimum connected coalition. This means that agreement will be forged between the fewest possible actors that can achieve a majority. Based upon coalition theory, Hagan *et al.* theorize that the reason that coalitions strive to have as few members as possible in a deal is that an agreement needs to accommodate the interests and needs of each additional actor (the 'size principle'). With more actors the compromise moves further and further away from the interests of any one particular actor, creating an incentive to minimize the number of actors in a coalition. Actors in a coalition also strive to create 'connected' coalitions, which means that like-minded actors tend to form coalitions. For example, two hawkish parties are more prone to forge a coalition than a hawkish and a soft-line party.

Hagan *et al.* then ask two questions: Is the pivotal actor (i.e. the actor without which no coalition is possible) on board? And is there willingness amongst the actors to compromise? If the answer is yes to both questions, then we should expect that a decision will be a broad compromise amongst the coalition actors; otherwise the outcome will be a deadlock.

Political institutions: bureaucratic and governmental politics

Bureaucratic and governmental politics are models of the 'pulling and hauling' of governmental decision-making that were originally formulated by Allison and Halperin and have been the subject of numerous reformulations (Allison, 1971; Halperin, 1974; Rosati 1981; Bendor and Hammond 1992; Welch 1992; Allison and Zelikow 1999; Preston and 't Hart 1999; Hermann *et al.* 2001). Allison together with Zelikow reformulated the original bureaucratic politics model in a 1999 revision of Allison's classic *Essence of Decision*, renaming it 'governmental politics'. The key difference between bureaucratic and governmental politics models is that the focus of governmental politics is upon minister-level actors (termed 'chiefs' by Allison), whereas bureaucratic politics can be better understood as the lower-level (termed 'Indians'), intra-ministerial struggles between bureaucrats. At the heart of the two models is the argument that foreign policy decisions are the result of political battles between different decision-makers, each with their own parochial interests and perceptions of the national interest. Instead of structural realism's view that foreign policy is a rational cost–benefit analysis of different options by decision-makers that share the same goals, the bureaucratic/governmental politics models see decisions as the result of internal bargaining games among decision-makers with differing preferences, and where the policy that is a result is a compromise that reflects the preferences of the actors with the strongest bargaining advantages. Actors are not irrational in these models, but the sum total of the bargaining games within governments that produces foreign policy outcomes that do not reflect the intentions of any individual player (Welch 1992). The decision-making *process* within government, and the preferences and power of the players in the game, is therefore viewed as an important intervening variable between system-level or state-level theories of national preferences and foreign policy decisions.

While bureaucratic and governmental politics have been the focus of

---

Box 5.2   Core propositions of Allison and Zelikow's governmental politics model

1. Policies are the result of political battles instead of a coordinated governmental strategy.
2. Actors perceive issues differently.
3. Preferences matter, with where you stand depending upon where you sit, although there are also differences between 'Chiefs' and 'Indians'.
4. The relative power of actors and who participates depends upon which action-channel is being used.

Source: Based on Allison and Zelikow (1999).

---

much research, most of the formulations of the models are *not* theories per se, but are instead descriptive models of decision-making processes (Bendor and Hammond 1992: 317–18; Caldwell 1977: 95). This is especially the case with Allison and Zelikow's governmental politics model, which lists 17 factors that should be investigated to explain why a given policy resulted from a particular political game – the most important of which are depicted in Box 5.2, which is a simplification of the model.

Bendor and Hammond (1992: 318), in a withering critique of Allison's original 1971 model of bureaucratic politics (which has become even more complex in the 1999 revision), state that the model 'is simply too thick. It incorporates so many variables that it is an analytical kitchen sink. Nothing of possible relevance appears to be excluded'. The analytical utility of the model is reduced by this complexity, as the very purpose of an analytical model is the same as a map. A good map reduces the level of detail by focusing on the key features of the terrain, giving us an overview that allows us to navigate effectively while being manageable to use.

Additionally, none of the propositions is a theoretical one that is a predictive statement that explains a particular event or class of events. As discussed in Chapter 1, explanatory theories in political science link independent variables (causes, X) with dependent variables (effects, Y), where a change in or occurrence of X is expected to cause/produce a change in Y. Some theorists have however attempted to push the two models in a more theoretical direction by transforming propositions into hypotheses (see Chapter 10).

Common to both models is the concept of 'action-channels', defined by Allison and Zelikow (1999: 300–1) as a 'regularized means of taking governmental action on a specific kind of issue ... Action-channels structure the game by preselecting the major players, determining their usual points of entrance into the game, and distributing particular advantages and disadvantages for each game'. This concept attempts to capture both formal institutional procedures for taking decisions such as the National Security Council in the US, and the politics that take place outside of formal channels.

Where the two models diverge concerns which decision-maker is in focus, with governmental politics concentrating on decision-making at the highest level, whereas bureaucratic politics can be interpreted as the lower-level intra-ministerial games between civil servants. Governmental politics models are applicable when major issues are being discussed at the highest level, especially during crisis situations, whereas bureaucratic politics models analyze issues of lower salience and which concern more routine decision-making. Most existing case studies of both models are in effect only studies of foreign policy decision-making at the highest level, and therefore only study governmental politics. Examples include Allison and Zelikow's case study of the political games within the US and Soviet governments during the Cuban Missile Crisis, Yetiv's (2004) analysis of the Gulf War in 1990–91, and Mitchell and Massoud's (2009) study of the US decision to invade Iraq in 2003.

The core of the governmental politics model is the proposition that battles between 'chiefs' within action-channels are a key factor in explaining the content of foreign policy decisions, with the outcome the product of the clashes between actors with different preferences and bargaining advantages. Yet Allison and Zelikow's model of governmental politics is weak on both the sources of actor preferences and their bargaining advantages.

First, in the original model put forward by Allison in his 1971 book, he posited that actor preferences are determined by the organizational self-interest of the department that they represent ('where you stand depends upon where you sit'); an idea reiterated in his 1999 book with Zelikow. Yet this begs the question: Why should ministers who are politically appointed and who have upwardly mobile career ambitions bind themselves to represent the bureaucratic self-interest of the department or ministry that they are in charge of? In the US, the preferences of central decision-makers such as the Secretary of Defense and Secretary of State are usually not linked with the organizational self-interest of the Department that they are in charge of; instead they reflect factors such as partisan orientation, individual ideology or career motivations. For instance, in Allison and Zelikow's analysis of the Cuban Missile Crisis, very few of the elite-level participants took positions that reflected where they sat. The best example was Secretary of Defense McNamara, who was an ardent *opponent* of military action against the Soviet missiles in Cuba; exactly the opposite of what we would expect if we assume that McNamara's preferences are determined by crude organizational self-interest (advocating a military solution that favors his own organization).

The 'where you stand depends upon where you sit' proposition is arguably more applicable when describing governmental politics in corrupt, non-democratic systems. In this type of system, ministers are able to enjoy the 'spoils' of office. Therefore, increasing the budget of their ministry enables ministers to extract more resources from the ministerial budget for their own personal gain, giving them a self-interest in promoting outcomes that favor their own ministry.

In democratic systems, the argument that ministers follow organizational self-interest is more realistic, however, when dealing with routine, technical matters. Principal–agent theories of bureaucracy suggest that there are often informational asymmetries, where ministers are dependent upon the information and expertise of the civil servants that they are in charge of. As the classic BBC TV series *Yes Minister* illustrates, this dependence can be exploited by civil servants, allowing them to subtly (and not so subtly) provide information framed in such a manner that it pushes the minister toward supporting the parochial self-interests of the bureaucracy (see www.bbc.co.uk/comedy/yesminister/). Yet this effect should not be exaggerated, especially when ministers have access to multiple sources of information (news media, discussions with other ministers within a governmental cabinet, meetings with foreign colleagues, etc.), and therefore most likely is only relevant in quite technical and routine matters.

Returning to the theoretical model itself, the key to explaining what foreign policy decisions come out of the pulling and hauling of governmental politics are the bargaining skills and advantages that individual players have. However, as Allison and Zelikow describe them, these factors are quite idiosyncratic in any particular case, preventing us from developing an actual theoretical model of bargaining power that can predict a priori who wins or loses. While the advantages that decision-making rules grant specific actors within the chosen action-channel can be theorized upon (e.g. having veto power is, other things being equal, a strong bargaining advantage), a large element of bargaining skills and advantages is made up of factors such as experience in intragovernmental political games and as sheer force of personality. These factors are only apparent post hoc, making it impossible to predict outcomes based upon the institutional positions and preferences of players prior to a bargaining game. For example, in the internal deliberations during the Cuban Missile Crisis, despite having a relatively weak formal role within the national security apparatus, Robert Kennedy was trusted by his brother, and the president gave him a strong informal role that granted him bargaining advantages that enabled him to steer the debates and engineer a consensus (Allison and Zelikow 1999).

Beyond this vacuous core at the heart of the governmental politics model there is also the problem that Allison and Zelikow do not take into account the strong hierarchical relationship between a president and his advisors in the specific US context. Basically, they discount the constitutional fact that the president is, in the words of George W. Bush, the 'Decider-in-Chief' in foreign policy crisis situations. In their case study of the Cuban Missile Crisis they sidestep the question of whether there actually was a 'bargaining game' underway between President Kennedy and his advisors, or whether the case was really just about the decision-making process of the president, where the role of the other players is merely to present information about the consequences of different courses of action and different interpretations of the choice situation. Yetiv (2004), in an analysis of Bush Sr's decision to intervene in the Persian Gulf War in 1990–91, finds no evidence that the president bargained with his senior staff. Bush took the decision that Iraq had to be expelled from Kuwait and did not 'bargain' with his advisors. Instead, the internal debates dealt with finding the best way that this could be done by considering the costs and benefits of different options. However, the outcome did not represent a 'collage' of views, but instead the views of the 'Decider-in-Chief'. This would suggest that operational codes might provide more analytical leverage in explaining outcomes in these types of situations (see Chapter 4 for more on this theory).

Taken together, the governmental politics model can be better thought of as a *framework* for descriptive case studies, offering a set of questions that can be asked of a given case. This does not mean that the model has no analytical utility, but merely that it should not be treated as a predictive theory that offers clear hypotheses of cause and effect. On the other hand, scholars that do use the governmental politics model would tend to agree with neoclassical realists, who contend that any given historical case is so complex and events are so contingent upon idiosyncratic, case-specific factors that it is impossible to predict events using parsimonious theories. In the trade-off between explanatory richness and theoretical generalizability using a parsimonious model, both sets of scholars choose explanatory richness. They contend that the aim of the scholar should be to 'understand' what factors were the most important in driving events in a given case and therefore we should use 'theory' as a set of questions that concentrates our attention on what the model predicts are the most important factors, instead of relying on a parsimonious model with poor explanatory power.

After Allison and Zelikow decided to rename Allison's original 'bureaucratic' politics (model III in Allison's book) as 'governmental politics' it has become rarer to find examples of the use of the term 'bureaucratic' politics in the literature. As stated before, bureaucratic

Table 5.4   *Bureaucratic politics theory*

What is being explained?	How decisions are affected by the 'pulling and hauling' between different bureaucratic actors
Type of theory	Analytical model that can be used heuristically, but that does not provide 'testable' hypotheses beyond the 'where you stand is where you sit' argument. However, Welch has tried to use the theory in a more explanatory fashion
Core argument	The preferences of bureaucratic actors are affected by parochial, organizational self-interest ('where you stand depends upon where you sit'). Decision-making is a bargaining situation between different bureaucratic actors, whose power is determined by the institutional position
Hypotheses	Welch has described four theoretical hypotheses that can be seen as the essence of the bureaucratic politics model: 1. Player preferences should correlate highly with their bureaucratic positions 2. Player perceptions of problems should correlate highly with their bureaucratic positions 3. Player influence in bargaining games flows from their bureaucratic positions 4. A decision-making process should be understood as a bargaining situation where players 'pull' and 'haul' to promote their organizational interests, with the net result not reflecting the intentions of any particular player (Welch 1992: 128)
Example (Mitchell and Massoud 2009)	US decision-making during the post-invasion of the Iraq War (2002–03) Mitchell and Massoud find substantial evidence for bureaucratic in-fighting between the Departments of Defense and State. Defense was put in charge of planning for the post-invasion situation despite State having extensive expertise and already developed contingency plans. Throughout 2003 Defense 'did everything it could to protect its influence when it came to the control of postwar Iraq' (p. 276)

politics refers to decision-making at lower levels of government than the elite level, including both battles within individual ministries or departments and in the coordination of policies across ministries or departments.

In contrast to the model of governmental politics, the bureaucratic politics model has as its core several propositions that can be formulated as clear theoretical hypotheses, enabling the theory to be used in an explanatory fashion. Welch (1992) has helpfully formulated four hypotheses that can be seen as the essence of the bureaucratic politics model (see Table 5.4). Notice that each of these hypotheses has a different dependent variable (effect) that it attempts to explain; for instance that player preferences (effects) should be the product of player bureaucratic positions (causes). Linked together, they form an explanatory model of the sources of actor preferences, perceptions, power and the nature of bureaucratic/governmental politics. These hypotheses can then be tested empirically in case studies, attempting to discover whether evidence supports them, bringing this more stringent variant closer to an explanatory theory.

The proposition that 'where you stand is where you sit' leads to a hypothesis that posits that civil servants within government tend to advocate the parochial interests of the bureaucratic organization that they belong to in interdepartment battles. The key to bureaucratic politics is therefore the behavioral assumptions that are supposed to drive civil servants, yet the proposition that 'where you stand is where you sit' needs to be fleshed out. Allison's original 1971 formulation uses a relatively primitive model of bureaucratic self-interest that does not reflect the state-of-the-art in organizational theory. More sophisticated theories suggest for example that bureaucratic actors will attempt to maximize their ability to perform what they perceive to be their core tasks, for example by protecting their 'turf' (Dunleavy 1991). An example of turf wars was the interdepartmental battles between the FBI and CIA over who should monitor foreign terrorists operating in the US, preventing the two organizations from cooperating in tracking the 9/11 terrorists as they entered the US (9/11 Commission 2004: 263).

While it is a stronger theory than governmental politics, there have been few empirical case studies that have utilized the bureaucratic politics model. One reason is that the battles at the bureaucratic level are about less important issues, such as which instrument should be chosen for implementing a policy choice made at higher levels. Another reason is due to the methodological challenges involved. Bureaucratic politics is notoriously difficult to study empirically, requiring a detailed record of discussions at the technical level between bureaucrats (Michoad 2002). Further, evidence of actual bureaucratic in-fighting is difficult to find, given that these types of squabbles rarely make it into the minutes of meetings and other documents, making the researcher excessively dependent upon participant interviews. This does not mean that studying bureaucratic politics is impossible. Case studies can be developed using interview data and archival material, and broader quantitative tests of the hypothesis that 'where you stand depends upon where you sit' can be undertaken using data that measures the positions of different ministries on a range of issues, attempting to detect whether ministries take positions that reflect organizational self-interest. But given the sizeable effort needed by scholars to overcome the daunting methodological challenges involved, most have decided that, while important, there are other more important phenomena that can be studied that involve much lower investments of effort.

The implementation of foreign policy: how organizations matter

Allison in his classic 1971 book also developed another model of foreign policy decision-making that focused upon how organizations matter; a model that has also been updated in Allison and Zelikow (1999). Seeing foreign policy actions as organizational output, the organizational model explains two different phenomena. First, it explains how organizational capabilities, while empowering states to act, also constrains what options are available. The basic point is that if you only have a hammer to implement policies, you will tend to confront foreign policy problems in ways that allow you to use the hammer, irrespective of whether a given problem would be better solved by a screwdriver. For example, a country with a well-developed diplomatic corps but that lacks effective covert capabilities or offensive military forces will tend to choose 'diplomatic' solutions to foreign policy challenges, irrespective of whether some problems might be better served with more coercive tools.

Second, the organizational model can explain why policies that were intended to have a particular effect often end up having a very different one. The key insight here is that we cannot reason backwards from an implemented policy to what the policy was *intended* to do; often there is not a strong connection between the two.

The central thesis of Allison and Zelikow's organizational model is that organizations empower governments by enabling policies to be implemented in the first place, but that the existing capabilities of governments also affect what policies are chosen. While the overall organizational model also resembles a 'kitchen sink' analytical model, there are several of the core propositions that draw upon established theoretical conjectures from organizational theory that can be converted into theoretical hypotheses in a manner similar to the bureaucratic politics model.

The term bureaucracy has negative connotations for many, begging the question of why governments create bureaucratic organizations in the first place. Organizations are created to simplify the complex tasks of government that require the coordinated behavior of a large number of individuals. Coordination is achieved through the creation of standard operating procedures (SOPs) for the most important tasks of a given organization. SOPs are created to save time and resources, as they free the civil servant from undertaking a comprehensive analysis of how best to complete a given routine task. One of the most SOP-laden private organizations is McDonald's. McDonald's has developed a very detailed SOP for exactly how one of its hamburgers should be made, including precise rules for how many seconds the burger patty should be fried on each side, when condiments should be added, etc.

The SOPs free the individual worker from making time-consuming decisions on a case-by-case basis, allowing the output of burgers of a homogeneous quality in an astonishingly short amount of time. Rigid SOPs also allow McDonald's to hire relatively low-skilled workers instead of trained chefs.

While the output of large bureaucratic organizations such as the Pentagon is naturally much more complex than producing hamburgers, governmental organizations are also very reliant upon SOPs to simplify routine procedures in ways that allow numerous individuals to coordinate their behavior in a more cost-effective manner. The positive side of organizations is that they enable government to accomplish collective tasks. For example, an intelligence organization like MI6 allows the UK government to gather more information and analyze it with greater expertise than any individual could muster. Yet blindly applying existing SOPs to new tasks can result in output that is ill-matched to achieve the objectives. One oft-quoted caricature of SOP-following behavior in the military that does contain a kernel of truth is: 'If it moves, salute it; if it doesn't move, pick it up; if it is too big to move, paint it.'

In governmental organizations, sets of rehearsed SOPs for producing actions are clustered together in programs for properly dealing with different contingencies. As the complexity of action increases, the greater the importance that programs have for organizational behavior. The importance of programs increases even more during a crisis, where there is less time to match complex problems with solutions and there is a more intense threat to core goals (see pp. 115–16).

Organizations are created to solve specific tasks such as territorial defense or diplomacy, but over time complex organizations can develop a life of their own. This organizational 'life' is termed an 'organizational culture' within organizational theory. Organizational culture can be defined as 'relatively stable propensities concerning priorities, operational objectives, perceptions, and issues' of an organization (Allison and Zelikow 1999: 168). While it is possible for an organization with simple tasks like McDonald's to codify detailed rules that describe individual behavior in all possible situations, prescribing the contractual obligations of individuals is simply not possible for organizations that face a multitude of often ill-defined public objectives and a complex environment. Therefore, organizational cultures arise to enable cooperation between individuals within an organization.

Culture is the result of the way that an organization has defined success in operational terms, the specific technologies an organization uses in performing its tasks, the distribution of rewards in the organization, and the professional norms of personnel (Allison and Zelikow 1999: 167). For example, some university departments have cultures that prioritize providing high quality teaching to students, often due to

---

Box 5.3 Why no camouflage?

US analysts during the Cuban Missile Crisis were puzzled as to why the Soviets did not attempt to camouflage the missiles being installed in Cuba, as it made the detection of the weapons much easier. US analysts inferred that the Soviet's must have *intended* the US to detect the weapons. In fact, the Soviet forces were merely following existing SOPs regarding standard missile deployment, and *did not intend* that the US spotted the missiles. The Soviet deployment SOP for missiles had been developed and adapted for conditions in the Soviet Union, where the dense forests made camouflage unnecessary. But the lack of camouflage was not suited to the sparse forests of Cuba, making the missiles naked to the US surveillance planes that the Soviets knew were flying over Cuba (Allison and Zelikow 1999). Had the Soviets adapted the SOP for deployment to local conditions, the US might not have known about the weapons until they were fully operational, at which point it might have been too late for the US to protest and stop the deployment.

---

an incentive system for personnel that rewards quality teaching (and punishes poor teaching), but also due to professional norms about quality teaching that have been nurtured in the department. Other departments prioritize academic research over teaching, often due to a combination of more research-oriented professional norms and a reward system where advancement and tenure is only achieved by publishing in prestigious journals and university presses.

Taken together, organizational culture shapes how organizations implement policies, determining which set of SOPs (programs) are chosen to tackle a given problem. In theory, well-functioning organizations should be flexible and adaptive, able to discern when to use an existing program or develop a new procedure that is better adapted to solving a given task. In reality, organizations tend to fight 'the last war', drawing upon past experiences of what programs worked (and did not work) to deal with new contingencies.

Why do organizations not automatically update their organizational culture so that the performance of tasks optimally matches the contingencies of new environments? Here there are two different answers according to which branch of organizational theory one draws upon. Rational institutionalists argue that, because developing and changing an organizational culture involves significant transaction costs, rational individuals will be reluctant to expend the resources necessary to change the culture to match a new environment, except in very unusual circumstances. Moreover, such a culture can even prevent the organization from detecting that a new environment exists. For example, after World War I navies throughout the world had organizational cultures

Table 5.5   *Organizational politics theory*

What is being explained?	How organizational capabilities affect what options are chosen
Type of theory	Analytical model
Core argument	• Organizational capabilities affect what options are chosen • Implemented policies often diverge from what was intended
Hypotheses	• Of which organizations does the government consist? • What capabilities and constraints do these organizations' existing SOPs create in producing information about international conditions, threats and opportunities? • What capabilities and constraints do these existing SOPs create in generating the menu of options for action? • What capabilities and constraints do these existing SOPs establish for implementing whatever is chosen? (Allison and Zelikow 1999: 390)
Example (Author's research)	The organizational model and the US invasion of Afghanistan in 2001

The implementation of the US intervention in Afghanistan in 2001 illustrates how the availability of instruments affects the policy chosen, and that this can result in unintended consequences that risk undermining the very rationale behind the original decision. After the 9/11 attacks by al-Qaeda, the Bush administration asked the Taliban regime in Afghanistan to both hand over the perpetrators and stop giving al-Qaeda sanctuary. Once the Taliban refused to stop harboring al-Qaeda groups, the Bush administration took the decision to topple the Taliban regime by force. However, the US lacked the organizational capabilities to invade Afghanistan by itself, as they could not get land troops for an invasion through Pakistan or another neighboring country, and there were no bases from neighboring countries that could logistically support a risky airborne invasion. The US was forced to rely upon air power, covert action and materials supplied by the CIA to support Afghan allies on the ground. These allies were the Northern Alliance, which was a loose group of various brutal warlords that had lost the struggle for control of Kabul to the Taliban regime prior to 2001. One of the primary reasons for this was that they represented the Tajik minority, whereas the Pashtun majority supported the Taliban. Once the Northern Alliance toppled the Taliban regime they took control of Kabul, bringing an unpopular Tajik-dominated governmental coalition to power whose ethnicity was the very reason that the Taliban regime had come to power in the first place. The intention of the US intervention in Afghanistan had been to remove the safe haven for al-Qaeda offered by the Taliban regime that threatened US interests. An optimal solution could have involved a US-led invasion of Afghanistan with ground troops that removed both the Taliban *and* the Northern Alliance warlords. Thereafter a broadly representative Afghan national government could have taken charge. While it was by no means certain that this solution would have succeeded in fulfilling US objectives, the strategy chosen by the US due to a lack of organizational capabilities undermined the goals that the policy was intended to achieve. This has resulted in a weak and unpopular Afghan regime supported by large numbers of US troops that became embroiled in a bloody internecine power struggle, costing US and NATO countries thousands of lives and billions of dollars that favored the use of proven technology (battleships), with 'battleship admirals' reluctant for obvious reasons to admit that they needed to undertake a costly reorganization (both in terms of retraining personnel and in the acquisition of new weapon systems) to adapt to the new circumstances brought about by the development of naval airpower, in which only a handful of cheap naval bombers could sink even the strongest battleship, making carriers more important than the increasingly redundant and obsolete battleships.

Sociological organization theory adds an additional layer to this explanation. The argument is that the culture of an organization pervades it, affecting the behavior of individuals by both providing a system of incentives for certain forms of acceptable behavior, but also through the socialization of individuals into the culture of an organization, resulting in rule-following behavior over time. The later aspect of culture draws upon similar role-following models of social action as social constructivism to theorize about how an organizational culture affects the behavior of individuals. Organizational culture therefore creates a form of 'stickiness' that makes organizations reluctant to adapt their routine tasks to new circumstances, irrespective of whether this is due to a rational assessment of the costs of change or whether it is the product of rule-following behavior.

Table 5.5 illustrates the core argument of the organizational politics model, along with a set of questions that can be asked in case studies. This is followed by an example of the organizational model applied to US decision-making about invading Afghanistan in 2001.

Social constructivism: different logics of action

Mainstream social constructivists argue that most foreign policy decisions are not dominated by rational, cost–benefit calculation as assumed by the RAM. Instead, they contend that there are two different logics of action, depending upon how deeply embedded the rules and identities are. At the level of conscious thought is the thesis that a *logic of appropriate behavior* structures which choices are made, capturing a form of normative rationality where options are chosen when they match the normative identity of an actor (March and Olsen 1998: 951; Finnemore and Sikkink 1998; Checkel 2004). At a deeper level is the theory of a *logic of habit or habitual action* (Hopf 2010). Here the argument is that most choices are made more-or-less automatically, never even reaching the level of conscious decision-making. Habits evoke and suppress actions and are ready-made responses to stimuli from the environment.

When actors are deciding in issue areas where there are embedded norms and rules in the identities of actors, decision-making is theorized to be dominated by the logic of appropriate action (March and Olsen

1998). March and Olsen distinguish between the logic of behavior underlying the RAM, which they term the 'logic of consequences', and the logic of appropriate action, where decisions are not just based upon a calculation of the utility of different material options. Instead, decisions in the logic of appropriate action are taken based upon intersubjectively held norms that become embedded as part of the identity of individuals that then form prescriptions for appropriate behavior. When these norms are highly embedded, the logic of appropriate action can explain why certain foreign policy options that strongly clash with actor identities become viewed as so morally 'inappropriate' that they are never even discussed by decision-makers.

When acting based upon the logic of consequences (the RAM), actors rationally calculate the optimum strategy to maximize the fulfillment of their material interests, based upon the expected utility of different strategies. In contrast, when following the logic of appropriate action, human actors follow norms that match particular identities with situations (March and Olsen 1998: 951; Finnemore and Sikkink 1998; Checkel 2004). For instance, during the Cuban Missile Crisis, when top US officials were discussing whether the US should undertake a surprise air attack upon Soviet installations in Cuba, the US under secretary of state George Ball responded that 'it's the kind of conduct that one might expect of the Soviet Union. It is not conduct that one expects of the United States' (Allison and Zelikow 1999: 118). Note especially the reference to US identity by Ball.

Through processes of socialization and social learning, these norms become an *internalized* duty and an obligation which actors are assumed to act in accordance with (Checkel 2004; Finnemore and Sikkink, 1998). An everyday example of the impact of logics of appropriate action is why (most of us) do not rob banks. If you have abstained from bank robbing due to a rational calculation, where the expected profit does not exceed the risk of going to jail or even getting killed in the robbery, your behavior would have followed a logic of consequences. If on the other hand you have never seriously contemplated robbing a bank, ask yourself: why? Most likely, you have never seriously calculated whether robbing the local bank would pay because you never even considered it, as this action is so contradictory to your identity as a law abiding citizen (in most circumstances) that you see it as a 'wrong' action that is morally repulsive.

Socialization occurs for example when actors learn 'social norms' through their childhood that then form the bounds of 'rational choice' as adults, ruling out serious consideration of morally abhorrent actions such as murder, rape or armed robbery. In the same manner, logics of appropriate behavior are theorized to form strong norms in the international system that become ingrained through interaction between states to such a degree that actions such as dropping a nuclear bomb

Table 5.6 *The social constructivist theory of a logic of appropriate action*

What is being explained?	Why decision-making is dominated by a logic of appropriate action when deeply embedded norms exist
Type of theory	Analytical tool
Core argument	When the logic of appropriate action dominates decision-making, actor decisions are based upon habitual compliance with embedded norms for appropriate behavior. Actors become socialized into a community of actors holding an intersubjective norm that becomes part of the interests and even identity of the actor, producing decision-making dominated by the logic of appropriate action
Hypotheses	Actors that are socialized (logics of appropriate action) make different decisions than non-socialized actors (RAM)
Example (Tannenwald 1999)	The US and the norm of nuclear non-use
	In a comparative case study, Tannenwald (1999) investigates four cases of use and non-use of nuclear weapons (Japan (1945), Korea (1950–53), Vietnam, 1991 Gulf War). She investigates whether there is evidence of decision-making in the four cases that is dominated by a logic of appropriate action, expecting to see 'taboo talk', examples of which include 'we just don't do things like this' or 'this is simply wrong' in internal governmental deliberations. She finds that in the Korean War, the emerging norm of non-use had an inhibiting effect, shaping how US leaders defined their interests. By the time of the Vietnam War the norm was so entrenched that US decision-makers did not even contemplate using nuclear weapons even though their use could arguably have staved off defeat, and possibly even resulted in a military victory. Decision-making during the 1991 Gulf War illustrates that the norm is so deeply entrenched with US decision-makers that it is virtually unthinkable that the US would drop a nuclear weapon on an adversary unless it was retaliating against a nuclear strike upon itself

go from being 'acceptable' (e.g. they were used by the US at the end of World War II to prevent the massive loss of life that would have been involved in an invasion of Japan) to something that is morally abhorrent (Tannenwald 1999).

The core argument of the social constructivist theory of decision-making and the logic of appropriate action is illustrated in Table 5.6. When actors have become socialized into a community of actors that hold an intersubjective norm, decision-making becomes dominated by a logic of appropriate action instead of the rational calculations in the RAM. Scholars have used the theory to investigate both global and regional norms, including norms against land-mines (Price 1998), the non-use of nuclear weapons (Tannenwald 1999) and European citizenship norms (Checkel 2001).

At an even deeper level is the logic of habit. Hopf (2010: 542) theorizes that social structures are the primary source of habits for individuals and can be learned either through instrumental calculations or through socializations to normative standards. Once embedded, they form cognitive structures beyond conscious thought that result in certain patterns of perceptions and practices that are automatically and unconsciously evoked in specific circumstances. Note that we are beyond discussions of rationality, be it bounded or normative, here. Rationality is in play only when actors engage in a deliberate consideration of alternatives.

Hopf contends that a large part of what states do is dominated by logics of habit. For example, a certain type of policy from both the US and Soviet Union became habitual during the Cold War, with each state so used to the other being viewed as an enemy that hostile relations became a matter of habit – and like most habits were difficult to break. Despite numerous attempts during the Cold War by leaders to break this habit by thawing relations in periods of détente, old habits reasserted themselves and pulled the states back into more hostile relations.

Habits can be broken when they are reflected upon at the level of conscious thought, although it usually takes some form of strong shock to do it. Habits within the Cold War complex of relations between the two superpowers were first truly broken after the collapse of the Soviet Union in 1991, although many individuals on both sides still habitually view the other as an adversary (so called 'Cold Warriors').

Habits are not necessarily negative, and Hopf contends that a large amount of the cooperative behavior found in foreign policy is the product of habits. For instance, he contends that the US cooperates with Britain in the World Trade Organization without any reflection of the costs and benefits or norms. He writes that 'the US automatically cooperates with Britain because the people making the decisions have stereotyped Britain as a friend or partner, and so respond to Britain's actions, even if objectively ambiguous or possibly non-cooperative, as if they are naturally benign' (Hopf 2010: 550).

Part III
What States Do

Chapter 6

Security Policies

Are all types of foreign policy issues the same? As seen in Figure 6.1, we have now reached the final stage of foreign policy making – what states do. The next three chapters introduce theoretical debates about the different dynamics that drive policy-making in three different types of foreign policy: security, diplomacy and economic. While the three types of policies are strictly split into three chapters for heuristic reasons, based upon the core theoretical debates in each subject, in reality they tend to overlap considerably. For example, the substance of many diplomatic negotiations is trade or security policy. This chapter deals therefore quite narrowly with security policy.

Security foreign policies deal with what traditionally is defined as security studies, where states attempt to counter external threats to their core values. States remain the central actors in world affairs, and despite the revolutionary developments in the interconnectedness of the world economy due to globalization (see Chapter 9), there is little evidence suggesting that the traditional focus of states upon security concerns has been supplanted by political economy calculations (Ripsman and Paul 2010).

Security foreign policy studies may be defined as the study of the threat, use, and control of military force. It explores the conditions that make the use of force more likely, the ways that the use of force affects individuals, states and societies, and the specific policies that states adopt in order to prepare for, prevent or engage in war (Walt 1991: 212). The security behavior of states depends upon the level of relative

Figure 6.1 *Foreign policy at Stage Three: what states do*

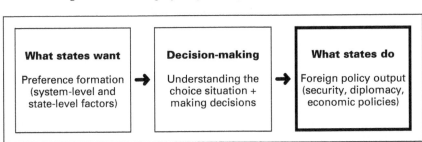

power the state has, ranging from a hegemonic great power, to major powers, to minor powers (Gilpin 1981). It varies also according to state type, with large differences according to whether a state is satisfied with the status quo, or whether it is a declining state trying to maintain a crumbling status quo, or whether it is a rising power that wants to challenge the status quo (Gilpin 1981).

I will present competing theoretical answers to the following questions: Why do states choose to go to war? Why do states choose different military/strategic options when faced with the same environment (strategic culture)? How and when can balancing behavior prevent war? Can states be deterred from going to war? Once armed conflict starts, how can it be resolved?

War and security foreign policies

Explaining why states choose war as a foreign policy instrument has been a central area of empirical and theoretical scholarship in security studies. The following review will concentrate upon realist explanations of war that build upon RAMs and the criticism from cognitive theorists who contend that war is more often the product of misperceptions and miscalculations (see Chapter 4).

War can be defined as 'a substantial armed conflict between the organized military forces of independent political units' (Levy 1983: 51). Interstate wars should be distinguished from intrastate civil wars between armed groups within a state. There are also large differences in the causes and consequences of wars depending upon whether they are minor skirmishes over territory between two states or are major regional or even global conflicts over dominance of the system (either regionally or globally). Some of the theories below are able to explain both minor and major wars (e.g. expected utility theory), whereas others focus upon major regional/global wars (e.g. balance-of-power theory).

There are (at least) five different explanations for the causes of war:

1. War is a natural product of the anarchical system.
2. Major wars occur when there are dramatic shifts in the relative strength of great powers (hegemonic stability theory).
3. Major wars occur to prevent the rise of a hegemon (balance-of-power theory).
4. More general 'rationalist' theories of the expected utility of war.
5. Minor wars are diversionary tools to distract the public from the poor domestic performance of the government.

The discussion of these five theories is followed in the next sections by theories that explain ways in which war can be prevented (balancing, deterrence and coercive diplomacy, and democracy) and conflict resolution.

First, a core realist argument shared by both structural realism and neoclassical realism is that war in general is a product of the anarchical international system. Basically, war is used as a tool of foreign policy because there is no higher authority preventing states from doing so. In plain English, states can bully other states with force because there is no one stopping them from doing it. In offensive structural realism, the primary tool for states to gain power relative to their rivals is through war or the threat of war (Mearsheimer 2001). Whereas defensive structural realists believe that the predominant form of state behavior is balancing (see pp. 39–42), offensive realists see a world of conflict in which great powers engage in a continuing struggle for hegemony.

A related realist explanation sees war as less intentional in that it can be the result of an arms race gone crazy, where a spiral of conflict has been spawned by the 'security dilemma'. This is 'a structural notion in which the self-help attempts of states to look after their security needs, tend regardless of intention to lead to rising insecurity for others as each interprets its own measures as defensive and the measures of others as potentially threatening' (Herz 1950: 157). A classic example of a security dilemma is the arms race that preceded World War I, where European great powers were locked in an increasingly risky arms race, with an ever more fragile peace that was eventually shattered by a minor crisis between Austria–Hungary and Serbia.

Yet anarchy and the resulting insecurity created are not in themselves sufficient to explain why 'rational' states would choose the risky and costly option of war over a negotiated agreement. Structural realists point to two different competing explanations for major regional or global wars.

The first explanation is based upon *hegemonic stability theory* and the power transitions that occur as the result of dramatic shifts in the relative power of states (Modelski 1978; Gilpin 1981). Hegemony is usually defined as one great power that controls or dominates the lesser states in a system, although 'no state has ever completely controlled an international system' (Gilpin 1981: 28). Peace reigns during periods in which one great power enjoys hegemonic status; examples include the UK in the 19th century and the US after the end of the Cold War. When the material power resources of a challenger state come close to the dominant state, the challenger will start to make demands to change the status quo of the international system. If these are not accommodated, the challenger may resort to war to achieve its demands. Key here is the question of the level of risk-acceptance of the rising and declining powers. Risk-acceptant challengers will be more prone to engage in war to push for a revision of the status quo; and risk-acceptant declining powers are more prone to resist accommodation to the challenger's demands (Kim and Morrow 1992). However, there is little empirical evidence that major wars are caused by power transitions (Kim and Morrow 1992; Mansfield 1988). Indeed, historically most major wars have begun as smaller wars unrelated to power transitions that later escalated as great powers intervened. This includes World War I, which started when Austria–Hungary declared war against Serbia, and World War II that was triggered by the smaller-scale German–Polish war (Kim and Morrow 1992).

A competing explanation is that major wars are caused by *other powers balancing* against attempts by a challenger to gain hegemonic preponderance in a regional system or the global system. For instance, the German drive to balance against British hegemonic dominance in the late 19th century through internal balancing (economic reforms, political unification) and external balancing (alliances) produced increased antagonism and conflicts between the two powers that ultimately resulted in World War I (Layne 1993). Here war is seen as either a means of enforcing a balance of power or an indirect product of security dilemmas that result from arms races fueled by balancing attempts.

The theoretical challenge facing this argument is to explain why states would resort to war against challengers when it is less risky and far cheaper for them to 'free ride', allowing other powers to balance against the challenger instead. While having interests in reaping the benefits of autonomy and independence that come from a lack of hegemony, each weaker power also has incentives to free ride by allowing others to pay the *costs* of balancing while they share in the *benefits* (no power achieves hegemonic status). As theories of collective action tell us, incentives to free ride result in the lack of provision of the collective good. Indeed, the historical record shows that challengers with hegemonic pretensions generally have more often *not* been met by a strong counterbalancing coalition, irrespective of the costs. Instead, challengers were balanced against through war only when the war was expected to be short and tolerable – World War I was expected to last only a few short weeks (Rosecrance and Lo 1996). Furthermore, the empirical evidence that suggests that *bandwagoning with* the stronger state is historically more common, especially as regards smaller states (Schroeder 1994). Prior to and during World War I, weaker states flocked to the stronger allied side instead of the weaker Central powers who lost the war. 'Bandwagoning' is defined as allying with a strong power instead of balancing against it as we would expect following Waltz. The term refers to a practice in early American politics where the strongest candidate would ride through town with his large bandwagon, collecting weaker candidates who would jump on board to join what was perceived to be the winning side. One can also think of bandwagoning as flocking toward the winner.

Expected utility theory builds upon the banal insight that states only go to war when they expect that the gains will exceed the costs, though it develops a more convincing theory by making explicit how states calculate costs and benefits along with the mechanisms that produce situations where the costs of war are lower than the expected benefits (Bueno de Mesquita and Lalman 1992; Fearon 1995). Expected utility theory can explain the paradox of why rational states choose to take the extreme risks associated with waging war over the alternative of less costly negotiated settlements. The theory can also be termed a rationalist explanation for war, and can be thought of as a form of RAM applied to security foreign policy (see Chapter 4).

Here it is important to explain the paradox of why, if the outcome of war was obvious from the start, a less costly negotiated settlement that reflects the expected outcome was not agreed upon at the beginning. Fearon argues that rational states prefer war over negotiated settlements in two situations: (1) when rational leaders are unable to locate a mutually beneficial negotiated settlement due to private information about their own relative capabilities and/or resolve and the incentives of both parties in misrepresenting this information; and (2) commitment problems resulting from the anarchical system.

First, in conflict situations state A can lack information about both state B's willingness to fight and/or its relative capabilities. For example, when Japan attacked the US at Pearl Harbor in 1941 the Japanese did not believe that the US response would be full scale war for control of the Pacific. The reason for these miscalculations is that leaders have incentives to misrepresent their true resolve, for instance by signaling that they are more committed to defending an interest than they actually are in an attempt to gain bargaining leverage. Given that leaders have incentives to misrepresent their resolve, other states will not always trust the veracity of the signals. During the July 1914 crisis, a key question for Germany was whether Russia would go to war to support Serbia or whether they would acquiesce in an Austro-Hungarian action against Serbia. Russia sent signals to Germany saying they would fight to support Serbia, but German officials believed it was a bluff. In the words of Secretary of State Jagow, 'there is certain to be some blustering in St. Petersburg' (quoted in Fearon 1995: 397). Events would show that Russia was not bluffing.

States can also disagree about their relative strength due to the possession of private information about their capabilities. This cause of war stems from a fundamental dilemma – to prevent war states must signal strength, but to avoid losing in war they must also jealously guard their military secrets (e.g. the exact placement of fortifications and the number of weapons possessed and their exact capabilities). The Russo-Japanese war of 1904 resulted from a refusal by Russia to compromise despite repeated Japanese offers. The Russian intransigence was based upon their overestimation of their military capabilities relative to those of the Japanese. If the Japanese told the Russians about their 'true' strength by revealing private information, either the Russians would not believe it or they would exploit the information in battle – either way the Japanese had no incentive to divulge their true strength.

Second, there can be commitment problems that can lead states to choose war over negotiated settlements. Due to anarchy, neither side trusts the other, making negotiated settlements over sensitive issues such as territory very difficult. Disputes over territory are the most common source of interstate conflict (Vasquez 1993; Vasquez and Henehan 2001). One historical example that illustrates the logic is the 1939 Winter War between Finland and the Soviet Union (Fearon 1995). Stalin made a relatively minor territorial demand of Finland, which feared that this was just the first step in a series of demands for territorial concessions. Given that the Finns did not trust the Soviet Union, they chose war over negotiation and compromise.

Furthermore, states can have incentives not to commit themselves to future policies. In particular, rising powers can have incentives to challenge other actors in the future, whereas existing powers can have incentives to exploit their current power superiority to launch preemptive wars (Gilpin 1981; Fearon 1995).

In order to harness expected utility, in practice you need to possess good information that enables you to reconstruct the expected utility calculation of leaders on both sides. In particular, what kind of situation do leaders think they are facing? How do they rank their goals (in technical terms, what is their utility function)? What options do they perceive are available? And how do they think others will react to the different options (Jervis 1989a)?

Expected utility theory has been subjected to strong critique from cognitive theories (see Chapter 4). The core of the critique has been focused upon the strong assumptions made about the rationality of leaders, where cognitive theorists contend that the single most important factor explaining why leaders choose war over negotiated settlement is misperception (Levy 1983; Stoessinger 1998). Common misperceptions include a leader holding an inflated image of him or herself, viewing the adversary's intentions in a too negative light, or holding incorrect views of his or her adversary's capabilities due to wishful thinking (Stoessinger 1998: 211). A famous example of misperception was Hitler's decision to invade the Soviet Union and his fateful misperception of Soviet power based upon his beliefs in the inherent inferiority of the Slavic nations, best indicated by Hitler's decision not to issue winter uniforms to his soldiers invading the Soviet Union in 1941.

Finally, minor wars can be chosen as diversions in order to bolster public support for a regime. Here the idea is that leaders can use adventurous foreign policies to divert public attention away from (a) unpopular domestic policies, (b) a poor domestic situation (low or negative economic growth, high unemployment and inflation) or (c) from domestic unrest. War or the threat of war causes the public to 'rally round the flag' in support of their leaders (Levy 2003; Brulé 2008). There are for instance numerous historical examples of what is termed 'jingoism', where elites use aggressive foreign policies (including war) to promote domestic patriotism.

Probing deeper into the relationship in the US context, some scholars have recently suggested that the president's relations with Congress is an important intervening factor between unpopularity and military action (e.g. Brulé 2008). A president, who is unpopular due to poor domestic economic or political conditions, but has the support of Congress, is likely to choose to pass domestic legislation that attempts to improve the situation. In contrast, when an unpopular president is unable to act domestically he or she can choose to use force abroad to distract voters from domestic woes. Presidents tend to choose wars when (a) the economy is doing badly, (b) when they are in the later stages of the electoral cycle, and (c) when their general support in Congress is low (Wang 1996). However, other studies have not found an impact on the level of Congressional support. Howell and Pevehouse (2005) in a study of US military operations from 1945 to 2000 find that congressional support does not matter in minor conflicts, suggesting that presidents enjoy relatively free hands in such military actions. The picture is quite different as regards the major use of force, where the level of partisan support matters greatly for the president's use of force.

Why states prefer certain military/strategic options over others: the role of strategic culture

Why do two states in comparable strategic environments choose very different options? Theories of strategic culture attempt to explain why states choose differently by investigating state-level factors. Strategic culture can be thought of as a set of shared beliefs and assumptions derived from common experiences and accepted narratives that shape collective identity, influencing which security foreign policy tools are viewed as appropriate for achieving security objectives (adapted from Glenn 2009: 530). The theory is closest to mainstream constructivist work on national identity, which as we saw in Chapter 3 has a degree of overlap with some forms of neoclassical realism, in particular in the work by Barkin and Sterling-Folker. Where the two theories diverge is whether culture is 'ideas all the way down' (as in constructivist thought) or whether ideas and identities are secondary to material factors (neoclassical realism). In constructivism a security culture forms an ideational milieu which limits choices.

The theory investigates how the domestic cultural context impacts upon the identification and choice of preferred military options by states. Johnston (1995: 46–7) helpfully suggests two sets of assumptions that form the basis of a given strategic culture: (1) basic assumptions about the orderliness of the environment, and (2) assumptions as to which strategic options are viewed as most effective in dealing with threats. Each of these assumptions can be further split into both basic assumptions and more operational ones regarding:

1. The frequency of war in human affairs (inevitable or aberration).
2. The nature of the adversary (zero-sum or positive).
3. The effectiveness of force.

High values on all of the assumptions together result in what Johnston terms a 'hard realpolitik' strategic culture, where a state is predisposed to choose foreign policy security strategies involving the use of offensive military strategies, whereas at the low end are states that tend to choose diplomatic options, given that they believe that threats can be easily managed using negotiations involving trade-offs and compromises. Taken together, these assumptions at both the basic and operational levels result in a shared set of values that is theorized to be embedded in the political mindset of a given state, affecting the choice of security policies.

The strategic culture of a given state is expected to be evident in key texts and can be tested using analytical tools such as content analysis, cognitive mapping and symbol analysis. The case of Japan can be used to demonstrate the impact of strategic culture, where norms of appropriate actions were institutionalized after World War II, resulting in a strategic culture favoring economic rather than military options (Katzenstein and Okawara 1993). In terms of the assumptions espoused by Johnston, we would suggest that Japan scores low on all of these, resulting in a diplomacy-biased strategic culture.

Preventing war: creating stable balances of power

Defensive structural realists argue that a stable balance of power can in theory prevent wars between major powers (Waltz 1979). Bipolar systems like the US–Soviet rivalry during the Cold War are seen as the most stable systems, whereas a multipolar system is more prone to war given that it is more difficult to assess clearly whether the system is in balance. With states constantly switching alliances to balance against perceived imbalances, the power of specific alliances is less predictable, raising the risk of miscalculations that can lead to war.

Prominent defensive structural realists such as Kenneth Waltz and Stephen Walt believe that the international system pressures states to undertake moderate forms of behavior, termed 'balancing', in order to preserve the balance between great powers. Balancing has two elements: an internal one that describes state strategies – such as the modernization program of Japan in the late 19th century (the Meiji Restoration) – that are designed to increase the capabilities of a state, and an external foreign policy element involving alliances with other states to balance against a common foe. Weaker powers will always fear the strongest power in the system as, regardless of what the strongest power might say, the weaker state can never be sure whether the great power will exploit its own power to dominate the weaker state or even threaten its very survival through military intervention. Therefore weaker states have a strong interest in balancing against stronger powers.

State security policy is relatively defensive as effective balancing is relatively swift and easy to achieve due to the ease of forming alliances. Further, the so-called offense/defense balance in warfare has historically been tilted toward defense, with an effective defense costing far fewer resources than an offensive military force that can threaten other states. A commonly cited maxim states that offensive forces need to outnumber defenders by a ratio of 3 to 1 to succeed. Counterbalancing against expansion by great powers is even easier in the nuclear age, as it is relatively inexpensive to build a credible nuclear deterrent that prevents aggression (Waltz 1990). Great powers are therefore relatively assured that they will not be attacked by other powers. These factors make offensive strategies of expansion and aggression that aim to upset the balance of power difficult and often even counterproductive (Waltz 1979: 126–7). Foreign policy is therefore dominated by moderate, status quo-oriented defensive strategies, with states striving to achieve what can be termed the 'appropriate' amount of power necessary to ensure survival and protect state autonomy from the domination of others (Waltz 1979: 204). Note that the term 'appropriate' is a very ambiguous term, and Waltz has never clearly defined how we can empirically evaluate this prediction.

As discussed in Chapter 2, offensive structural realists are generally more pessimistic about the creation and maintenance of stable balances of power, which are difficult to achieve due to the difficulties for states to calculate with any degree of accuracy when the 'appropriate' level of power has been reached that can ensure state survival and autonomy. Alliances entered into by a state are at best very temporary marriages of convenience.

An analysis of state security foreign policy better captures real world events when it incorporates the distinction between regional and global balances of power. Many realists distinguish between the global and regional level. John Mearsheimer argues that *global* hegemony is impossible given geographic factors. In particular, oceans are a strong limiting factor that prevents even the greatest power from dominating globally. Due to the stopping power of water, states tend to focus upon threats from regional great powers and are most concerned with preventing regional hegemony. Therefore, despite the US being the greatest power today, Mearsheimer expects that India would be more concerned with balancing against rising Chinese power than against the US superpower. *Regional* hegemony is only possible when geography blesses a potential hegemon with no neighboring great powers, as was the case for the UK in the 19th century and the US today. The US acts as an 'offshore' balancer, attempting to prevent any one power from achieving regional hegemony that would limit its influence in the region (Mearsheimer 2001). Furthermore, while structural realists like Waltz see balancing behavior as being close to a law of nature, the historical record suggests that, more often than not, states either attempt to hide from growing powers or even to ally with them through bandwagoning (Schroeder 1994).

Neoclassical realists contend that there are (at least) two reasons why states can fail to balance against external threats. First are cognitive factors relating to misperceptions of the external environment (see pp. 111–15). Second, even if state leaders are able to perceive correctly the strong systemic pressures they face, domestic politics can play a role. It is by no means certain that domestic elites share their views, nor can leaders be assured that they will be able to mobilize the necessary domestic resources to counter effectively a threat or seize an opportunity. The key factors here are the level of autonomy of the foreign policy decision-makers from domestic pressures to pursue a foreign policy strategy of their own choosing, and their ability to extract resources from the state to follow the strategy.

There is a difference between a strong and weak state. In a strong state, the executive is better able to respond effectively to systematic pressures than one in a 'weak' state which is highly constrained by domestic (societal) pressures. While structural realists ignore these differences for parsimony reasons, assuming that states can mobilize their latent power, neoclassical realists provide a toolbox to analyze these differences (see Chapter 3).

Neoclassical realists contend that national resources have to be extracted from society, which means that, despite possessing large latent resources in the form of national wealth, a weak state may not be able to convert them into more tangible power resources such as military equipment due to domestic factors. For instance, in some states the demands by key constituencies for domestic spending can crowd out military expenditures, as was the case for most of the Cold War in Europe, where many NATO countries spent much lower percentages of the national manufacturing base on the military than the US, despite the massive threat posed by Soviet forces on the other side of the Iron Curtain. Another example was the dormancy of US power in the 1880s and 1890s, where a decentralized and divided state was unable to convert the rising US material power into influence abroad (Zakaria 1998).

Schweller (2004) has for instance developed a neoclassical realist theory of underbalancing that investigates the roles of domestic politics and executive strength to explain when and why underbalancing against external threats occurs. Schweller explores how variation in state coherence matters for the ability of a state to respond to systemic threats. State coherence is determined by four different factors: (1) the level of elite consensus about the systemic challenges facing the state; (2) the level of government vulnerability to being removed from office; (3) the level of social cohesion; and (4) the level of elite cohesion. As was seen in the US prior to the Pearl Harbor attack of December 7, 1941, US elites did not agree that there was a strong external threat. Therefore, there was little chance that they would support the introduction of policies that potentially could have enabled the US to balance effectively against the Japanese threat and so prevent the attack from happening. Further, Schweller posits that domestically weak governments also have to take into consideration the political costs of foreign policy strategies, suggesting that timidity is the result. States that have fragmented societies are also more likely to underreact to external threats. Finally, high levels of elite polarization make effective balancing strategies less likely. All of these factors played a role in the lack of British balancing against the rising German threat in the 1930s. Despite the massive rearmament by Hitler's Germany, British 'elites were paralyzed by the threat of social unrest and fears that the domestic political system could not stand the strains of rearmament' (Schweller 2004: 189). British 'balancing' against Germany first occurred in the aftermath of the German seizure of the rest of Czechoslovakia in early 1939, after which Britain together with France gave security guarantees to Greece, Poland, Romania and Turkey in the event of German invasion.

Preventing war: deterrence and coercive diplomacy

Rational deterrence theory deals with foreign policies of threat and rewards that can deter an adversary from going to war. The aim of deterrence is to persuade an opponent not to take military action by convincing it that the costs and risk of doing so will outweigh the expected gains. In this respect rational deterrence theory is analogous

---

Box 6.1 Nuclear deterrence as a game of Chicken

Nuclear deterrence formed the core of rational deterrence theory during the Cold War. The basic conundrum facing both the Soviet Union and the US was how one could convince the other party that one would commit self-destruction to protect vital national interests. If the Soviet Union decided to invade West Berlin, would the US initiate nuclear strikes in retaliation, full knowing that this would most likely result in the total annihilation of both states in a nuclear conflagration? However, the US could not hope to defend the 'island' of West Berlin with conventional forces, making it dependent upon the threat of nuclear retaliation to deter a Soviet attack. Yet how could the US convince the Soviets that they would commit suicide in order to protect West Berlin?

The logic of convincing one's enemy that a conventional attack upon a vital interest will result in a nuclear response that destroys *both* parties can be best analyzed by applying the Game of Chicken. The Chicken Game involves two cars driving directly toward each other (illustrated in the classic movie *Rebel Without a Cause*). The first driver to swerve to avoid collision is a 'chicken'. If both drivers continue, the result is mutual destruction (both drivers die). The basic problem in the Chicken Game is how does one convince one's opponent that you are prepared to commit suicide in order to win the game? One way to do this is to throw one's steering wheel away in full view of the other driver, locking the car on a straight course in the hope that the demonstration of irrevocable commitment will convince the other driver to swerve. However, if both parties do this at the same time, or the other driver fails to notice that you have thrown your wheel out, this tactic for creating a 'credible commitment' is a sure-fire recipe for mutual death.

During the Cold War, massive efforts were made by both sides to convince the other that they were actually prepared to do the unthinkable to protect vital national interests. This resulted in the development

➡

---

to expected utility theory – both of which focus upon the calculation of the costs and benefits of military action versus its alternatives based upon the goals of actors (i.e. utility functions), and both utilize the RAM of decision-making (see Chapter 4). In contrast, Prospect theory would suggest that attempts to deter an adversary are more likely to be successful if the adversary sees itself in the domain of gains than the domain of losses (Levy 1992b: 289). This is particularly the case regarding deterring an adversary from initiating an action instead of compelling it to undo what has already been done. In the case of the latter, the adversary will take its gains as the new status quo due to the endowment effect, turning any attempt to restore the previous status quo into a domain of losses for the adversary.

In a situation with two rational actors – initiator and defender – the

➔

of the doctrine of Mutually Assured Destruction, a doctrine that came to be known by its appropriate acronym – MAD. In the MAD doctrine, a violation of a vital interest by one's opponent would be met with swift retaliation. Given that both parties had counter-strike capabilities, MAD meant that the costs of threatening the opponent's vital interests were so high that it would be irrational to do so.

The inherent logical problems with the 'rational' logic of nuclear deterrence were best expressed in the 1964 Kubrick movie *Doctor Strangelove*. In the movie, the Soviet Union built a nuclear doomsday device that would be automatically triggered if a military attack was initiated upon the Soviet Union. This deterrent would be completely credible as it was analogous to the driver in the Chicken Game throwing the steering wheel out of the window. Unfortunately, human error entered into the equation on both sides, resulting in an unplanned annihilation of humanity. On the US side, a rogue commander sent a B-52 to attack the Soviets. Once it is discovered, the US tells the Soviets what has happened. The Soviets then inform the US that the stakes are even higher. They had not yet informed the US that the doomsday device existed, even though the machine had gone into operation – if the US bomber strikes the device would be triggered. Despite cooperating in trying to recall or shoot down the bomber, they do not succeed, with the result that the Soviet's 'credible commitment' doomsday device destroys the world.

The movie illustrated the all too real paradox of nuclear deterrence – an automatic system that is completely credible will result in the destruction of the world due to inevitable human error sooner or later, but if the system is not automatic the deterrent threat is not very credible, as no *rational* human being would actually push the button that would destroy the world, and who would trust a madman with custody of the button?

defender seeks to prevent an attack by the initiator upon its own interests in an area by formulating a commitment to defend it (Achen and Snidal 1989). To be effective, the defender's commitments must be: (a) clearly defined in terms of which behavior is unacceptable; (b) clearly communicated by the defender; (c) the defender must have the means to punish violations and the commitment must be deemed sufficient to achieve its aims by the initiator; and (d) the commitment must be seen as credible in the eyes of the initiator (Lebow 1981: 85–9; Achen and Snidal 1989). Credibility of a commitment is linked with the state possessing a clear national interest in an area that can be seen by an opponent (Craig and George 1995: 191). For instance, Hitler did not believe that the Allied guarantee to aid Poland was credible as he believed that Poland was of little value to the allies.

Deterrence policies can be very attractive as a cost-effective tool of foreign policy. When they succeed the defender has protected a vital national interest with little or no cost, and no force is used. In contrast, the actual use of force often increases the determination of an opponent (Schelling 1966).

As with expected utility theory, rational deterrence theory has come under harsh criticism from cognitive theorists who contend that we should not assume that leaders are fully 'rational'. Instead, in most empirical cases where rational deterrence theory predicts that deterrence policies would succeed, the theory actually fails as leaders misperceive and miscalculate (Lebow 1981; Lebow and Stein 1989; Jervis 1989a). Jervis contends that leaders almost never understand each other's goals, fears and beliefs, and almost always miss or misperceive signals that in theory are clear commitments that should deter an opponent (Jervis 1989a).

Beyond signaling commitments, states can engage in coercive diplomacy, which can be defined as an even more muscular foreign policy of threats and limited force aimed at coercing an 'opponent to call off or undo an encroachment – for example, to halt an invasion or give up territory that has been occupied' (Craig and George 1995: 196). The Cuban Missile Crisis is one illustrative example of successful coercive diplomacy, where the US naval blockade, backed up by threats of air strikes and invasion, resulted in the removal of Soviet missiles from Cuba. Coercive diplomacy works best in theory when the issue is not purely zero-sum. The prospect of joint gains enables a negotiated settlement to be reached. In the Cuban Missile Crisis, a major concern of the US was to preserve its strategic superiority in missiles, whereas Soviet leader Khrushchev was most interested in security guarantees for Cuba (Gaddis 1997). Through a carefully formulated compromise, the US signaled it respected Cuban sovereignty while the Soviet Union removed its missiles from Cuba (sweetened by the tacit promise that the US would withdraw similar missiles from Turkey). If the situation is pure zero-sum, neither party has incentives to compromise, making war more likely (Craig and George 1995).

Preventing war: strong liberal theories on transformations due to democracy and interdependence

Strong liberal theories suggest that war as an instrument of security foreign policy is becoming increasingly obsolete due to the expansion of the democratic and liberal economic zones of peace. Mutual democracy and/or high levels of economic interdependence are theorized to result in more pacific relations between states, reducing the risk of war.

In the following I will review both the democratic and liberal economic peace literatures.

Strong liberal theorization on the democratic peace has exploded in the last two decades. In the words of Bruce Russett, the finding that democratic states do not go to war with each other is 'the closest thing we have to an empirical law in the study of international relations' (quoted in Owen 1994: 87). This does not mean that democracies do not go to war with non-democratic states; only that mutual democracy is seen as sufficient to produce peace between two countries. Foreign policy-making between two democratic states becomes transformed, with factors intrinsic to the democratic political system resulting in the non-violent resolution of conflicts. I now offer a short introduction to the voluminous debate, focusing upon the two variants of the theory: institutional and normative.

The institutional variant of democratic peace theory contends that democratic institutions constrain the ability of governments to wage war (also termed a 'structural variant'). The primary mechanism is the democratic *accountability* of leaders that want to be re-elected. While a capricious dictator can (in theory) freely start a war, democratic leaders are ultimately accountable to voters through free and fair elections, and are open to criticism of their actions in the free press. As voters at the end of the day are the ones that pay for foreign wars with their blood and treasure, voters will tend to be opposed to foreign wars (see p. 72).

The accountability constraint can be even stronger when executives need to secure the approval by a legislature for a foreign war. Besides the direct effect from democratic accountability, some scholars argue that democracies are slower at mobilizing for war due to the need to build domestic consensus, making it more likely that leaders can find a peaceful settlement to their differences in the build-up to war. Finally, given that leaders need to build domestic consensus and are accountable to domestic voters, if a democratic state mobilizes for war the other democratic state, aware of the difficulty of mobilizing in a democracy, will see the mobilization as a clear and credible *signal of resolve* and will back down in disputes unless it is equally resolved, which is almost never the case (Fearon 1995; Schultz 1998). Due to signaling, two democratic states avoid war caused by misperceptions of resolve.

The institutional variant has been the subject of much criticism. The most damaging is that the mechanisms of accountability do not explain the puzzle of why democracies only refrain from war with each other; democracies are otherwise just as likely to go to war as non-democracies (Farber and Gowa 1995). If the domestic unpopularity of war makes it hard for democracies to go to war, we should expect that this public aversion would be the same irrespective of the regime type of the target state. Further, Rosato (2003: 594) makes the point that in many ways non-democratic leaders are actually more 'accountable' than democratic leaders, as they are more prone to be removed or even killed after losing a war or engaging in a costly foreign war. Finally, some realist scholars have argued that the democratic peace theory is actually reversed, in that democracy is only possible in 'safe neighborhoods' where there are few severe conflicts of interest (Farber and Gowa 1995). Democracy and peace co-vary, but peace is created by common interests, not democracy.

The other variant of democratic peace theory is a normative variant. Politicians in democratic systems are used to negotiating and compromising with each other in non-violent fashion. For instance, it is very rare for democratic politicians to use force against each other during law-making, although there have been some isolated instances in weak democracies (certain Asian states) or during extreme political crises. For example, a US senator drew a pistol on another in 1850 on the floor of the Senate during a heated debate on slavery in the West.

When facing conflicts with other democratic states, democratic norms of compromise and peaceful resolution of conflict are theorized to become externalized as democratic leaders from both states reflexively view each other as democratic politicians who are used to negotiating and compromising. In contrast, when facing a non-democratic opponent, a democratic state will not trust or respect the non-democratic leaders, and therefore violent conflict can occur (Rousseau *et al.* 1996). Some theorists go so far as to conclude that democratic states are actually more prone to engage in 'crusading' wars against non-democratic states due to a lack of respect for non-democratic regimes that are seen to repress their population (Rosato 2003).

The normative variant of democratic peace theory can explain the puzzle of why democracies do not go to war with each other, but are just as prone to go to war with non-democracies as other states. Yet there are anomalies that are still difficult to explain. For example, if democracies externalize norms of peaceful conflict resolution, why did the US engage in violent *covert* actions against other democracies during the Cold War, including assisting coups in Iran (1953) and Chile (1973) against democratic regimes (Rosato 2003: 590)? Another major problem in the literature has been how we can measure democratic norms. As good quantitative measures do not exist, most quantitative studies of the democratic peace thesis only test the institutional variant despite qualitative evidence that shows that the normative variant has the strongest explanatory power. For example, Owen (1994) in a qualitative study found strong evidence for the impact that democratic (liberal) norms had on liberal elites acting within a democratic political system.

Turning to liberal economic peace theory, the idea that trade results in more peaceful foreign policies has a long history in liberal thought, stretching back at least to the writings of Kant and Montesquieu. The basic argument is that 'the greater the amount of trade, the higher the price of conflict, and the less the amount of conflict that is demanded' (Polachek 1980: 60), although many liberal scholars now accept that this relationship is conditional upon how evenly the dependence upon trade is distributed. In situations where both states are equally dependent, we should expect more pacific relations, whereas if one party is much more dependent upon the relationship than the other, this dependency can be a source of power that can be exploited by the less dependent party (Keohane and Nye 2001). Asymmetric dependence can therefore result in more conflictual relations and even war (Moravcsik 1997).

Economic ties are theorized to (1) constrain state behavior due to the pressure from powerful, affected, domestic constituencies, (2) change state goals over time due to the growth of pro-interdependence domestic constituencies and (3) make it easier for states to signal their true level of resolve in crisis due to the opportunity to exchange greater information, making war due to misunderstandings less likely.

The dynamic in theories of economic interdependence is that large volumes of trade and investment remove the incentive for states to engage in conflict. Societal actors such as competitive exporting firms have strong self-interests in trade and they lobby governmental authorities to adopt policies that protect their trading relationships. Governments, in order to maintain the support of important societal groups, will adopt foreign policies that protect beneficial trading relationships (Mansfield and Pollins 2001: 841). Governments can also be dependent upon the continued willingness of foreign investors to buy government bonds in order to finance public spending. Taken as a whole, a society would incur significant exit costs if economic ties with partners were severed, making the state reluctant to engage in conflicts with the partner state (Crescenzi 2003).

More recent theorization has argued that it is not only exit costs that matter, but that as the major source of interstate conflict and war is a misunderstanding about the resolve of the other party in crises, trade or capital flows can be manipulated by a state in order to signal resolve. Here it is the very fact that reducing trade has costs for a state that matters for the strength of the signal of resolve. By using 'costly' signals instead of 'cheap talk', states can avoid the uncertainty that can lead to war (Gartzke *et al.* 2001).

Realists rebut the liberal 'trade produces peace' thesis with several arguments. One oft used argument is that high levels of trade did not prevent World War I and other major conflicts. Second, many realists argue that high levels of trade actually can create *more* insecurity, as the gains of trade are usually not evenly distributed amongst states, creating shifts in the distribution of power that can result in interstate insecurity and conflict (Gilpin 1981; Grieco 1988; Gowa 1994). This line of theorization is inspired by mercantilist ideas from the 17th and 18th century (see Chapter 7).

Further, if one state is more dependent upon an economic relationship this creates vulnerabilities that the less dependent state can exploit as a source of leverage over the other. Waltz (1979: 138) has argued that 'close interdependence nears closeness of contact and raises the prospects of occasional conflict'. The reason for the increase in conflict is that 'close interdependence is a condition in which one party can scarcely move without jostling others; a small push ripples through society. The closer the social bonds, the more extreme the effect becomes, and one cannot sensibly pursue an interest without taking others' interests into account. One country is then inclined to treat another country's acts as events within its own polity and to attempt to control them', with conflict as the inevitable result (Waltz 2000: 14).

Finally, a further realist argument is that 'trade follows the flag', meaning that the causal relationship is reversed (Keshk *et al.* 2004). When governments have few conflicts with each other's trade we see that trade flows increase, but when there are serious conflicts of interests that can potentially result in war, trade flows decrease. Therefore, finding trade is correlated with peace does not mean that X_{trade} produces Y_{peace}; instead the connection can be the reverse, with X_{peace} producing Y_{trade}.

Liberals have responded to these arguments by developing more conditional theories about when we should expect a liberal peace caused by interdependence to exist. Moravcsik (1997) has argued that whether trade promotes peace depends upon the pattern of costs and benefits of foreign trade upon powerful domestic groups. Others have argued that the liberal peace only works for developed states (Hegre 2000), or that trade inhibits conflict only under the auspices of preferential trading arrangements (Mansfield and Pevehouse 2000).

Another response to the realist critique has been that many liberals have accepted that asymmetric interdependence, where one state is more dependent upon a relationship than the other, can be a source of power for the least dependent state (Baldwin 1980). Keohane and Nye (2001) discuss how vulnerability of a given state to costs imposed by external events can affect levels of state power. Therefore, high levels of dependence upon economic relationships with other states can be a significant external constraint upon state foreign policy. For instance, during the 1973 Arab–Israel war, OPEC countries exploited the dependence of Western European countries upon Middle Eastern oil by threatening to cut supplies to countries that supported Israel in the conflict. This resulted in countries like West Germany not allowing the US to use West German bases to resupply Israel (Young and Kent

2004: 432). The US, in contrast, was not as vulnerable to this threat as it only imported 5 per cent of its oil from the Middle East.

Conflict resolution and the termination of international conflicts

Rationalist explanations see war itself as a bargaining process (Fearon 1995; Schelling 1966; Wagner 2000). Therefore, when two states in armed conflict both perceive that the benefits of a negotiated settlement or otherwise stopping a war are greater than the value of continued conflict, they will stop the conflict. When conflicts are caused by private information about resolve and/or capabilities, wars are often relatively short affairs as the level of certainty of information increases over time (see pp. 55–6). Each battle reveals information about the 'true' capabilities and resolve of the parties. Once the relative balance is obvious, settlement can be reached based upon the relative capabilities and resolve of the two parties. In this type of conflict, third-party intervention in the form of *mediation* is particularly effective when the efforts of the parties involved in a conflict has reached an impasse, or what can be termed a 'hurting stalemate'. Mediation involves non-coercive, non-binding third-party intervention in conflicts. Early theories saw the neutrality of mediators as vital for their ability to broker a resolution of a conflict – with the mediator being perceived as an 'honest broker'. Young wrote that 'the existence of a meaningful role for a third party will depend on the party's being perceived as an impartial participant' (quoted in Carnevale and Arad 1996: 40). A broad consensus today is that neutrality is not always a quality, depending upon whether the costs of continued conflict (a hurting stalemate) are seen as greater than any biases from the mediator (Touval and Zartman 1985). Further, mediators sometimes succeed because they have ways they can twist the arms of protagonists to push them toward a deal (Carnevale 2002). However, most scholars agree that it is important that both parties trust the mediator.

One of the functions of mediation is to facilitate communication between adversaries by acting as a trusted go-between, collecting information from each party and sharing it to both (Touval and Zartman 1989: 177). Here the key to a mediator's success is that parties trust the mediator enough to disclose private information that enables resolution of the conflict (Carnevale and Arad 1996). Mediation does not affect the distribution of gains from a final outcome, which only reflects the relative capabilities and resolve of the parties.

Conflicts caused by commitment problems are more difficult to resolve. In conflicts over zero-sum issues such as territory or vital economic resources, wars can degenerate into 'absolute' or total war, where the aim is not to reach a negotiated settlement but to destroy the ability of the adversary to resist. In zero-sum issues, the gain of one party is inversely related to the losses of the other party, making conflict an all-or-nothing dispute. Mediation in this type of dispute involves tactics aimed at offering the parties compromise solutions that transform a zero-sum issue into a positive-sum issue. This includes tactics where the mediator attempts to either sweeten a deal through side-payments (carrots) or where the mediator threatens action against one or both parties (sticks) in an attempt to change their valuation of a negotiated settlement. Success here requires the mediator to possess significant resources (Carnevale and Arad 1996; Pruitt and Kim 2004). A prime example is the US role as a mediator between Israel and Egypt. As a superpower, the US was able to offer significant sticks and carrots to convince both parties to accept a deal. In this type of mediation, neutrality can actually be a drawback, as a disinterested party will lack the resources necessary to push the parties toward a mutually acceptable outcome.

Additional tactics include the formulation of 'issue linkages' that attempt to transform an issue from a zero-sum dispute on one dimension into a positive-sum dispute in multidimensions, where each party concedes in sub-issues that are less important and gains in others. This can naturally only succeed where it is possible to divide an issue into subcomponents where governments have complementary interests (Gilady and Russett 2002: 402). Mediators can assist by formulating compromises that transform the issue in ways that enable the resolution of a conflict (Touval and Zartman 1989).

If we open up the possibility that cognitive and social-psychological factors matter (see Chapter 4), dispute resolution can be seen as potentially easier during early stages of conflict but which becomes even more difficult over time than we would expect following rationalist theories. Cognitive theories contend that misperceptions and miscalculations are more prevalent than rationalist theories accept, meaning that we should expect that many conflicts are caused not just by rational, cost calculations, but instead are due to misperceptions of the objective situation. If this is the case, conflict resolution in the form of mediation that provides neutral communication about intentions can be an even more effective tool to resolve conflicts than otherwise expected to be following RAM-based models of negotiations.

However, social-psychological approaches to conflict would suggest that as a conflict escalates, and in particular when it continues over extended periods of time, psychological attitudes of the parties to the conflict will become increasingly negative, creating self-reinforcing negative images of the Other that make resolving a conflict very difficult (Pruitt and Kim 2004). Parties also can become 'entrapped' during a conflict. 'Entrapment is a process in which Party, pursuing a goal over a period of time, expends more of its time, energy, money, or other resources than seems justifiable by external standards (Pruitt and Kim 2004: 165). An example of this was the reasoning given by supporters in the US of the Vietnam War. While opponents argued that US lives should not be spent on a peripheral conflict, supporters contended that withdrawal would mean that the US had sacrificed lives in vain. Instead of withdrawing from an unwinnable war, the US continued throwing away even more life and treasure until the conflict came to an inevitable conclusion (Pruitt and Kim 2004: 166). When parties are trapped in a conflict spiral, social-psychological approaches theorize that it takes many 'positive' actions that are clearly communicated as such to overwhelm the strongly negative views held by the Other.

Chapter 7

Diplomacy

The term 'diplomacy' is for some synonymous with foreign policy itself (e.g. Kissinger 1994). As used here, the definition is narrower, referring to the range of *non-violent* foreign policy actions, including the use of declarations, meetings and negotiations with representatives of other foreign policy actors. Without diplomacy, interstate relations would be almost impossible. For many, diplomacy is the defining feature of what can be termed a more *mature*, anarchical international system (Bull 1977). For example, before the advent of international rules and norms of diplomatic protocol that offered so-called 'diplomatic immunity' to the official representatives of other states, it was a very dangerous business being a foreign emissary – even resulting in being taken hostage or killed.

Diplomatic relations between states play a crucial role in managing and preventing conflicts, negotiating agreements and ensuring communication between states. There are five main functions of diplomacy (the first four are from Bull 1977: 163–6):

1. Exchange of information between states (communication).
2. Gathering of intelligence about foreign countries.
3. Negotiation of international agreements.
4. Minimization of the effects of 'friction' in international relations caused by interactions.
5. Representing the state in world affairs, including in international organizations (Jönsson 2002).

Diplomacy is performed by professional civil servants and political representatives (usually foreign ministers and prime ministers or presidents) who are official agents of states and international organizations with standing in world politics (Bull 1977). Most countries also have a permanent network of embassies that house their professional diplomats around the world; or for smaller states in their most important countries for their foreign policies. A new phenomenon is the sharing of embassies amongst EU countries that will be discussed below.

Of all of the functions of diplomacy, bargaining and negotiations have spawned the most scholarly interest, in particular the question of what constitutes power in interstate negotiations. There are a range of different theoretical approaches to the study of negotiations: from formal game theoretical models to constructivist models of identity reconstruction through social interaction within negotiations. In the following I will explore several of the key insights from mainstream negotiation theory and how they apply to the study of negotiations in foreign policy-making. I also introduce the literature on two-level games, which is an analytical framework for studying interstate negotiations and the interplay between international and domestic pressures. Two-level games theorization also provides insights into the sources of power in negotiations, in particular the thesis that strong domestic constraints can be a bargaining asset in international negotiations. Finally, the literature on the impact of culture on negotiations is discussed.

Negotiations as a form of diplomacy

Negotiations and bargaining between states take place in situations where there is a common interest in some form of negotiated deal, but where there also is conflict about how the deal should look. 'Without common interest there is nothing to negotiate for, without conflict there is nothing to negotiate about' (Iklé 1964: 2). Reaching agreement for the fulfillment of common interests is often termed 'creating value', whereas the conflictual element of negotiations is termed 'claiming value', where the parties to a negotiation haggle over who gets the most gains out of a deal. This overlaps with the distinction between zero-sum and positive-sum issues, where zero-sum issues involve dividing a pie (claiming value), whereas positive-sum issues deal with making a pie bigger (creating value).

Negotiations are often used to resolve problems relating to *policy interdependence*. This refers to the situation where achieving the goals of one state are dependent upon the policies of other countries. The crucial link that creates dependencies between states is the concept of *policy externalities*, defined as the costs and benefits that domestic policies have upon other countries. One example of negative policy externalities is the impact that the lax environmental policies in the UK in the 1970s and 1980s had for other European countries. Acid rain created by British industry and energy production fell predominately in Norway and Sweden (and notably not in the UK), resulting in the acidification of lakes and severe damage to forests. Neither the Norwegian nor Swedish governments were able to achieve their preferred goal of clean lakes and healthy forests by themselves; instead they were dependent upon Britain changing its air quality policies. However, the problem for these two governments was that they were in a highly asymmetric bargaining situation, where the costs of imposing higher air quality standards in the UK would fall solely upon British industry and energy consumers, while the benefits of abatement would occur in Scandinavia.

Other forms of policy externalities include the effects of domestic trade policies, as for instance imposing tariffs on imports is a *negative* policy externality for other countries, whereas a unilateral reduction in tariffs by country A is a *positive* policy externality for countries exporting to country A. Another form of policy interdependence is *security interdependence*, where the defensive actions of state A in building missiles can threaten the security of state B. During the Cold War the US and Soviet Union were locked in a pattern of strategic interdependence due to the threat of mutual destruction by the thousands of nuclear weapons that they had aimed at each other (Keohane and Nye 2001: 8).

Policy interdependence therefore can create incentives to coordinate policies at the international level. In terms of foreign policy this means that when a state is dependent upon another in order to achieve its preferred policy goals, we should expect a foreign policy directed at coordinating policies with the other state, usually conducted through negotiations. For example, the mutual insecurity created by the increasingly dangerous nuclear arms race in the 1960s and 1970s created a strong incentive for the US and Soviet Union to coordinate their nuclear policies through negotiations, resulting in a series of arms control agreements.

When state goals are incompatible, or when costs and benefits fall highly unequally upon the parties, it is difficult (or even impossible) to reach agreement on the coordination of policies. In the case of the UK and air pollution, the impasse in the negotiations between the UK and Scandinavian countries was first breached when materially stronger states became involved in the process in the 1980s; especially after Germany started pushing for international reductions in air pollution after it discovered that German industry was also responsible for acid rain pollution that affected not just Scandinavia but also German forests (Levy 1995).

Levels of policy interdependence also affect levels of state power. Whereas state power in structural realism is seen as solely a product of *possessing* material capabilities, liberals hold that it also can be affected by how dependent upon an agreement a given state is relative to others. In an interstate negotiation, the state that is least dependent upon an outcome is the strongest, other things being equal. As theorized by Keohane and Nye (2001), levels of state power vary across issue areas depending upon both material power resources and levels of policy interdependence. In an issue such as fishing, small states like Iceland and Denmark can possess significant issue-specific power due to their large fishing stocks that other countries are also dependent upon gaining access to.

Box 7.1 How do we know transaction costs when we see them?

Transaction costs are defined as all of the 'costs' of negotiating a deal. Take a negotiation on a transatlantic free trade deal between the EU and the US as an example. These negotiations would involve a lengthy diplomatic process at multiple levels between the two parties, including at the civil servant, ambassadorial, ministerial and heads of state levels. Some of the costs of negotiation are sunk costs, such as the costs of maintaining permanent diplomatic representation facilities that the EU has in Washington DC and that the US has in Brussels. More direct transaction costs relate to all of the hours of preparation of positions at the civil servant and political levels on both sides prior to and during the negotiations. During the actual negotiations, armies of civil servants on both sides would be engaged. As these civil servants could be employed doing other tasks (or not hired in the first place), there is a considerable administrative sticker price associated with negotiations. The infrastructure of negotiations is often expensive, with numerous civil servants flying across the Atlantic, along with the costs of secure communication, meeting facilities, etc. Further, high-level political involvement is often vital in the endgame of negotiations to reach a final deal on politically sensitive matters such as free trade. As the time of leaders such as the US president and the president of the EU Commission is very valuable, this represents a very significant cost. Taken together, the transaction costs of transatlantic negotiations would be very high, although the potential gains from a liberalization of transatlantic trade could be far greater.

The central question that negotiation analysts ask is: Based on theory X, who should we expect to win in a given negotiation? The realist school (both structural and neoclassical) theorizes that powerful actors always win negotiations, with power defined for instance as the aggregate power resources described in Chapter 2. If a regional great power like Russia and a small state like Moldova are locked in a negotiation, we should expect that the final outcome will closely reflect Russian preferences. Realist theories also believe that negotiations are relatively 'efficient', meaning that there are usually no 'gains' left on the table. Furthermore, the transaction costs of negotiation are viewed as low *relative* to the gains of agreement. This means that while there are often sizable costs involved in negotiating a deal, the expected gains easily outweigh these costs.

Liberal theorists contend that aggregate, structural (military) power cannot be translated into power across the board. In trade negotiations between the EU and the US, despite the US scoring much higher on all dimensions of military might, the EU possesses considerable 'issue-specific' power due to the size of its economic market. The US cannot reasonably employ its military resources as a bargaining tool in trade negotiations; for example threatening to invade Belgium with the 101st Airborne Division unless the EU removes restrictions on imports of US genetically modified agricultural products. The liberal argument is therefore that power is not 'fungible' across different issues. Power in security affairs does not necessarily transfer into power in economic issues and vice versa.

Habeeb (1988) has introduced a helpful distinction of types of power resources that underlie liberal theorization on negotiations, drawing on the notion of policy interdependence. The first type of power is *structural power*, which is akin to the structural realist conceptions of power seen as an aggregate measure of an actor's resources and potential capabilities (Habeeb 1988: 17). This forms the basis for the second type of power, *issue-specific power*, which is determined by a party's domestically derived *dependence* upon an agreement. Another way of thinking about dependence is whether a party to a negotiation has a viable alternative to a negotiated agreement, defined as the party's 'best alternative to a negotiated agreement' (BATNA). A state that is vitally dependent upon securing access to another state's market has a low BATNA, while a large, self-sufficient state would have a high BATNA, as they are not dependent upon gaining access to other markets.

BATNA determines the issue-specific power of an actor. Moravcsik (1998: 63–4) summarizes this well when he states that

> governments that have poor unilateral alternatives to agreement (in other words, those relatively dependent on foreign governments) find their bargaining power is weak and must make concessions and compromises. By contrast, governments with attractive unilateral alternatives and whose policy shifts are highly valued by other governments (e.g. access to large protected markets or satisfactory macroeconomic performance) are more likely to secure concessions and compromises. In sum, those who more intensely desire the benefits of cooperation will concede more to get them.

To measure issue-specific power you therefore need to ask yourself whether there are viable alternatives to a negotiated deal available for each party.

Behavioral power relates to the process in which each actor uses structural and issue-specific power resources to alter the issue-specific power balance (Habeeb 1988: 23–4). A negotiation process involves 'moving from one issue-power balance (the pre-negotiation balance) to another issue-power balance (the outcome balance) by the mutual practice of tactics' (Habeeb 1988: 24). Behavioral power relates to tactics such as threatening to veto any but the most favorable agreement, building a coalition that alters the issue-specific power balance, or finding an alternative that lessens one's dependence upon agreement. Lax and Sebenius (1986) discuss an example of naval base negotiations between Malta and the UK in 1971. The UK had used Maltese bases since World War II, but due to technological advances was less dependent upon the bases. In negotiations for improving base rental terms, Malta was therefore in a weak initial position given the low dependency of the UK upon a deal. Malta then attempted to increase the UK's dependence by making overtures toward the Soviet Union about their having a naval base in Malta. The use of behavioral power by Malta created pressure upon the UK and its NATO allies to deny the Soviets these bases, resulting in a significant shift in dependence of the UK upon a deal. The final agreement resulted in a quadrupling of base rental payments and supplemental aid from other NATO members.

In a two-party negotiation, liberals argue that the final deal will reflect the issue-specific power balance, which in turn is a reflection of the dependence of the actors on a deal. If two parties have equal levels of dependence (issue-specific power) then they will meet in the middle and 'split the difference'. It is important to note that smaller states can 'win' over larger states in negotiations, depending upon their issue-specific power and whether they succeed in shifting this balance through the use of behavioral power.

In liberal theorization, negotiations are also seen as having low transaction costs relative to the gains of a negotiated deal. Negotiations are viewed as being inherently 'efficient'. While the parties to a negotiation do engage in a 'negotiating dance' of offers and counter-offers in an attempt to change their own and the other's issue-specific power through the use of behavioral power, negotiations are seen as relatively predictable based upon prior issue-specific power balances. The negotiation *process* itself plays a negligible role in determining outcomes (Moravcsik 1999).

However, based upon numerous case studies of negotiations, a distinct 'negotiation-analytic' approach has developed that postulates how the negotiation process matters for outcomes. Here transaction costs are perceived to be sizable, and negotiations are not inherently 'efficient'. Gains can be left on the table due to the 'fog of negotiation' (Hampson 1995; Sebenius 2002). Drawing on cognitive psychological theories (see Chapters 4 and 5), 'negotiation-analytic' approaches contend that actors are 'boundedly rational' and therefore face a range of challenges in complex negotiations. Here behavior power, or the use of tactics, can in theory be much more significant.

This approach argues that international negotiations are not what can be termed an 'efficient market' where the demand for an agreement is easily coupled with a mutually acceptable legal text. International negotiations have high transaction costs due to the many issues that are often under negotiation. Further, the 'larger the number of participants, the greater the likelihood of conflicting interests and positions, and the more complex the interconnections among the parties' (Touval 1989: 163). There are therefore often laborious efforts involved in first identifying often poorly understood problems created by interdependence between states, and then finding and reaching mutually acceptable solutions in the form of contractual agreements. This can lead either to less efficient deals being agreed or even to bargaining failure.

There are several ways in which complexity in negotiations can be managed in order to increase the efficiency of negotiations (i.e. to ensure that no 'gains' are left on the table). One way that this can be done is by adding and subtracting issues in a negotiation in order to find viable deals (Sebenius 1983). *Adding issues* can create a bargaining set where none existed when they were negotiated separately, linking two previously unrelated issues together into a package deal. This tactic can succeed when parties value two issues differently. For example, in negotiations between Egypt and Israel at the Camp David meetings in 1978 that aimed to negotiate a peace settlement, the issue of whether Israel should relinquish territorial control of the Sinai back to Egypt as it had been prior to the 1967 war was at an impasse (Fisher and Ury 1991). However, an agreement was made possible by adding the issue of demilitarization to the negotiations. Israel was not concerned about possessing territory per se; instead it was vitally concerned about security and the threat that Egyptian forces in the Sinai would pose to Israel. Egypt was preoccupied with regaining territorial sovereignty over the Sinai. Linking territorial sovereignty with the military status of the region resulted in a viable deal that brought peace between Egypt and Israel. Issues can also be *subtracted* when there is no bargaining set in one issue but where there is one in another linked issue.

Coalitions can also be built to simplify multiparty negotiations by structuring the negotiation into manageable groups (Hampson 1995). In the successful negotiations on liberalizing trade that created the World Trade Organization during the Uruguay Round of trade negotiations (1986–94), the final deal was facilitated by the development of fluid coalitions, including the Cairns group (agricultural exporting nations organized by Australia), the Rio group (informal discussions between industrial and developing countries) and the de la Paix group (Switzerland and a number of other smaller countries) (Hampson 1995: 189–91). Another function of coalition is to forge a viable compromise starting with a core (a single hegemon or group of states) that expands into a winning coalition (Zartman 2003). Expansion can take the form of either 'snowballing', where newly added parties shape the deal, or 'bandwagonning', where they merely join 'a moving machine' (Zartman 2003). Finally, complexity creates a *demand for leadership* in negotiations, defined as actions aimed at helping the parties in a negotiation to overcome high transaction costs, enabling the achievement of mutually acceptable outcomes that would otherwise not be reached. Here transaction costs relate both to (1) the 'information costs' of understanding complex problems created by interdependence and finding and reaching mutually acceptable solutions in multiparty negotiations; and (2) two collective action problems – agenda failure and the 'Negotiator's dilemma'. Agenda failure occurs in multiparty situations where each party has equal agenda-setting opportunities, resulting in each party suggesting its own preferred outcome. A solution to this problem is to delegate agenda control to one actor (Tallberg 2006). Another problem occurs when negotiations have a distributive dimension (claiming value). In the Negotiator's dilemma, sincere cooperative moves such as the disclosure of one's true bottom-line in a negotiation would be exploited by other actors that are not so forthcoming (Lax and Sebenius 1986). Yet creating value is often impossible when each party exaggerates its bottom-line, removing the possibility of joint gains that facilitate agreement.

Leadership involves setting and shaping agendas in ways that maximize the possibility for joint gains, inventing novel solutions to overcome bargaining impasses and brokering deals (Young 1991: 293–4). Leaders can facilitate negotiations by shaping the agenda, deciding what issues should be discussed and when, and proposing a focal point around which negotiations can coalesce (Tallberg 2006). The Negotiator's dilemma can be alleviated by delegating brokerage functions to a leader. If each party trusts the leader to be fair, they will be more willing to divulge their true bottom-line, enabling the leader to formulate an acceptable compromise that divides gains in an equitable manner. Finally, a leader can assist the parties in making sense of negotiations through the provision of expert information and by drafting texts that propose solutions to common problems.

Smaller states or secretariats of international organizations are often delegated leadership functions in international negotiations, helping the parties to find a mutually acceptable agreement. The reason for this is that they are often more trusted to act in a relatively neutral manner, as the scope of interests of great powers is far broader than the usually minimal reach of small state interests.

When leaders are delegated strong powers in a negotiation (e.g. the power of the chair), the leader can exploit them to craft a deal that more closely represents his or her own preferences in the process, within the limit created by the need for the deal to be still acceptable to a winning coalition of parties (usually *all* parties in international negotiations). For example, in the EU's enlargement negotiations with ten applicant states, the Danish government in the fall of 2002 exploited its delegated leadership function of holding the Council Presidency to push the final deal closer to its own preferred outcome of enlargement with all ten countries while minimizing the budgetary implications of enlargement by not offering monetary concessions to the candidate countries (Tallberg 2006).

Two-level games

Robert Putnam (1988) introduced the idea of two-level games played by leaders in foreign policy in an influential article. The basic idea of two-level games is that an executive negotiating a deal with a foreign country is playing two interacting games that have to be balanced: a domestic game to secure ratification of a final deal, and an international game to secure the best possible deal. In the middle of these two levels is the executive who negotiate deals and who also has his or her own views about what type of deal is most favorable to the national interest and to his or her own private interests in securing a deal that maximizes his or her chances of re-election (Milner 1997: 34–5).

Level 1 of the two-level game is the international level, where 'national governments seek to maximize their own ability to satisfy domestic pressures, while minimizing the adverse consequences of foreign developments'. Level 2 is the domestic level, where 'domestic groups pursue their interests by pressuring the government to adopt favorable policies, and politicians seek power by constructing coalitions among these groups' (Putnam 1988: 434). Each state is assumed to have a 'win-set', defined as 'the set of potential agreements that would be ratified by domestic constituencies in a straight up-or-down vote against the status quo of "no agreement"' (Moravcsik 1993: 23).

Win-sets (also termed 'reservation curves') can be depicted graphically in a so-called Edgeworth box, which depicts a two-party, two-issue negotiation on trade issues (Figure 7.1). The most preferred outcome for state A is Am, where state A's tariffs are high and state B's tariffs are low, and vice versa for state B. The win-sets represent the minimum deal that can be domestically ratified. If state A agrees to a deal at point 1, this will not be ratified domestically, whereas a deal at point 2 within the overlap of the two win-sets (bargaining set) will be ratified by both states.

The theoretical hypothesis that has attracted the most attention is a conjecture that was originally formulated by Thomas Schelling. The 'Schelling conjecture' posits that domestic weakness can be a bargaining asset in certain situations. An executive who is forced to secure a very preferential deal due to hawkish domestic constituencies can

Figure 7.1 *A two-party, two-issue negotiation in issue space*

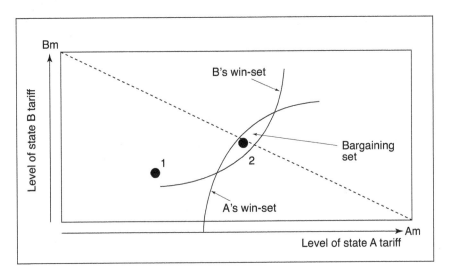

exploit having his or her hands tied domestically as a bargaining strength in the level 1 game, saying to his or her counterparts that 'I would love to agree to deal 1, but it would never be passed by my legislature'. In the words of Schelling (1960: 19), 'the power of a negotiator often rests on a manifest inability to make concessions and meet demands'. Domestic constraints are related to how an international deal is ratified domestically, which affects the placement of the win-sets of actors (Milner 1997). More domestic constituencies have to be satisfied when a deal has to be ratified with large majorities in the legislature (e.g. two-thirds majority as in the US Senate), whereas fewer are required when using a simple majority.

Figure 7.2 illustrates the hypothesized effect of a strong domestic constraint. The bargaining situation at the start of a negotiation is illustrated with bargaining set I, depicting the overlap between A's and B's win-sets (A has win-set I). Here we should expect agreement 2 to be accepted.

If state A *ties its hands* by changing how the final deal will be ratified, by for example committing itself to ratification through the legislature, this can result in a shift from win-set I to a new, more restrictive win-set (shift inwards) for state A that is closer to Am, assuming that the legislature has more restrictive preferences than the government. A real-world example of this is the US in climate change negotiations during the 1990s, where the Clinton Administration faced a Congress that held more restrictive preferences. This is depicted as a more restrictive win-set (win-set with domestic constraints). The result of tying hands would be a shift in the agreement from point 2 to 3,

Figure 7.2   *The impact of a domestic constraint*

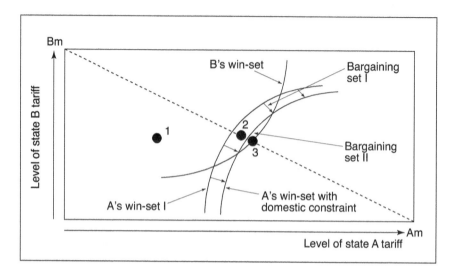

shifting the deal closer to state A's preferred outcome. In this example, tying hands increases the utility of the deal for the constrained state in this circumstance, whereas it decreases the utility of the final deal for state B (point 3 is farther from Bm than point 2).

A key factor in determining whether domestic constraints grant bargaining advantages is the credibility of the threat of non-ratification. Tying hands only works when other states believe that a country will actually carry out the threat of non-ratification. In negotiations between democracies it can be difficult for an executive to exaggerate the level of domestic constraints, as other states can read in the media whether there is strong domestic opposition or not. In negotiations with autocratic leaders it can be more difficult to evaluate claims, although very little research has been done to test whether such leaders are more successful in claims of the tightness and inflexibility of their domestic constraints. In general, however, the Schelling conjecture has not found much empirical support, with a few notable exceptions such as negotiations within the EU.

The preferences of the negotiator and domestic constituencies matter (Milner 1997). In theory, the situation in Figure 7.2 could be the opposite, with the government favoring a more restrictive deal, whereas the legislature that has to ratify it favors a more lax deal. Here the outcome would shift from point 3 to point 2 if the agreement had to be ratified domestically, shifting gains away from state A.

Win-sets can also be shifted when executives loosen domestic ratification requirements or by buying off domestic constituencies ('cutting slack') (Moravcsik 1993). In the US, presidents have often sought so-called 'Fast Track' authority in negotiating international trade deals, where Congress grants the president a mandate for the types of agreements they will consent to. In return, Congress promises that they will not amend the final deal and will decide on it within a shorter time frame, making it more likely that a trade deal will survive Congress. An example of 'buying off' constituencies was during the SALT I negotiations with the Soviet Union, where President Nixon bought support from the military for reductions by agreeing to back the production of a new nuclear armed submarine (Trident) (Mayer 1992: 806).

Executives can also target the domestic constituencies of state B to shift the win-set of that state. This can involve targeted issue linkages or side-payments to particularly powerful domestic constituencies in state B that shift what can be ratified by that state, or through the use of 'reverberation', where the actions of state A alter the expectations of agreement held by domestic groups in state B (Mayer 1992; Moravcsik 1993).

The two-level game model can be used to analyze a range of international negotiations in which domestic constraints and the international game interact. In particular, the model draws our attention to the impact that domestic constraints have upon negotiations, and how these constraints can be manipulated to either facilitate agreement ('cutting slack') or to achieve a better negotiated deal ('tying hands').

Negotiations and culture

Culture can be defined as 'a set of shared and enduring meanings, values, and beliefs that characterize national, ethnic or other groups and orient their behavior' (Faure and Sjösted 1993: 3). Weiss (1994) has suggested five ways that culture can affect negotiations through its impact on negotiating actors: (1) how they understand the negotiations; (2) their orientation toward time; (3) their risk averseness/acceptance; (4) their protocol and proper behavior; and (5) their decision-making style (formal or informal). This can result in a situation where the very rules of the negotiating game are not common knowledge and significant cultural differences can exacerbate conflicts and prevent intercultural communication.

Cohen (2001) suggests a broader difference relating to whether the culture is a high context or a low context society, defined in terms of the degree of collectivistic nature of the culture. In high context culture, speech is about preserving and promoting societal interests, meaning that language is often more about pleasing others and evasion than what can be thought of as 'painful precision', making it hard for diplomats from high-context cultures to deal with those from low-context ones, where there is a 'get to the point' understanding of communication and language. For example, when Americans (low-context) negotiated with Egypt (high-context), they found that Egyptians hated to say no, and therefore negotiations would tend to drag on endlessly. If consent was reached, it was not certain whether it was a genuine consensus or merely pleasing but insincere behavior on the part of the Egyptians (Cohen 2001).

This example illustrates the fact that the concept of culture is notoriously fuzzy, making any form of determinate predictions based upon a theory of culture nigh impossible (Bercovitch and Elgström 2001). Often theories degenerate into cruder forms of national stereotyping that oversimplify a very complex reality. An additional challenge is that the concept of culture is almost impossible to measure in practice, especially in quantitative terms. How can we create an objective indicator for a low-context or high-context culture?

That said, culture plays an important role in negotiations across cultures, affecting how actors perceive issues and the intentions that they attribute to other actors, along with patterns of communication during negotiations that are important to be aware of. The most productive uses of the concept would focus on limited applications, attempting to develop mid-range theories for how particular aspects of 'culture' impact upon negotiation processes.

Chapter 8

Economic Foreign Policies

Economic foreign policies include the use of a range of different policy instruments, from trade policies (decreasing or increasing tariffs or non-tariff barriers), to economic aid (often military), to various forms of economic sanctions (trade, financial and monetary), to foreign developmental aid. The use of economic foreign policy instruments to promote political objectives is often termed 'economic statecraft'. This has arguably played a more prominent role in foreign policy-making since the end of the Cold War (Ripsman and Paul 2010).

In this chapter I discuss the following questions: What do states want in foreign economic policies as regards trade? What do we know about trade-related foreign policy-making? Further, what motivates states to give economic aid, to institute sanctions and to give foreign developmental aid?

Realists hold that national power is based upon the ability of states to raise armies and purchase military capabilities. Therefore, states are obsessed with economic gains relative to their competitors. This has led realists to espouse mercantilist theories of international economics, where states will strategically protect their home market from external competition. Other forms of economic foreign policy can also be motivated by the egoistical strategic concerns of states, where even policies such as foreign development are viewed as tools to further strategic interests.

Liberal theorists build upon international economic theories of free trade, although most liberals do not argue that states always want free trade. As is recalled from Chapter 2, liberal theories at the system level are unable to explain what types of economic foreign policies states support beyond the simplistic assertion that they will increasingly support free trade policies as they become ever more integrated into the world economy. More useful are liberal state-level theories that investigate societal input by developing theories that explain the variance in what states want in economic foreign policies by looking at the domestic winners and losers from freer trade and the supply-side of what types of political institutions are most prone to supplying free trade policies. As will be discussed below, liberalism at the state level lacks a strong theory of domestic politics that can explain how demands are translated through the political system into state economic foreign policies.

For liberals, foreign development aid is seen in a somewhat more positive light. For example, they hold that as economic growth increases in developing countries due to aid, they become increasingly integrated into the world economy, creating markets for the products from donor countries, creating strong self-interest amongst donor states to give aid. More critical are Marxist theories, where the basic argument is that economic foreign policies involving promoting free trade and economic interdependence are in effect imperialistic foreign policy, where the core (rich) countries systematically exploit the periphery (poorer) countries.

Trade policies

Trade policy is a key economic foreign policy that can have substantial effects upon other countries. Bilateral trade agreements are for instance commonly used instruments by states to cement close relations with foreign partners. For example, the United States–Australia Free Trade Agreement that went into force in 2005 was used by the US to strengthen the bilateral relationship. In the debate on the FTA in the House of Representatives, members used arguments such as 'strengthening an alliance that is as strong as any in the world' and 'it will expand one of the most important bilateral relationships that exists' (*Washington Post*, July 15, 2004, p. E02).

What factors determine whether a country liberalizes its trade policy, lowers tariffs, quotas and other barriers to free trade, or introduces protectionist policies that block free trade? I now review the debates on free trade, introducing economic realist theories (mercantilism), liberal free trade theories (that explain why free trade can be mutually beneficial and why there is a variation in the level of protection in different states due to variance in the demand for and supply of protectionism) and Marxist theories of trade and underdevelopment.

Economic realist theories

Economic realists draw their inspiration from the mercantilist school of international economic theory. Mercantilism developed in 16th and 17th century Europe – a period of extreme strategic competition, where the economic wealth of states was vital to their ability to wage war (Kennedy 1987). Mercantilists theorized that the possession of silver and gold was the route to national wealth. Therefore, each state aimed to create a positive trade balance by strategically protecting against competing imports, attempting to export as much as possible, while imposing restrictions on the movement of precious metals abroad. Colonial policies were also a vital element in the mercantilist strategy, as the strict regulation of colonial economies could be used to create favorable trade balances, with the colony exporting raw materials that could be processed into manufactured goods in the home country and re-exported for consumption in the colonial market. Further, colonies also served as the source of precious metals, fueling for instance the rise of Spain in the 16th century. Importantly, exchanges between colonies and the mother country involved no precious metals being transferred to foreign states. Taken together, the result was expected to be the accumulation of precious metals that could be used to buy strength on the battlefield. To paraphrase Clausewitz, mercantilists viewed economic competition as a continuation of war by other means, with an extreme focus upon gains relative to one's competitors and the use of economic activity as the basis for political power.

However, while mercantilist ideas about the possession of precious metals as the source of national power have been largely discredited, the mercantilist focus upon relative gains and the strategic function that trade policies can play as a way to improve one's position has served as the theoretical inspiration for structural realists such as Mearsheimer and Waltz. Looking at international trade, realists theorize that states focus on maximizing their relative economic gains and industrial power *vis-à-vis* competitors, as any economic advantage gained by the other party will be quickly translated into military power that will be used against oneself (Gilpin 2001). The logic can be seen in the following quote from Mearsheimer (2001: 401):

> Of course, China's prospects of becoming a potential hegemon depend largely on whether its economy continues modernizing at a rapid pace. If that happens, and China becomes not only a leading producer of cutting-edge technologies, but the world's wealthiest great power, it would almost certainly use its wealth to build a mighty military machine. Moreover, for sound strategic reasons, it would surely pursue regional hegemony, just as the United States did in the Western Hemisphere during the nineteenth century. So we would expect China to attempt to dominate Japan and Korea, as well as other regional actors, by building military forces that are so powerful that those other states would not dare challenge it. We would also expect China to develop its own version of the Monroe Doctrine, directed at the United States. Just as the United States made it clear to distant powers that they were not allowed to meddle in the Western Hemisphere, China will make it clear that American interference in Asia is unacceptable ... This analysis suggests that the United States has a profound interest in seeing Chinese economic growth slow considerably in the years ahead ... So it is not too late for the United States to reverse course and do what it can to slow the rise of China.

Liberal free trade theories

Economic liberals reject mercantilist ideas that markets should be subservient to political control. Liberalism builds upon the insights of Adam Smith's 'invisible hand', where market forces left alone are able to produce such wealth that they far outweigh concerns of relative gains. Starting with Ricardo's theory of 'comparative advantage', economic liberalism has developed a sophisticated set of theories that explain why free trade is mutually beneficial to all states, bringing great benefits through specialization and the resulting efficiency gains.

One of the most influential models of free trade that can explain why trade is mutually beneficial was developed by two Swedish economists in the 1930s, and is based upon differing factor endowments. Factors are the inputs required to produce a good, including labor, capital and land. The Heckscher-Ohlin model illustrates how freer trade can in theory benefit two countries with different levels of factor endowment: one that can be seen as a developed economy where capital is plentiful but labor is relatively expensive, and a developing country where capital is scarce but labor is plentiful. In the developed economy it is expensive to produce labor-intensive products such as clothes but relatively cheap to produce capital-intensive products such as high technology products (biotechnology, medicinal products, etc.), whereas the opposite is the case for the developing country. As a labor-intensive product would be relatively more expensive to produce in a developed country, the developing country can sell its labor-intensive products for a higher price in the developed country than it would get domestically, and vice versa. In this situation it is mutually advantageous for both countries to engage in specialization, with exporting firms enjoying higher prices and a larger market for their goods, and consumers reaping the benefits through lower prices for products. Free trade is however not just a win–win situation, as there are domestic groups that lose out in the short term. For instance, workers in labor-intensive sectors in developed countries lose their jobs as firms move abroad to developing countries where labor is cheaper, although the model assumes that these workers will be able to shift (relatively) effortlessly from labor-intensive to capital-intensive sectors.

Marxist theories

Marxist theories build on the argument that the capitalist economy system, where workers sell their labor to capitalists, who own the means of production, involves the exploitation of workers in a system of unequal exchange. Paradoxically, while Marx believed that capitalist production within developed countries resulted in the exploitation of workers by capitalists, he believed that the spread of the capitalist system to countries like India was beneficial for them, as these countries were at a lower stage of economic development (e.g. a feudal mode of production).

Later theorists have drawn upon the idea of exploitation of workers and transferred it to international economic relations, theorizing that international trade involves the exploitation of workers in peripheral countries by capitalists in core developed countries, resulting in the underdevelopment of the periphery. Free trade is therefore seen as a form of economic imperialism, where value is transferred from the poor in the periphery to make the rich in the core even richer. Marxist theories of economic foreign policies such as Wallerstein's model developed below are system-level theories, but they develop theories to explain why promoting free trade in economic foreign policies is an exploitative foreign policy.

How does an economic foreign policy that promotes free trade result in exploitation? The argument is based upon Marx's theory of surplus value, even though most Marxist theories of trade and imperialism do not explicitly cite it. Marx developed a complex theory of wages and prices that distinguishes between the use value and exchange value of goods, the latter of which is the price of the good on the market. In a capitalist system, workers are forced to sell their labor, with the wage they receive being the value of labor power that reflects the value of the commodities that a worker needs to survive. The value of labor is lower than the value created by the worker. As workers do not own the means of production, they only receive their wage, and the extra value created by the worker is the surplus value that goes to the owner of the means of production (capitalists). In hourly terms, a worker might receive a wage that reflects three hours of labor, whereas the worker actually produced value corresponding to four hours of work. The value of the extra hour is the surplus value that falls to the capitalist, and is seen as the exploitation of workers in Marxist theory.

Theorists such as Andre Gunder Frank and Immanuel Wallerstein have translated the Marxist idea of exploitative capitalist exchange to the realm of international trade (Frank 1969; Wallerstein 1974, 1980). Exploitative chains of production between capitalists and workers are expanded internationally through the investment in periphery countries by capitalists from core countries. The reason that production is moved from the core to the periphery is that labor is cheap.

An example of Marxist theories of economic foreign policies involved in promoting trade is shown in Figure 8.1, which depicts Wallerstein's world-systems theory. The main argument is that core countries promote free trade in order to incorporate peripheral countries in an exploitative international commodity chain, where surplus

Figure 8.1   *Wallerstein's world-systems theory of trade and imperialism*

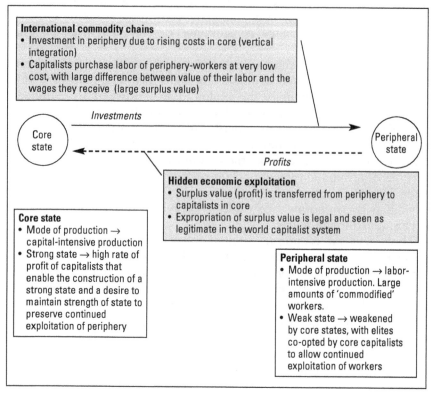

International commodity chains
• Investment in periphery due to rising costs in core (vertical integration)
• Capitalists purchase labor of periphery-workers at very low cost, with large difference between value of their labor and the wages they receive (large surplus value)

Investments

Core state

Peripheral state

Profits

Hidden economic exploitation
• Surplus value (profit) is transferred from periphery to capitalists in core
• Expropriation of surplus value is legal and seen as legitimate in the world capitalist system

Core state
• Mode of production → capital-intensive production
• Strong state → high rate of profit of capitalists that enable the construction of a strong state and a desire to maintain strength of state to preserve continued exploitation of periphery

Peripheral state
• Mode of production → labor-intensive production. Large amounts of 'commodified' workers.
• Weak state → weakened by core states, with elites co-opted by core capitalists to allow continued exploitation of workers

Source: Based on Wallerstein (1974, 1980, 1989).

value (profit) is extracted from peripheral states. Capitalists in core countries face rising wage costs in their own countries and therefore shift production to periphery countries where wages are much cheaper. Wallerstein argues that in many periphery countries, wages of individual workers are even below the value of the commodities the worker needs to survive. The only way that these workers can survive is by pooling income within a large household.

Core capitalists are then able to expropriate legally the surplus value they extract from peripheral workers as profit that is transferred back to the core, making the core even richer and locking the periphery in a cycle of underdevelopment and exploitation that results in them becoming ever poorer. This exploitative cycle is strengthened by the strong political institutions that form the superstructure in core countries and the weak state structures in peripheral countries, ensuring that there are no barriers to the extraction of surplus value. Therefore, according to Wallerstein, economic foreign policies of core countries therefore aim to increase free trade in order to promote the uneven exchange inherent in the world capitalist system.

*   *   *

Before we turn to the predictions the various theories make for when states want to adopt free trade, a few words are in order about the history of the relationship between development and trade. From the 1950s to the 1970s, many developing countries criticized developed countries such as the US for forcing free trade upon them, basing their arguments on Marxist and other critical theories of free trade. These theorists suggested that developing countries should adopt a policy of *import-substitution*, where high tariff barriers were used as a shield behind which the developing country could build a manufacturing base instead of relying on exporting primary products and importing manufacturing products. Supporters of import-substitution argued that the developed countries were saying 'do as I say, not as I have done in the past', as countries such as Germany and the US both began their industrialization behind high tariff barriers. The policy was especially popular in India and Latin America, but the results were very mixed. In particular, protection of an industry could not automatically create a competitive sector if there were more fundamental reasons behind the lack of success, such as a lack of skilled labor or an adequate infrastructure.

The success of the East Asian economies in the 1970s and 1980s showed that there was another, potentially more viable, path toward industrialization and development: the developmental state and export-oriented industrialization. Countries such as Japan, South Korea and Taiwan used a combination of protection for infant industries until they were internationally competitive and a central role for the state was established for guiding investment in education and infrastructure in order to create the structural conditions for an internationally competitive economy (Gilpin 2001: 316–33).

Wallerstein expected that countries that are most deeply integrated into the capitalist world-system will become increasingly poor and underdeveloped, though historical developments have shown the exact opposite is the case. Countries such as North Korea and Somalia are non-integrated into international commodity chains, whereas the East Asian states like Taiwan and more recently China have developed through intense integration into international commodity chains through high levels of foreign trade and investment.

*   *   *

When should we expect states to adopt free trade policies? The simple realist answer is that free trade policies will rarely be adopted, and only in sectors that are marginal to the net growth of the state's economy.

In more strategic sectors, we should expect to see that states will carefully protect their economies, attempting, through a series of measures, including barriers to trade and the support of sectors, to build a stronger economic foundation than their rivals. In contrast, the liberal answer is that we should expect a steady march toward free trade, with increased trade creating even greater absolute gains for states that give them greater incentives to push for more free trade, and so on.

This simplified dichotomous either-or answer naturally does not reflect reality. More interesting and analytically useful are theories that can contribute to an understanding of the conditions in the international economic system under which free trade is possible, along with the domestic, state-level factors that produce differing levels of free trade.

At the system level, the economic variant of hegemonic stability theory develops the argument that free trade is only possible when a hegemon or leader exists in the international economy. The basic problem of free trade is that it can be seen as a public good, defined as a 'good' where everyone gains from taking part, but where members of a group cannot be excluded from the group despite not paying for it. A classic example is a lighthouse, where all ships benefit from not colliding with a rock, but one cannot exclude non-payers to a lighthouse from the good it provides. This creates incentives for actors to free ride, meaning they consume the good while not paying for it. Unless there is a leader, such as a hegemonic state, that shoulders the burden of providing the public good, public goods will tend to be undersupplied.

Realist variants of hegemonic stability theory hold that public goods such as free trade will only be provided by a hegemon that has interests in supplying the good or can force other states to share the costs of paying for it (Snidal 1985; Gilpin 2001). Gilpin contends that the US created an international liberal economy order after World War II to strengthen the anti-Soviet alliance and to allow American firms to exploit their competitiveness internationally. One example of how the American economic hegemony manifested itself was through the use of the dollar backed by gold as the international reserve currency. In contrast, in periods when there is no hegemon the international liberal economic order will break down, with the prime example being the Great Depression in 1929–39 (Kindleberger 1973).

Liberal theorists contend that while hegemony or leadership *can* be necessary for the survival of open markets, the provision of public goods can also be maintained by international institutions. Institutions can take up the slack after hegemony, enabling decentralized cooperation to take place that ensures that vital public goods are produced in the international economy (Keohane 1984).

As discussed above, in Marxist theories free trade is a foreign policy of economic imperialism, where core countries are theorized to have strong interests in incorporating peripheral countries in the exploitative system. If strong states are able to develop in peripheral countries, we should expect these countries to resist free trade, instead concentrating on domestic development through protectionist measures and measures that restrict the repatriation of profit by capitalists from core countries.

As regards variation in the level of free trade at the state level, realist theory provides us with fewer answers. Liberal theory in contrast enables the analyst to open up the black box of the state in an attempt to explain the *variation* in free trade policies. The following provides an analytical framework that can explain variations in free trade policies based upon a combination of demand and supply.

On the demand side, there are two overall liberal models of the demand for freer trade that theorize which societal groups 'win' and 'lose' from international economic competition. The first model is the *factor of production* model, based upon the Heckscher-Ohlin model. In a country that is rich in labor but poor in capital relative to the world economy, producers of labor-intensive products will support liberalization as they have a comparative advantage relative to their foreign competitors, whereas producers of less-competitive capital-intensive products will lobby for protection (for example for trade barriers against competing products). Therefore, the factor of production model suggests that we should expect that countries will support free trade in products that are produced using factors (labor, capital) that they are rich in, but will support protectionism for products made using factors that they are poor in.

The second model is the *sectoral model*, which contends that we need to lower the level of analysis from factors, investigating variations in the international competitiveness across *sectors*. A country can have an internationally competitive banking sector (capital-intensive), whereas other capital-intensive sectors are not as competitive. Internationally competitive producers favor liberalization, whereas uncompetitive import-competing producers will pressure for protection (Moravcsik 1998: 38–9).

Which factors then determine the level of free trade supplied by a government? Some liberals have suggested that we should expect that the level of protection will reflect the preferences of the median voter (Mayer 1984). However, the 'benefits' of protectionist policies often have large benefits for only a few voters (for example those in import-competing firms as suggested by the sectoral model), whereas the benefits of freer trade will benefit a large number of voters. Why then are protectionist policies that benefit the few adopted?

Olson's (1965) theory of collective action can partially explain this, arguing that small and cohesive groups with strong interests in protection are better able to organize effectively to lobby for their interests in contrast to larger groups with more diffuse interests such as consumers.

This is one reason why, for example, small groups of farmers in both the EU and US (under 2 percent of the work force) have been able to lobby politicians to adopt protectionist measures for agricultural products. As the benefits fall intensely on them, they have interests in creating strong organizations to pressure politicians, whereas the costs of protectionism are spread among all consumers.

Liberal theorists have also attempted to understand how *political institutions* influence the degree to which decision-makers are insulated from the demands for more/less free trade from domestic groups, thereby increasing or decreasing the level of free trade supplied in trade policies. Three factors have been identified that can hypothetically explain this variation in supply. First, it has been theorized that politicians representing smaller electoral districts are more prone to capture by interest groups favoring protectionism (Rogowski 1987). This means that an executive such as the US president should be better able to ignore domestic pressures for protection than are legislators (Baldwin 1986; Milner and Rosendorff 1997). The logic behind this is that an executive with a nationwide constituency will concentrate upon national economic welfare, whereas legislators with smaller constituencies will be more prone to being influenced by particular industries or interest groups from their constituency. Second, the administrative capacity of the state also matters. In weak, underdeveloped states, it is much more administratively difficult to collect income or other forms of taxes, whereas revenue from import taxes is easy to collect, resulting in more protectionism (Rodrik 1995). Finally, a related argument is that the supply of free trade policies is lower in autocratic states than in democratic ones. Autocratic leaders are more 'rent-seeking' (read 'corrupt') than their democratic counterparts. When a large, import-competing firm attempts to lobby an autocratic leader it can buy off the leader directly in ways that are illegal in democratic states where the rule of law is prevalent (Wintrobe 1998).

Economic sanctions and aid: the sticks and carrots of economic statecraft

Beyond trade, states also wage foreign economic policy through the targeted use of economic sticks and carrots. This involves using economic sanctions, aid and other economic incentives to change the political behavior of another state.

Economic statecraft can be aimed at *changing the domestic politics* of the target state. For example, the 1974 Jackson-Vanick amendment in US trade policy was targeted at encouraging the protection of human rights within the Soviet Union. The amendment denied Soviet Union trade benefits with the US unless the Soviets changed their policies regarding the emigration of Soviet Jews (Walt and Mearsheimer 2007). A more recent example was the increase in aid to Egypt following the overthrow of the Mubarak government in the spring of 2011 (*Washington Post*, May 8, 2011). Using US$1 billion in debt relief as the primary instrument of aid, the US government intended to support the consolidation of the domestic democratic reforms in order to avoid a roll-back.

Economic statecraft in the form of sanctions can also be aimed at *changing the foreign policy behavior* of the target state. For example, one of the aims of US sanctions against Libya and Iran in the 1990s and 2000s was to stop the two states from supporting international terrorism.

Economic statecraft can have *direct effects*, where it convinces leaders that the costs of changing their domestic or foreign policy behavior are lower than the costs of the sanctions or benefits of the promised aid. *Indirectly*, economic statecraft instruments such as sanctions can also generate popular pressures for change that can even result in the overthrow of a regime (Pape 1997).

For sanctions to work, the costs for the target state to change behavior have to be lower than the costs that the sanctions impose. For economic carrots (aid), the equation has to be tipped toward the benefits of the economic aid to be greater than the costs of changing policy.

Skeptics argue that sanctions are ineffective signals at best, and can even be counter-productive policy instruments at worst. In a study of 115 cases of the use of economic sanctions from 1914 until 1990, Pape (1997) finds that sanctions only succeeded in 5 percent of the cases, suggesting the conclusion that economic statecraft is not a reliable alternative to military force. Often the impact of economic sanctions is minimal in comparison to the political costs of changing policy. This is particularly the case when sanctions are imposed unilaterally by one country, enabling the target country to shift trade to other more willing partners (Drezner 2000).

For sanctions to have an effect the regime needs to be vulnerable to the pressure, which often is not the case (Nincic 2010). For example, despite sanctions being imposed upon Libya since the early 1980s, it was first in the 1990s that the Libyan economic crisis made the regime more vulnerable to the effects of the sanctions (Jentleson and Whytock 2005/06). Furthermore, in today's globalized economy, economic sanctions often only impact the population and not elites, who have ways to gain clandestine access to products from the world market. During the UN sanctions of Iraq in the 1990s, the population became increasingly malnourished while corrupt elites thrived.

Sanctions can even be counter-productive. While they might be intended to weaken support for a regime, through rally-round-the-flag effects, they often result in an otherwise unpopular leader gaining popularity in the eyes of the people as he or she stands up against foreign pressure (Pape 1997; Nincic 2010). On the other hand, positive inducements in the form of economic aid can potentially be more effective, as they do not produce rally-round-the-flag effects, but the regime still needs to be vulnerable to pressure for them to work effectively (Nincic 2010).

Proponents of sanctions contend that they can work when they impose significant costs, especially when they are imposed multilaterally or internationally in ways that effectively cut off a regime from the global economy (Drezner 2000; O'Sullivan 2003). Multilateral sanctions prevent the target state from switching trade to other countries. But even proponents admit that sanctions usually cannot stand alone, but need to be coupled with other policy instruments such as the credible threat of military force to form an effective strategy to change the behavior of a target state (O'Sullivan 2003; Jentleson and Whytock 2005/06).

The political institutions of the target state also determine whether economic statecraft will be successful or not (Blanchard and Ripsman 2008). Drawing on liberal, state-level theories, Blanchard and Ripsman theorize that the target state's level of 'stateness' can buffer leaders from domestic pressures to comply with sanctions. The level of 'stateness' is determined by three factors: (1) the level of autonomy of the executive to choose foreign policies when faced with domestic political opposition; (2) the capacity of the state, in particular the policy resources available to the state, to co-opt or coerce key societal groups; and (3) the perceived legitimacy of the leader's right to rule amongst the population. When each of the three factors are high, leaders are better able to resist complying in the face of strong domestic opposition, or are able to comply when there are strong domestic forces pushing toward non-compliance.

Foreign developmental aid

This chapter on economic foreign policy ends by looking at developmental aid as an increasingly important element of state foreign policy-making. If we look at the organizational charts of the foreign ministries of most countries in the world and the size of the developmental aid budgets in comparison to the diplomatic tools of foreign policy, it becomes apparent that developmental aid should be seen as a key element of state foreign policy. In this section I investigate the debate on why states choose to give foreign developmental aid as an instrument of foreign policy.

While most states officially proclaim that their developmental aid is aimed at promoting economic growth and alleviating poverty in the developing world, historically aid has been motivated more by strategic objectives of the state than altruistic goals (Alesina and Dollar 2000; Bearce and Tirone 2010). For example, one of the lessons that many states drew from the terrorist attacks on September 11, 2001 was that authoritarian regimes in the Middle East and North Africa offered young people few opportunities, resulting in their dangerous radicalization. There were two underlying reasons for this. First, authoritarian systems tend to result in underdevelopment and poverty, reducing employment opportunities. Second, authoritarian systems also are prone to corruption and cronyism, again reducing the opportunities for youths to get ahead unless they are well-connected. As a result, since 9/11 the developmental aid of many states has become conditional upon the target state either being democratic or adopting democratic reforms, suggesting that states are pursuing strategic objectives instead of altruistic goals.

Many scholars who have studied the effects of aid have suggested that it is an ineffective tool to foster economic growth and development (e.g. Boone 1996; Easterly 2003). The only measurable effect of aid is that it increases the size of government in the target country (Boone 1996). Other scholars have however found a robust correlation between aid and economic growth (Burnside and Dollar 2000; Hansen and Tarp 2001).

These contrasting results can be explained when we investigate the motivations behind aid. If we distinguish between developmental aid and what can be termed 'non-developmental' aid (i.e. aid more motivated by political and/or strategic concerns than an interest in promoting development), a strong and robust correlation appears between developmental aid and economic growth (Minoiu and Reddy 2010).

The logic behind this correlation is further explored by Bearce and Tirone (2010), who argue that while aid is usually conditional upon a state reforming its economic and political policies that will create favorable conditions for development, when states have strategic interests in giving aid the threat of revoking it is not credible. Therefore, target states will only reform policies when the donor state has few strategic interests attached to the aid.

During the Cold War, as the majority of aid that was given was strategically motivated by the goal of keeping countries within one's own block, aid had little effect in promoting growth – although it did achieve its primary strategic objective of ensuring that the target state did not ally with the other side. After the Cold War, states have fewer strategic objectives that they try to realize with developmental aid, resulting in aid that has stronger effects in promoting development.

Chapter 9

A Transformation of State Foreign Policy-Making?

Are we witnessing fundamental shifts in the nature of foreign policy due to globalization and the rise of new types of foreign policy actors in world politics today? Is the state-centric analysis of foreign policy presented in the rest of this book outdated? Do we need new theoretical tools that will enable us to analyze foreign policy in a less state-centric world?

I first introduce the debate on what globalization is and how it can potentially transform foreign policy. Building upon the argument that we are not witnessing anything new, globalization skeptics still view the state as the most important actor in international politics. At the other extreme are theorists who contend that studying foreign policy using state-centric theoretical tools misses the most important developments. However, a scholarly consensus is emerging that these extremes are oversimplified, and that in reality states are still the central actors in world politics, but at the same time business is not as usual. Transformations in three types of foreign policy are catalogued, including security, diplomatic and economic.

This section is followed by a discussion of whether foreign policy-making is possible beyond the state. I focus on what can be termed a 'most-likely' case of non-state actors in foreign policy: the EU. In a world of increasingly strong regional international institutions such as the African Union and the EU, are we seeing the rise of a new form of foreign policy actor in world politics? I debate whether the EU has developed a degree of 'actorness' that enables us to speak of a form of foreign policy identity 'beyond' the state.

Globalization and the end of the state-centric world?

As with any contested concept in political science, that of 'globalization' has many different definitions. The myriad uses of the concept can be reduced to two overall types. The *weak version* defines globalization as a form of increased *internationalization* and cross-border transactions between states (Hirst and Thompson 1999; Keohane and

Nye 2001). Here there is not a real difference in kind between economic and social transactions of previous and modern eras, only an increase in the *quantity* of interaction (Hirst and Thompson 1999). The *strong version* of globalization focuses on the *trans*-border nature of transactions; what can be termed the rise of 'supra-territoriality' where borders are not merely crossed or opened but are instead *transcended* (e.g. Strange 1996; Scholte 1997). For instance, Held *et al.* (1999) defined globalization as 'a process (or set of processes) which embodies a transformation in the spatial organization of social relations and transactions – assessed in terms of their extensity, intensity, velocity, and impact – generating transcontinental or interregional flows and networks of activity, interaction, and the exercise of power'. Here a qualitative change in kind is taking place, with the emergence of genuinely borderless economies, making the state an increasingly obsolete institution. In this conceptualization of globalization, states are no longer the most important actors in world politics, or at least are weakened very substantially.

In both definitions, globalization is produced by technological changes involving the radical fall in the costs and speed of transportation and communication, enabling the movement of persons, goods, capital and ideas across borders at ever increasing levels. For example, satellite television has made international media markets increasingly interconnected with global news cycles.

Academic fashion dictates that scholars sometimes are tempted to exaggerate empirical developments in order to position themselves better. For example, immediately after 9/11 many researchers argued that world politics had changed so fundamentally due to the terrorist attacks that existing theoretical tools were no longer appropriate (Smith 2002). In the same manner, growth in globalization in the 1990s and early 2000s led many academics to argue that existing theories were outdated, while at the same time they not surprisingly contended that the new theoretical set of tools they had pioneered were able to make sense of the new empirical reality. One prominent scholar of globalization went so far as to write that 'social scientists, in politics and economics especially, cling to obsolete concepts and inappropriate theories. These theories belong to a more stable and orderly world than the one we live in. It was one in which the territorial borders of states really meant something. But it has been swept away by a pace of change more rapid than human society had ever before experienced' (Strange 1996: 3–4).

Today an academic consensus has begun to form around a more pragmatic middle ground (e.g. Sørensen 2004; Ripsman and Paul 2010). Globalization is primarily seen as an increase in cross-border transactions, although the Internet and other forms of communication have created certain transborder spaces where the state holds little sway. The demise of the state is viewed as exaggerated by these scholars.

That the state is still the central actor in world politics does not necessarily mean that state foreign policy-making is the same today as it was 50 years ago. However, it does mean that the theoretical tool-kit that has been developed by generations of IR and FPA scholars is still applicable in describing, understanding and explaining foreign policy developments. I will now discuss the implications that globalization has had for the foreign policies of states in the security, diplomatic and economic realms, introducing the debate between realists scholars and others that posit that there is nothing new under the sun, and strong liberal scholars who theorize that globalization has resulted in a *transformation* in the way states conduct foreign policy.

Globalization and security policies: new threats?

Has globalization resulted in a changed nature of national security? Here it is important to distinguish between the significant effects that globalization has had for the security of strong, developed states and the relatively insignificant effects it has had upon the security policies of weak, underdeveloped states. Another important distinction is whether the state is in what can be termed a cooperative regional system, where there is a stable security environment such as Western Europe, or a more competitive, dog-eat-dog anarchical system where there are protracted conflicts and enduring militarized rivalries (Ripsman and Paul 2010). As regards strong, developed states, the core debates on whether globalization has transformed the nature of national security focus upon (1) whether interstate wars have become obsolete and (2) whether globalization has spawned a host of new threats from non-state actors that have usurped the threats from other states.

First, the globalization thesis in its most extreme variant suggests that interstate wars have become increasingly obsolete, with the nature of conflict shifting instead to intrastate wars and low-intensity conflicts like the 2008 Georgian–Russian war. The implications of this shift would be that the nature of external threats facing states has changed, making preparation for major interstate war unnecessary.

One reason for the change is theorized to be technological change, with increasingly devastating weapons making war so costly that it becomes irrational. However, the threat of the extinction of the human race in a nuclear conflagration did not stop the US and Soviet Union from threatening each other with war during the early periods of the Cold War, although one can make the argument that after the near miss in the Cuban Missile Crisis the risk of extinction pushed the two parties toward accommodation and ultimately to a peaceful resolution of their rivalry. Additionally, while there have been no wars between major powers since World War II, major powers like China, Russia and the US maintain large nuclear and conventional arsenals that make little sense outside of the context of being at least prepared for threats from other major powers.

It is true that there has been a marked decrease in the incidence of interstate wars since the end of the Cold War. In the period 1990–2007 there have been only nine interstate wars, defined as conflicts resulting in over 1,000 casualties, whereas there have been 62 recorded intrastate wars (Sarkees and Wayman 2010). However, there are numerous reasons that we cannot take these figures to mean that the nature of warfare has changed due to globalization. The key point here is that we cannot hold 'everything else equal', enabling us to measure the impact of globalization in isolation from other major trends. For example, the end of the Cold War removed a strong source of conflict amongst states, especially in the so-called Third World, where the US and Soviet Union fought numerous proxy wars.

Second, the collapse of the Cold War resulted in the emergence of a unipolar international system, where the US has been in a hegemonic position at the global level in relation to all competitors. Hegemonic stability theory (see pp. 153–4) suggests that hegemony should produce relative peace amongst states. How far the US is ahead of potential rivals can be seen in Figure 9.1. The figure is a depiction of the relative power of major states using the relative shares of three indicators for each state: economic capabilities (GDP), military expenditure and military personnel. The figure shows that the US in 2009 had roughly 40 percent of the total economic power of the seven major powers, but on the core realist indicator (military expenditure) it had 70 percent of the total spending. The only indicator where other powers were even close was in military personnel, although having a large but underequipped army like China does little to enhance one's ability to project power beyond borders. Realists submit therefore that the reason for the lack of interstate war since the end of the Cold War is the simple fact that the US is so far ahead in terms of military power (Wohlforth 1999). However, realists argue that this has not changed the nature of security policies, and we should expect that when states such as China have caught up with the US, we will see the re-emergence of interstate war, even potentially between major powers (Mearsheimer 2001; Gray 2005).

Strong liberals contend that a crucial transformation has occurred due to the increasing levels of intersocietal interaction and communication that produce a sense of community between states that makes war between them unthinkable (Deutsch *et al.* 1957; Deutsch 1968). Proponents of this position argue that the result is a zone of peace and security amongst strong developed states where the purely anarchical

Figure 9.1   *The relative distribution of three indicators of power, 2009*

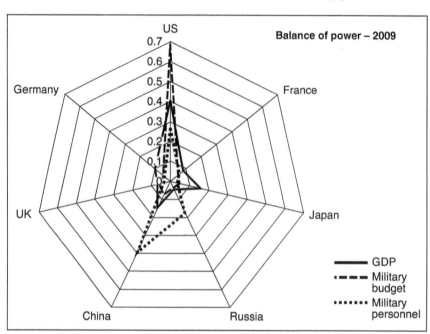

Note: the figure depicts the relative share of each power of the sum for each of the indicators.
Source: Based on data from the International Institute of Security Studies (2010).

system has been replaced by a dense cobweb of relations. Therefore, cooperative regions where a zone of peace reigns exist in Western Europe and North America, where concerns about relative gains are less important and cooperation is more prevalent than realists would expect (Goldgeier and McFaul 1992). In these cooperative regions, interstate war and the use of military threats have arguably become obsolete as tools of foreign policy.

The second argument is that while the traditional threat of being invaded by rival states has retreated, this has been replaced by new transborder security threats from non-state actors spawned by the increasing ease of movement and communication, including threats from international terrorism and drug trafficking – threats that states are not well-equipped to face (Creveld 1999; Carter 2001/2002). The attacks on 9/11 by al-Qaeda reminded the West of the vulnerability of open, integrated societies to terrorist threats – a threat that also existed in the 1970s and early 1980s but that had happily been forgotten. Deterrence and other forms of classic security foreign policy do not work against these new threats, as there is no clear 'homeland' of terrorist groups that can be threatened in order to deter attacks. Therefore, globalization theorists contend that new security instruments are necessary to deal with these new threats, creating new state responses along with adapting international organizations to counter these new threats.

Realists would suggest that these new threats spawned by globalization have not replaced the traditional security concerns of states. States still spend exorbitant amounts on conventional and nuclear arsenals to protect their vital interests from states; in particular the US (Ripsman and Paul 2005, 2010). Indeed, for realists the focus on security threats emanating from non-state actors is taking one's eye off the ball. Al-Qaeda is not seen as an existential threat to the US and US national interests, nor is it going to bring down Western civilization. Realists point to the fact that the response to 9/11 from the US and its allies was to attack states (Afghanistan and Iraq), not al-Qaeda. For realists, the real threats come from other states (Mearsheimer 2001).

Realists admit that there has been an increase in asymmetric warfare since the end of the Cold War, where strong states have faced unconventional forms of warfare such as terrorist attacks. Gray gives the example that all of the belligerents fought by the US since 1989 were 'third-rate or less' (Iraqis, Panamanians, Taliban, Serbs, Somalis, etc.) (Gray 2005). The aftermath of the 2003 Iraq War is illustrative here. The US won a crushing victory, but most of the opposing Iraqi force had simply vanished into the broader population as they had no hope of victory in a conventional battle against US forces. As became clear in the coming months and years, Iraqi forces slowly re-emerged to wage a bloody asymmetric campaign against US forces.

However, there is little evidence that suggests that the new threats have resulted in the decline of the centrality of the state as a security actor. After 9/11 there has been an increase in the spending by states on internal security to counter these new threats, along with many countries introducing dramatic new restrictions on personal liberties in the name of counter-terrorism (Ripsman and Paul 2010). Further, many European states have shifted their military spending from large conventional forces aimed at countering threats from other states to smaller, more mobile, intervention forces that can be sent to different hot-spots around the world to counter the instability that stems especially from intrastate conflict in the developing world.

The security picture in weak, developing states is, on the other hand, dire. The key security threats do not stem from other states, but from opposition groups within the country that erupt in violent, *intra*state conflicts. Yet these intrastate conflicts are not related per se to globalization; indeed it can be paradoxically argued that it is the *lack* of the globalization of states such as Somalia, which is effectively isolated from economic interdependence, that push them into bloody civil wars. Globalization, and especially the integration of a state's economy in the world market, has brought economic benefits for many countries throughout the world – in particular in East Asia. Beyond poverty and weak state structures, another cause of many of the intrastate conflicts since the end of the Cold War is the turbulence and instability that resulted from the dissolution of great empires and state federations (Dawisha and Parrott 1997; Gray 2005). This has been particularly evident in the wars in the former Yugoslavia and the former Soviet Union.

There is also little evidence that globalization has had an impact on the security concerns of states in anarchic, competitive regions of enduring rivalry such as the Middle East or South Asia (Ripsman and Paul 2010). Here other states are still the focus of security strategies. For example, Iran and the potential of Persian hegemony in the Gulf region is the focal point for security policy for countries such as Saudi Arabia.

Globalization has arguably only had effects for the security policies of strong, developed states in cooperative regions. It has spawned new security threats from non-state actors, although there is considerable debate about whether this has transformed the nature of state security foreign policy or whether security policies are still 'business as usual', where states worry most about existential threats from rival powers. Evidence suggests however that the state is still the central actor and is resilient and adaptive to any challenges created by globalization in the security sphere (Ripsman and Paul 2010).

Globalization and diplomacy: a new global polity?

What impact has globalization had upon diplomacy and interstate relations? Realists argue that we are not witnessing anything new, and that past periods of high levels of interdependence have not resulted in a transformation in either the role of the state in global politics or the way in which foreign policy is conducted. In contrast, proponents of the strong version of globalization see a fundamental transformation of the nature of traditional political foreign policy and a retreat of the state as the most important actor. Scholars such as Rosenau (2003) point to the diminished capabilities of the state to govern and cope with the dynamics of change, making state foreign policy increasingly irrelevant (see also Scholte 2000).

More moderate (weak) liberal theorists contend that globalization has had effects upon the way in which states conduct diplomatic foreign policies, though the state is still seen as the most important actor. Globalization, and especially increased economic and social interaction across borders produced by technological change, has increased the geographic scope of public policy. Problems that could be tackled domestically before have become more complex and transborder in nature, creating severe policy interdependence problems.

Weak liberals point to three changes that globalization and the resulting increase in policy interdependence have had upon political foreign policies: (1) the increasing use of intergovernmental organizations and multilateral cooperation; (2) the rise of 'trans-governmentalism'; and (3) the increasing importance of non-state and other actors in transnational networks in foreign policy.

Keohane and Nye in *Power and Interdependence* (2001) pointed to the impact that policy interdependence has upon interstate relations. Their claim was that as interdependence has increased between states, this has created pressures for them to cooperate even more to tackle these new challenges through mutual policy adjustment. The result has been an increase in interstate relations and a large rise in the number of intergovernmental organizations that aim to solve interdependence problems of various kinds – in particular at the regional level. In other words, as policy interdependence increases, so does the relevance of multilateral cooperation, cooperation within existing institutions, and new, purpose-built, intergovernmental institutions for facilitating mutually acceptable solutions to the problems created by interdependence.

More far-reaching effects upon the conduct of foreign policy due to increases in policy interdependence spawned by globalization – effects that have given rise to the phenomenon of 'trans-governmentalism' proposed by Slaughter (2004). Trans-governmentalism refers to relations between sub-units of government between states, be they legislative, bureaucratic or judicial. Instead of traditional diplomacy between two states that is channeled through foreign ministries and embassies, trans-governmentalism refers to *direct* relations between sub-units, operating on the basis of shared interests. For instance, international immigration issues are often dealt with through direct contacts between justice or home affairs ministries in different states. Judges in different states also engage in direct relations and transjudicial dialogue, resulting in a diffusion of legal principles and ideas from one jurisdiction to another (Slaughter 2004). The result of trans-governmentalism is a form of disaggregated state foreign policy, where traditional foreign policies conducted by foreign ministries are undertaken in parallel with the operation of looser trans-governmental networks that combine policy expertise and domestic, hands-on powers that can arguably solve policy interdependence problems more effectively than traditional tools of a unitary state foreign policy actor.

Finally, some strong liberal theorists suggest that we are witnessing a more fundamental transformation of state foreign policy as it becomes increasingly enmeshed in global public policy networks compromised of governmental officials, international organizations, firms and non-governmental organizations (Reinicke 1998, 2000; Ougaard 2004). In the global polity, transnational networks allow the mobilization of resources toward common policy objectives in domains outside of the hierarchical control of governments (Stone 2002: 131). In this perspective, focusing solely upon state actors will overlook a substantial amount of what is going on in foreign policy-making in a global polity (Ougaard 2004).

Both weak and strong liberal scholars agree that there have been changes in the conduct of political foreign policies, with an increased use of intergovernmental, trans-governmental and transnational networks to tackle problems raised by policy interdependence. The key disagreement relates to whether globalization has reduced the role of the state, with weak liberals subscribing to the argument that the key institution for global governance is still the state (Keohane and Nye 2001: 260; Sørensen 2004), whereas strong liberals contend that we cannot use traditional analytical tools to study diplomacy today (Ougaard 2004).

Globalization and economic foreign policies: the retreat of the state?

Most of the literature on globalization has dealt with its impact upon economic policies and the ability of states to govern the world economy. As with other areas discussed above, the primary debate on economic globalization is between globalization skeptics who contend that there is nothing new in what we are seeing, adherents of a weak version of globalization understood as an increase in interdependence that creates challenges for states, and a strong version where globalization has resulted in a fundamental transformation of economic affairs, with the retreat of the state and the diffusion of power to other actors in the global economy.

First, economic realists suggest that increased interdependence is nothing new; and even if it has a greater depth than previous periods of high interdependence, the state is still the most important actor. According to Gilpin (2001: 21), 'it is certainly true that economic and technological forces are profoundly reshaping international affairs and influencing the behavior of states. However, in a highly integrated global economy, states continue to use their power and to implement policies to channel economic forces in ways favorable to their own national interests and the interests of their citizenry'. Further, 'states are very concerned about relative gains and who produces what; for security and domestic reasons, whether an economy produces computer chips or potato chips is a major concern of every state' (Gilpin 2000: 350). Even in economic affairs, realists argue we are still living in a state-dominated world.

At the other extreme, proponents of the strong definition of globalization suggest that its impact has been the 'retreat of the state' from governance of the world economy (Strange 1996). In the words of Susan Strange (1996: 4), 'the argument put forward is that the impersonal forces of world markets, integrated over the postwar period more by private enterprise in finance, industry and trade than by the cooperative decisions of governments, are now more powerful than the states to whom ultimate political authority over society and economy is supposed to belong'. Within the global market, strong multinational companies that are involved in transnational production chains are key players. States are forced to play by the rules of the game dictated by markets (Held *et al.* 1999). The 'domain of state authority in society and economy is shrinking; and/or that what were once domains of authority exclusive to state authority are now being shared with other loci or sources of authority' (Strange 1996: 82). Here states are no longer the most important economic foreign policy actors, but have been relegated to a secondary role by market actors.

The more pragmatic middle ground of weak liberalism theorizes that what we are seeing is a dramatic increase in economic interdependence, which has resulted in some shifts in how economic foreign policy-making is conducted, though states are still the key actors (Keohane and Nye 2001). The scale of economic flows in the global economy makes governance of the global economy by states possible only through cooperation between governments. With the exception of states that are isolated from global markets and capital, individual governments are unable to govern markets effectively and unilaterally, creating an increased need to cooperate with other states in economic foreign policy-making. This takes place both within looser forms of intergovernmental cooperation such as the G20 group of the world's 20 largest economies, regional trade organizations like the EU, the North American Free Trade Association, and global organizations such as the World Trade Organization.

Weak liberals would point to the 2008 financial crisis, which illustrates both the impact of globalization and the still central role played by states in the global economy. What started as a meltdown in the subprime mortgage market in the US had severe global effects, resulting in bank crises and economic downturns throughout the world. Yet the actors that played the most central role in averting a global economic meltdown were states engaging in economic foreign policies. At the national level, governments bailed out failing banks and adopted huge financial stimulus packages. However, unilateral responses were not enough given the highly integrated nature of the global economy. Therefore, at the international level governments coordinated their efforts through multilateral intergovernmental forums such as the G20 group and international institutions such as the IMF and the World Bank.

The impact of globalization: much ado about nothing?

Realists argue that globalization is nothing new, and that it has no real impact upon how states conduct foreign policy. Advocates of a strong definition of globalization contend that everything is now new, requiring that we adopt a new set of theoretical tools to understand foreign policy-making in a new global polity.

Liberal scholars offer a more pragmatic middle-ground, although there is some difference between weak liberals such as Keohane and stronger liberal theories such as Deutsch's transactionalism (see Chapter 2). Taken together, some liberals argue that what we see is the creation of a new form of 'state': the postmodern state (e.g. Sørensen 2001). Postmodern states are integrated into security communities, which reduce the effects of anarchy, resulting in the emergence of zones of peace and security. Further, postmodern states are embedded in structures of *multilevel governance*, where issues are dealt with by political authorities at different levels and in different interlocking arenas, ranging from traditional intergovernmental cooperation to deeper forms of cooperation within supranational regional (the EU) and global institutions (the World Trade Organization).

Foreign policy-making beyond the state?

The definition of 'foreign policy' used in this book is limited to *public* collective actors. Actions by firms that are aimed at their own and foreign governments are instead defined as lobbying and other forms of relations with public authorities. Public collective actors are primarily states, but they can also, in theory, include international institutions. However, international institutions like NATO do not have their *own* foreign policy; instead they are forums where *states coordinate* their foreign policies toward achieving a common goal. Therefore NATO cannot be treated as an autonomous foreign policy actor, and any foreign policy actions are merely the product of what member states want. The only exception to this trend (at present) is arguably the EU.

Formally, the EU has two different types of common foreign policies depending upon the issue-area, with a strong economic foreign policy and relatively weaker diplomatic and security policies. In foreign economic policy (trade issues) the member states of the EU do not have their own independent policies. Here the EU acts in a manner similar to a federal system such as the US, with the supranational EU Commission representing the EU in external trade negotiations with other countries, based on a mandate given to it by governments acting within the Council of Ministers.

Within diplomatic and security-related foreign policy the EU has a

Common Foreign and Security Policy (CFSP). CFSP cooperation is *intergovernmental* and all important decisions are made unanimously. The supranational institutions of the EU (the Commission and European Parliament) have little if any role in CFSP. However, in recent years CFSP has developed tools and procedures that have arguably made it more than just the sum of the national foreign policies of the member states; most significant has been the creation of a permanent 'foreign minister' at the EU level (termed the High Representative) that is supported by a 'foreign ministry' of EU civil servants and a team of EU ambassadors who represent the EU in a number of countries throughout the world. The EU has also strengthened its common security policies in recent years, focusing on the ability to engage in peace-keeping and peace-making capabilities.

Some scholars have used the term 'civilian power' to describe the EU's overall foreign policy role (e.g. Sjursen 1998). The term refers to the fact that the EU is a strong economic actor in world affairs – it has a larger share of the world economy than the US – but it is very weak in traditional security policies, and large EU member states such as the UK have been extremely reluctant to let the EU take on a larger role in diplomatic relations with other countries.

The following will introduce the debate on whether the EU can be thought of as an *autonomous* foreign policy actor in world affairs. Are the EU's foreign economic and political policies merely the sum of member state foreign policies, or does the EU have a form of 'actorness' beyond the state (White 2004a)? In particular, this debate is centered on the question of whether we can speak of the EU having its own set of interests and identity, making its foreign policy more than just the sum of its states, enabling us to argue that it is distinct from those of the member states.

Is the EU an independent actor in foreign affairs?

Are we witnessing something new in world politics? Realists, not surprisingly, answer: no. They, and a variant of realist theorization used in EU studies that is termed intergovernmentalism, contend that the EU has *no autonomous interests or identity* in foreign affairs. Instead, it is seen merely as an institutional tool of the larger member states to pool resources to enable them to have a greater punch in world affairs, or to allow them to conduct policies that were otherwise not possible (Moravcsik 1998; Waltz 2000). For example, Germany in the 1990s used the EU's common foreign policy as a tool to assert its foreign policy interests through the use of a multilateral forum that is more acceptable for its neighbors than the same policies would be if they were made unilaterally by it (Ginsberg 1999). When the EU is able to find a common position, which only happens when all member states agree, this enables the EU to speak with a single voice that has a far greater impact than the individual voices of the member states. Realists suggest that the only way that the EU can become an autonomous foreign policy actor is if there is a fundamental shift in the external security environment caused by the emergence of a significant new external threat and/or a US decision to disengage from NATO and European security (Gordon 1997/98; Waltz 2000). The new threat would create strong common interests in creating an effective CFSP to balance against the new threat. However, realists suggest that this would not result in a new type of foreign policy actor beyond the state. Instead the smaller individual billiard balls would be replaced by a large EU billiard ball.

Strong liberal and social constructivist theorists counter by arguing that, despite the weakness of the institutional framework for the EU's CFSP, we are actually witnessing the gradual development of a form of 'actorness' in the EU that is created by the close interaction of national foreign policy civil servants from different member states, resulting in an incremental transformation of the foreign policy interests and perhaps very identities of the member states. The result is the beginning of what can be termed an *autonomous* EU foreign policy that is not merely the sum of member state interests and that does not necessarily replace member state policies, but instead represents a form of foreign policy *beyond* the state. These theorists contend that we are not witnessing a zero-sum game, where policies at the state level are merely replaced by EU-level policies. Instead we are seeing a positive-sum transformation, with policies being pursued at both levels.

Strong liberal theories such as neofunctionalism focus upon interactions that trigger *political spill-over* processes (Øhrgaard 2004) (see pp. 84–6). Neofunctionalists contend that governments and their civil servants change their perceptions about the utility of a common EU foreign policy in the course of their interaction with each other.

The key dynamic here is the instrumental calculation of the costs and benefits of increased coordination, following what was termed in Chapter 5 'the logic of consequences'. Earlier decisions to create contacts, consultations and procedures for the coordination of foreign policy can result in changes in the interests of participants. National civil servants involved in common foreign policy-making begin to perceive that EU member states either individually or in small groups are quite impotent in world affairs, whereas together they are quite strong (economic muscle backing). Perceptions of the benefits of the 'politics of scale' (Ginsberg 1999) will increase as more common foreign policies are adopted, creating a political spill-over process that results in increasing levels of foreign policy integration. Over time, the EU develops a form of 'actorness' as the interests of foreign policy civil servants are transformed through changed instrumental calculations.

Social constructivists also focus upon the interaction between civil servants, although the dynamics that produce a form of 'actorness' result from socialization and social learning instead of the more instrumental learning that occurs in neofunctionalist spill-over processes (Glarbo 1999; Tonra 2003; Jørgensen 2004a, 2004b). Instead of a rational, cost–benefit calculation, social learning results in the development of logics of appropriate action and even logics of habit if sufficiently embedded over longer time periods (see pp. 88, 118).

Glarbo (1999: 649–50) argues for example that 'social integration is emerging as the natural historical product of the day-to-day practices of political co-operation. Diplomats and national diplomacies have internalized, in particular, the formal requirements of a CFSP. On the level of foreign policy substance, a fully-fledged European identification is not yet discernible. But an institutionalized imperative of "concertation" is vividly evident from the interaction within political co-operation'. Tonra (2003) points out that national civil servants interacting with each other within the EU's CFSP engage in a form of social learning that rests on trust and shared core beliefs. Over time, national interests are transformed through social learning, creating a norm-based 'we feeling' amongst participants that transforms the nature of foreign policy-making in EU member state governments. Social interaction has therefore resulted in civil servants no longer thinking solely in terms of the 'national interest', but in terms of the 'national *and* European interest' (Larsen 2009).

Regardless of whether the transformation occurs through neofunctionalist spill-over processes based on instrumental calculations or through social constructivist interaction processes, there are some empirical indications that a change has taken place in foreign policy-making in Europe. For example, an indicator of the emergence of a form of 'actorness' is the increasing tendency of EU member states to vote together as a block in the UN General Assembly (Young and Rees 2005). Across a range of issues in the UN, member states hold increasingly similar views, suggesting that a convergence of national interests has occurred.

The degree of actorness of the EU varies though across different dimensions of its foreign policy. In economic foreign policy, while the domestic political context is important, member states are so intertwined economically within the Single Market that it makes little sense to speak about distinct national economies. This has resulted in a strong common economic foreign policy, where the EU has for the most part overtaken the economic foreign policy roles of the member states, although significant exceptions exist in the areas in which the EU does not have a common policy such as in taxation.

The situation is very different in political and security affairs. In security foreign policy, member states only engage in a loose coordination of policies due to the lack of common interests. Some member states are active participants in NATO whilst others are neutral. The best illustration of the distinctiveness of national security policies and lack of EU actorness in traditional security policies was seen in the split within the EU over the US-led invasion of Iraq in 2003 (Hill 2004).

Strong liberals and social constructivists agree that a degree of actorness has emerged in diplomatic foreign policies, although there is some difference in the degree to which it affects national foreign policymaking. Smaller states have seen their foreign policies fundamentally transformed, whereas for larger states the EU has become an overlapping network within which they articulate some of their foreign policies, while maintaining a distinct voice in other areas (Hill 2004; Larsen 2009).

However, despite individual member states retaining significant control over most areas of national foreign policy, there is a marked impact of the EU upon how they define their national interests. For example, British foreign policy is no longer recognizable as fully autonomous. Important elements are fully articulated within the EU (many aspects of economic foreign policies), whereas other areas are shaped by the context and processes within EU (traditional political foreign policies).

All of this said, there are few indications that the EU will become a fully autonomous foreign policy actor that replaces states. The EU is only slowly building up the traditional tools of state foreign policy; in particular in security affairs, where a very small common 'defense' force has been developed that in reality is a peacekeeping force that can be deployed for small scale post-conflict stabilization (e.g. Kosovo and Chad). Outside of economic policy, the common foreign policy institutions are merely intergovernmental, although some development of common representation of the EU has occurred through the creation of what can be termed an EU 'foreign minister' (the EU's High Representative) and the creation of a common EU foreign policy civil service, along with a set of EU ambassadors throughout the world.

Chapter 10

Analyzing Foreign Policy: Research Strategies and Methods

Students of foreign policy want to describe, understand, explain and predict events in the real world. This does not mean that the study of foreign policy is a purely empirical science devoted to description with little ambition to generalize and theorize beyond the particular. As has been seen throughout the chapters of this book, we do possess a range of theories that can be used as analytical tools to describe, explain and understand empirical foreign policy events. This concluding chapter provides students with a set of methodological tools that will enable them to study empirical events, using theories both as explanatory tools (analytical models) to understand events, and, for some theories, as critical theories to reflect upon inequalities in the social world.

The goal of most scientific research is *inference*, which is the process where we use known facts in the form of observable data to learn about broader phenomena that is not directly observed (King *et al.* 1994: 7–8). Inferences can be either descriptive or causal. Descriptive inferences focus upon what happened in an event, providing important knowledge regarding what actually happened in a particular episode. Causal inferences are made when we attempt to answer the question of why an event took place. Theories can suggest hypothetical answers to the question of why event X took place.

First I will describe how good research questions can be found, followed by a discussion of how one can choose an appropriate research strategy to study specific research questions. I then discuss two broad research strategies: one a more deductive, theory-testing strategy that can be used when studying well-researched questions, and a more inductive, theory-building strategy for less-well-studied questions.

Choosing research questions

Why did the Soviet Union decide to place missiles in Cuba in 1962? Why have EU member states chosen to develop a common foreign policy? Why did Germany adopt a cooperative, 'soft power' foreign policy strategy *vis-à-vis* its weaker, Central and Eastern European neighbors after 1989 instead of the 'power politics' strategy that its relative power enabled? Why did Israel decide to intervene militarily in Lebanon in 1982–83? Why did the US decide in the 1990s to intervene militarily in the conflicts in the Balkans but not in Rwanda? Do democracies adopt more peaceful foreign policies than non-democratic states?

The aim of research on foreign policy is to answer questions such as these. Yet there is a large difference in the scope of these different questions, ranging from those relating to explaining *particular* events to attempting to explain more *general* phenomena such as the impact of democracy upon foreign policy. Here the important question to ask yourself is whether you are interested in an event itself, or whether the event (or set of events) are part of a broader class of instances of a particular phenomenon (such as war or economic sanctions).

Research can be either case-centric or theory-centric. In case-centric analysis, the ambition is to understand why a particular outcome happened in a particular case, using theories as analytical tools instead of as predictive explanations that can be tested 'scientifically'. Scholars within this tradition contend that the world is very complex, and therefore we can at most hope to produce analytical models that assist us in understanding why an outcome happened (Jackson 2011). This position was termed the analytical position in Chapter 1. For instance, a typical case-centric question would be: why did the French government push so hard for a NATO-led military intervention in Libya in the spring of 2011? In this type of case study, the ambition is usually to provide a comprehensive, multifactor explanation that accounts for the important aspects of the case. Here the focus is on describing and understanding what caused individual events.

It must be pointed out that single case studies of exceptional events are legitimate areas of scientific research (Gerring 2006). We study US foreign policy decision-making relating to the escalation of the Vietnam War not solely because it represents a case of a general phenomenon such as misperception, but also because it is a historically important case in and of itself.

However, political scientists have traditionally held the ambition of going beyond describing why particular historical events occurred, aiming at building cumulative knowledge by generalizing the findings of a particular case to a broader set of cases of a given phenomenon. This is what can be termed *theory-centric* analysis. In philosophy of science terms, this involves an ambition at explaining events through the use of generalizable theories whose predictions can be tested against empirical reality; a position where theories are used as explanatory tools (Jackson 2011).

For instance, the Cuban Missile Crisis can be analyzed as a case of (extreme) crisis diplomacy, or as a case of crisis decision-making.

Another example could be findings of an analysis of US foreign policy toward Latin America, which can be generalized to broader trends in US foreign policy, or even more generally seen as a case of the foreign policy behavior of great powers toward weaker neighbors. These broader theoretical ambitions to generalize findings beyond the individual case is what differentiates political science research on foreign policy from the more policy-oriented foreign policy research done by think tanks, journalists and public intellectuals. Scholarship that aims to generalize beyond the individual case is termed 'nomothetic research', and concerns the causal relationships between variables and constructing broader explanations for important social behavior.

There are cases that are arguably unique, such as the case of common EU foreign policy making. As discussed in Chapter 9, the EU is the first example of what can be termed a 'post-national' foreign policy, where a strong regional institution has a common foreign policy in certain issues without being a state. Yet the case has broader implications, as it raises questions about whether the state-centeredness of realist theory is becoming out-dated, at least within the EU. Further, the case can be seen as only the most progressed example of the more general phenomenon of regional integration, enabling comparisons of the EU with cases such as the African Union. We can use the findings of studies of the EU to determine the conditions under which common policies are possible or not that can be used to analyze other cases of regional integration.

More general questions such as whether democracies have different foreign policies than authoritarian states (i.e. the democratic peace) are more typical research questions. In this type of question the goal is to contribute to an existing theoretical debate on the subject, although it can also involve starting a new debate if the question has not been previously investigated.

What are good research questions?

How can we evaluate whether a foreign policy research question is good or not? Often good research questions involve a 'puzzle' or paradox that is difficult to explain. For example, Janis's analysis of the Bay of Pigs decision starts with the paradox of how we can explain why a group of 'some of the most intelligent men ever to participate in the councils of government' could adopt a decision in which the 'major assumptions supporting the plan were so completely wrong that the venture began to founder at the outset and failed in its earliest stages' (Janis 1983: 14).

Finding paradoxes or puzzles is not a straightforward process. Often we stumble upon puzzles that we find difficult to explain when we are reading secondary, historical or journalistic accounts of events, or when we are reading the academic literature on a subject.

While deciding whether a research question is 'good' is ultimately subjective, King *et al.* (1994: 15–18) have suggested two criteria for evaluating research questions: (1) is the question 'important' in the real world? and (2) does studying the question contribute to an identifiable scholarly debate?

The first criterion involves evaluating the real world relevance of a research question. Basically, does studying the topic matter? Is the topic so trivial that it has no real world relevance? For example, a case study that attempts to explain why the Vietnamese governments voted for a UN Security Council Resolution imposing sanctions upon Eritrea in 2009 can be seen as a relatively trivial question (except for scholars and practitioners that are *deeply* interested in Vietnamese foreign policy). In contrast, a less trivial study would be to see the case as being only a part of a broader study of why the Security Council adopted the sanctions against Eritrea (or decides to impose sanctions in general), or as a case study of the broader phenomenon of how non-permanent members behave in the UN Security Council.

In the study of foreign policy there are a multitude of important research questions such as why wars occurred and how they can be avoided, or why governmental decision-making was poor in key historical cases like the escalation of the Vietnam War. However, if the research question deals with explaining a particular event it should be historically significant, although this is naturally subjective. For instance, it is obvious that exceptional cases such as the Cuban Missile Crisis or the Soviet decision to permit German reunification in 1989–90 are historically important in themselves and merit in-depth research.

Arguments for why a research question is important can be thought of as a form of literary 'hook', where the scholar attempts to convince readers that the topic is so important and interesting that they should continue to read the work. In other words, they attempt to answer readers' skepticism about why they should use their precious time to read the work. Good examples of arguments for why a research question is important can be found in the introductory section of articles in major journals and books published by university presses.

The second criterion is that scholarship on the question should contribute to an existing debate. As students of foreign policy we do not tread virgin ground; instead we follow in the footsteps of generations of able scholars. Therefore, as most topics have already been subject to some scholarship, our goal should be to attempt to contribute to the debates that already exist. For example, Ripsman and Paul in the preface to their book on globalization and national security make clear the importance of their work in the two first sentences: 'the onset of intensified globalization since the 1990s has affected every aspect of state functions, including national security. However, the extent of this impact is yet to be fully assessed' (Ripsman and Paul 2010: v).

In research areas where there is little pre-existing work, the objective of research is to provide good *descriptions of phenomena* that can serve as the building blocks for the formulation of theoretical explanations and causal inferences. This type of study is termed an inductive, theory-building design. One example of this type of research is what George terms the method of '*structured, focused comparison*' (see George and Bennett 2005). In this type of analysis, the scholar collects data on key variables across a range of cases, asking the same questions of each case. The method is 'focused' description, in that it only includes specific aspects of the historical cases that are of theoretical interest. Other forms of descriptive analysis involve: (1) creating *typologies* within a given phenomenon; for example dividing the broad concept of 'war' into a series of subtypes such as 'major international war', 'minor international wars', 'intra-national wars', etc.; (2) *empirical comparisons* such as: is the presidential post institutionally stronger in foreign policymaking in France or the US?; and (3) *empirical descriptions of developments* such as trends in Chinese foreign policy since 1945.

In areas where there exist good descriptions of phenomena (descriptive inferences), scholars can attempt to engage in *causal analysis*, attempting to infer what the causes of a given phenomenon are from observational data. When engaging in causal analysis, there are several ways in which good research questions can be found through surveying the existing theoretical and empirical literature studying a given phenomenon (adapted from King *et al.* 1994: 16–17 with the exception of number 6):

1. Investigate a hypothesis that has been suggested as important by other scholars, but that has not been subjected to systematic study.
2. Investigate whether a hypothesis that has been confirmed in existing research can be confirmed using new sources of evidence and/or different research methods than those originally used to test it.
3. Design research to illuminate or evaluate unquestioned assumptions in the literature.
4. Argue that an important topic has been overlooked and proceed to undertake a systematic study of the area.
5. Demonstrate that theories or evidence designed for some purpose in one literature could be applied in another literature to solve an existing but apparently unrelated problem.
6. Investigate the scope conditions for the applicability of a given theory by investigating whether it can be confirmed in different types of cases than were originally used.

Note that retesting well-established hypotheses is not included in the list. This does not mean that you cannot write a term paper that more-or-less replicates existing scholarship, but this type of question scores relatively low on originality, and would for instance not be accepted for publication in a serious peer-reviewed journal.

Where should you start when attempting to find a research question? The most important factor is that you are interested in studying a given topic, as this gives you the motivation to spend the time and effort that is necessary to write a good research paper. Ask yourself whether you are most interested in more empirical topics such as the foreign policies of a particular country or more theoretical questions like the impact of a particular independent variable such as stress upon the quality of decision-making (dependent variable).

Once you have decided upon a general topic, a practical next step is to survey briefly the academic literature. In particular, look for holes in the literature that relate to the six criteria listed above. One good source of inspiration is to look carefully at the conclusions of articles and books where authors discuss studies that could be done in the future.

Finally, throughout the research design process you need to think about feasibility in terms of the time and space available to conduct the study, and whether information is readily available or not. A comprehensive study of the situations in which force has been used in foreign policy-making in the 20th century is naturally not a feasible research question in the context of a 20-page term paper. An in-depth analysis of Iranian or Chinese foreign policy decision-making is difficult to conduct given issues of access and availability of information. Therefore, the formulation of research questions is often narrowed during the research process itself. You might start out your research interested in the phenomenon of crisis decision-making, but you will not be able to undertake a comprehensive, comparative analysis of all instances of this phenomenon, and therefore the research question will reflect your later choice of research strategy, in particular as regards the case selection strategy chosen, based upon whether you decide on a quantitative or qualitative methodology.

Most journal articles have very narrow research questions as pushing cumulative knowledge forward usually involves a very time-consuming research process. They are limited both in the form of the cases they choose and the breadth of the phenomena they investigate. Recent examples of good foreign policy research questions from one of the leading journals (*Foreign Policy Analysis*) include the following relatively narrow questions:

- Constructing the 'National Interest' in U.S.–China Policy Making: How Foreign Policy Decision Groups Define and Signal Policy Choices (Garrison 2007).
- Modeling Foreign Policy and Ethnic Conflict: Turkey's Policies Towards Syria (James and Özdamar 2009).

- Constituency Size and Support for Trade Liberalization: An Analysis of Foreign Economic Policy Preferences in Congress (Erlich 2009).

Choosing an appropriate research strategy

Once a research question has been chosen, the next step in the research process is to develop an appropriate strategy for answering the question. There are large differences in design depending upon whether your research question is case or theory-centric.

Case-centric research

If your research question is case-centric, the ambition is to build a plausible explanation of the outcome using theories as heuristic tools that can act as frameworks for analysis. Evans (1995: 4) states that 'cases are always too complicated to vindicate a single theory, so scholars who work in this tradition are likely to draw on a mélange of theoretical traditions in hopes of gaining greater purchase on the cases they care about'. When used in a heuristic manner, theories:

1. Indicate what sort of explanation is required. Are the important explanatory factors, for example, at the system or state level?
2. Provide conceptual categories that are used to navigate through the empirical material. For example, a structural realist analysis would focus our attention on power and its distribution in the system, whereas a social constructivist theory would analyze social interaction and norms.
3. Indicate what mechanisms, actors and chance factors are worth examining in the case. (Humphreys 2010: 263)

It is vital to make sure that you do not claim too much in case-centric research. You cannot 'test' the comparative explanatory power of theories in a stringent manner in a single case. However, you can assess whether there are 'big and important' aspects of the case that a given theory can account for or not when theories are used as analytical tools. You also cannot make claims that reach beyond the individual case based upon the findings. For example, based upon the finding that misperceptions did not play a significant role in explaining why the US believed that Saddam Hussein's Iraq had WMD in 2003, you cannot claim that the theory of misperceptions is incorrect; only that it offers little analytical leverage in explaining the particular case.

Beyond using theories in a heuristic manner, case-centric analysis employs what has recently been termed 'eclectic theorization', where one draws on elements from different theories to craft what is expected to be a stronger explanation of a phenomenon (Sil and Katzenstein 2010) (for a good discussion of how you can engage in theoretical synthesis, see Jørgensen 2010). The ambition of eclectic theorization is not to create new grand theories, but instead is a more pragmatic strategy aimed at capturing the multiplicity of mechanisms that produce *particular* historical outcomes, using parts of existing theories like Lego bricks to construct better accounts of cases. This is also why eclectic theorization is also termed 'problem-oriented research'.

Eclectic theorization can be thought of as the combination of different theories in a complex composite in order to craft a good explanation of a particular outcome (Sil and Katzenstein 2010). It 'offers complex causal stories that incorporate different types of mechanisms as defined and used in diverse research traditions ... seeks to trace the problem-specific interactions among a wide range of mechanisms operating within or across different domains and levels of social reality' (Sil and Katzenstein 2010: 419). According to Hirschman, 'ordinarily, social scientists are happy enough when they have gotten hold of one paradigm or line of causation. As a result, their guesses are often farther off the mark than those of the experienced politician whose intuition is more likely to take a variety of forces into account' (quoted in Sil and Katzenstein 2010: 413–14).

For instance, Schimmelfennig (2001) in an article in *International Organization* attempts to explain why countries like France that were opposed to Eastern Enlargement of the EU ended up not opposing it. He tests both realist, interest-based theories and social constructivist, norm-based causal mechanisms and finds them both 'wanting in the "pure" form'. In response he formulates a theoretical synthesis that attempts to 'provide the missing link between egoistic preferences and a norm-conforming outcome' by developing the idea of 'rhetorical action' (the strategic use of norm-based arguments) that can provide a sufficient explanation of the specific outcome in the case, combining social constructivist and realist elements in his model (2001: 76).

Theory-centric research

The emphasis of theory-centric research is upon analyzing causal relationships between variables, using theories as explanatory tools. When and why are interest groups (X) able to influence national preferences (Y)? Does Groupthink (X) produce faulty decision-making processes (Y)?

The first step in theory-centric research is to determine whether the research question has been extensively studied or not. If it has there should exist numerous competing theories that can be used as a starting point for a more *deductive, theory-testing research design*. On the other hand, when one confronts a little studied phenomenon it is usually more appropriate to adopt an *inductive, theory-building strategy* unless there are theoretical literatures in other fields that could hypothetically be applied.

Both of these strategies should be seen as ideal-types. In practice researchers often start by testing whether an existing theory can explain a set of cases (deductive, theory-testing), but once they find that there are important aspects of cases that cannot be explained using existing theories they then use more inductive, theory-building methods to account for significant anomalies. The next two sections detail these two overall research strategies. Within each of these strategies there are two overall categories of methods: quantitative and qualitative methods. Within these two categories there is a range of different methods, including statistical analysis, process-tracing, comparative and discourse analysis. Formal methods such as game theory are not discussed in the following, as they are much rarer than other methods in the study of foreign policy (though see Bueno de Mesquita *et al.* 1999; Bapat 2010).

In deductive, theory-testing studies, the variables need to be specified along with a hypothesized theoretical relationship of cause-and-effect linking them together (if cause–effect relationships are to be investigated). Theories were defined in Chapter 1 as reasoned and precise speculation about the answer to a research question (King *et al.* 1994: 19). Theories play a central role in causal analysis, although the precise role that they play is the subject of considerable debate (George and Bennett 2005; Friedrichs and Kratochwill 2009; Humphreys 2010).

The outcome or event that is in focus is usually termed the *dependent variable* (Y), although in a *single case study* of a significant historical case the 'event' does not vary, making it more appropriate to use the term 'outcome'. For instance, the Cuban Missile Crisis (luckily) only had the outcome of no war, and unless this crisis is compared with other crises with other outcomes there is no variance in the dependent variable. Factors that are hypothesized to be causes of the dependent variable/outcome are termed *independent variables* (Xs).

If causal analysis is being undertaken there have to exist plausible arguments for why a given independent variable or set of variables can hypothetically be the cause of a dependent variable. If we are interested in explaining why certain NATO countries have withdrawn their troops from Afghanistan while others have continued their presence (the dependent variable), a (hopefully!) implausible explanation of a continued presence could be that the prime minister enjoys the good photo opportunities created by his or her visits to the troops in the field (the independent variable). More plausible theoretical explanations could involve independent variables such as the level of public support for the mission or the degree of elite consensus behind the involvement (Kreps 2010).

There are three different types of focus in causal analysis. First, one can be interested in studying the *effects* of a given independent variable (X-centered analysis) (Gerring 2007). Much of the literature on the democratic peace investigates the effects of democracy (X) upon the war-proneness of states (Y). Scholarship on the importance of economic sanctions is also focused upon the independent variable (sanctions) and its effects upon state behavior (more cooperative or not).

The second type is scholarship that focuses upon the dependent variable and what *causes* result in variance of the dependent variable (Y-centered analysis) (Gerring 2007). Here the scholar wants to explain a puzzling outcome but has no preconceptions about the cause. Scholarship on why states cooperate with each other focuses upon the dependent variable 'conflict–cooperate' between states, attempting to identify what independent variables are the causes of variation in the dependent one.

The third and by far least common type of study is the investigation of the causal link or mechanism connecting an independent variable or set of variables with an outcome (X/Y-centered analysis) (Gerring 2007). This usually involves in-depth examination of a small number of cases in order to detect whether the observable implications of a hypothesized causal mechanism can be detected. For example, Owen (1994) used in-depth process tracing methods to detect whether the theorized mechanism linking democracy and more peaceful behavior toward other democracies was actually present in four historical cases.

Deductive, theory-testing research designs

Deductive, theory-testing research designs are used when there exists a substantial body of scholarship that has studied a phenomenon, enabling you to draw upon a set of theoretical hypotheses to investigate your research question. Here theories are used as explanatory tools.

The following will first discuss how you can find and choose theories, followed by a discussion of the conceptualization of key concepts and hypotheses. The section then introduces the two different overall categories of research methods (qualitative and quantitative methods), along with short summaries of the main research tools available within each method, including the techniques for case selection that are most applicable to the given tool. The section on deductive designs then discusses the operationalization of key concepts.

Finding and choosing theories

A deductive research design starts by cataloging the 'state of the art' in the literature, noting the main theoretical debates about hypothetical answers to the research question. A good shortcut is to first look at textbooks that review theories related to the phenomenon. Good textbooks should provide an overview of the lines of theoretical debate about the phenomenon you are going to research, enabling you to identify which theories can be used to provide hypothetical answers to your research question.

Once you have catalogued the main lines of debate in the literature you need to decide the number of theories you will utilize and how you will use them. There are several ways in which you can use theories including as:

1.   A critical analysis of the explanatory power of one theory.
2.   A test of two or more competing theories.
3.   The basis for a theoretical synthesis.

In theory-centric research, a critical analysis of the explanatory power of one theory is very common, especially when an author is proposing a new theory in an article or book. The author then proceeds to test the explanatory power of the new theory in an empirical analysis of a number of cases. The explanatory power of a theory cannot be strictly tested in a single case, although more pragmatically one can assess whether a given theory can explain the 'most important' aspects of a case.

This type of analysis is often very relevant for students writing term papers and other shorter works. Here it is vital that you ensure that your analysis critically examines the theory's ability to explain empirical developments across the cases. This can be ensured by carefully operationalizing the theory so that you clearly state what you expect to see in the empirical record if the theory is correct.

One pitfall of this type of study is that it can fall prey to *confirmatory bias*, where the researcher succumbs to the all too common tendency of the human mind to see what it wants to see. Most articles of this type tend not surprisingly to find significant support for the proposed new theory.

A strategy to avoid confirmatory bias is to take two competing theoretical answers to your research question and use them to structure your analysis. A competitive theory test creates a form of critical dialogue and debate in your analysis, unless you have a pet theory that you favor. As most scholars tend to prefer one type of theory, such as constructivism or realist theorization, over others, this type of analysis often tends to degenerate into what Checkel (forthcoming) has termed a 'gladiator approach ... where – like a Roman warrior on his chariot – one perspective went forth and slayed all others, with the latter presented in highly simplified form'. To avoid this both theories need to be treated to an equally critical evaluation. The results are usually in the form that independent variable X from theory A could account for more variation in Y (dependent variable) than independent variable Z from theory B.

Common to theory tests is that predictions of what we should expect to see in the empirical material have to be deduced from the theory. Testable hypotheses are derived from the theory that can be tested empirically across a range of cases using either comparative or large-*n* quantitative methods. However, this is often easier said than done, especially when we are attempting to explain particular cases. Here it is rare that a given theory is sufficiently detailed to be able to deduce exactly what we should expect to see in a given case (Humphreys 2010: 259). The best suggestion is to be relatively pragmatic in using theories as the basis of deductions about what caused Y to happen in most instances (Friedrichs and Kratochwill 2009).

The conceptualization phase: translating abstract concepts into systematized concepts

Before one can proceed it is important to define carefully the different theoretical concepts that one will be investigating; in other words, what exactly do the variables in the study mean? The meanings of concepts such as democracy and power are hotly contested amongst theorists. For most important political science concepts there are usually dozens of competing definitions. If you merely use the term 'power' without any further definition, readers can take this to mean that you are speaking about anything from the structural realist definition of power as being the possession of material resources to broader definitions such as structural forms of power, where the concept is defined as the ability to create or control the structures of international relations. Careful definition of key theoretical concepts is therefore critical to avoiding an ambiguous analysis with indeterminate conclusions.

The conceptualization phase involves the translation of an abstract concept such as democracy into a clearly defined *systematized concept*, usually by referring to how the concept is specified by a certain scholar or group of scholars (Adcock and Collier 2001). An example of a systematized definition of the abstract concept of power could be what Barnett and Duvall (2005: 49–50) term 'compulsory power', which they base upon Dahl's original systematized definition of power as the ability of actor A to get B to do something he or she otherwise would not do.

There are at least two dangers that one should be aware of in the translation of abstract concepts into systematized concepts. First, while you have a considerable degree of freedom in defining a concept, conceptualization should not be understood as merely 'anything goes'. Instead, it is important to remain as faithful as possible to the original definitions used by the scholars such as Dahl who developed a specific definition of a concept. Second, when defining a systematized concept it is usually necessary to flesh out the definition by specifying in considerable detail what the concept entails, including relating it to competing definitions. In relation to a systematized definition of power as 'compulsory power', it would be useful not only to define the concept in a sentence or two but also to contrast it briefly with other competing definitions of power such as structural power. If the concept has multiple dimensions, it is also important to delineate these.

Beyond creating clear definitions of dependent and independent variables, it is at this phase that the logical interrelationship of concepts with each other should be described if causal analysis is being undertaken. This usually takes the form of a paragraph or two of text that describes in linear fashion how a given independent variable or variables can hypothetically affect a dependent variable. Here is one example from recent FPA theorization that describes the causal logic linking constituency size (X) with support for free trade (Y):

> The ... literature on the presidential liberalism thesis ... holds that Presidents are naturally more liberal on trade policy than their protectionist colleagues in Congress. Typically, supporters of this thesis advocate delegating trade policy to the President in order to achieve free-trade. The causal logic of this thesis usually rests on the idea that the President's national constituency forces him to be more concerned with national welfare rather than the particularistic demands of individual industries or interest groups. Since free-trade increases national welfare while protectionism only helps particular groups, the President should support free-trade. Congresspersons, who often represent narrow constituencies, may be more supportive of particularistic demands as they may represent the particular industries that benefit from these demands. (Erlich 2009: 216)

The operationalization phase: measuring systematized concepts

After variables and their interrelationship have been clearly defined as systematized concepts the next step is to develop empirical indicators of these variables. If the focus of the research is upon studying the causal mechanism linking independent and dependent variables, the observable implications of the theory should also be developed. What you basically have to answer is: how do I know X when I see it? What types of empirical indicators reflect the presence/absence of a given variable?

For example, in a study of bureaucratic politics, part of the theory is the hypothesis that bureaucrats take positions (Y) that reflect the institutional self-interest of the department that they are part of (X) ('where you stand reflects where you sit'). This institutional, self-interest, independent variable can be further theorized as an interest in protecting the 'turf' of the department in inter-institutional battles within government. Operationalizing the self-interest variable then involves asking yourself: how do I know bureaucratic self-interested turf-protecting behavior when I see it? An answer to this could for example be that you expect to see that bureaucrats, when faced with a choice of different options on implementing a policy, will attempt to maximize funds and policy instruments that are available to perform their core tasks while minimizing the delegation of unattractive tasks and other disruptions that could hinder the effective delivery of their core tasks. Indicators for this could include statements in interdepartmental meetings advocating that department A be delegated task B instead of another department, provided that task B is related to the core tasks that department A delivers.

If you are testing the explanatory power of a theory, you should first ask yourself: what evidence would disconfirm it and what would constitute confirming evidence? This should be formulated as a set of observable implications of a theory. A good example is Janis's Groupthink theory, where he details a set of 'symptoms' of Groupthink that can be understood as observable implications of the existence of Groupthink in a given case (Janis 1983; see also pp. 125–32 above).

There is a difference between the type of indicators that we choose when we are using qualitative and quantitative methods. Quantification involves choosing numerical indicators, such as the size of military budgets or the number of times a speech uses conflictual and cooperative terms that then form the basis for numerical codings of variables. Qualitative measures are text-based indicators, often in the form of different 'types'. For instance, in a study of why states contributed to the 1991 Gulf War, Bennett *et al.* operationalize the independent variable 'collective action' as 'would a contribution from the country in question (including the use of military bases) be important to achieving the public good of expelling Iraqi forces from Kuwait?' (in George and Bennett 2005: 256).

When operationalizing variables and hypotheses a key concern is the *measurement validity* of our indicators. This is defined as whether we are actually measuring the systematized concept that we intended to measure (Adcock and Collier 2001). There are numerous ways in which we can attempt to test whether our chosen measures are actually valid, i.e. measuring what we want to measure. The most intuitive validation technique is termed *face validation*, where we present common-sense arguments for why a given indicator is actually measuring the systematized concept. In an operationalization of the structural realist conceptualization of power defined as the possession of material power resources, if we choose 'number of nuclear weapons possessed' as an indicator, we would need to be able to present coherent arguments for why this is a valid measure in comparison to other indicators. This could prove difficult given basic facts like Russia and the US both possess relatively similar numbers of nuclear weapons but have very different capabilities as regards the overall ability to project military force across the globe, suggesting that the indicator is not a particularly valid one.

Another particularly useful form of validation is termed *convergent validation*, defined as whether there is a correlation between an alternative established indicator and your indicator for the same systematized concept (Adcock and Collier 2001). This type is particularly used in quantitative analysis, where it is possible to test statistically correlation between two different indicators for the same systematized concept. Using the structural realist power example, if you have chosen to use military budget size as an indicator, your new indicator could be validated by testing how correlated it is with established indicators such as the widely used Correlates of War (COW) composite indicator of material capabilities (see www.correlatesofwar.org/).

The best starting point for operationalizing is to seek inspiration from established scholars writing within the subject you are studying, investigating how they operationalize key concepts and hypotheses. In many areas there already are good operationalizations of key concepts that can be used directly – there is no need to reinvent the wheel every time we do research.

It is also important not to create overly complex indicators that are unwieldy in practice. Parsimony is to be strived for, although not at the cost of measurement validity. For example, the structural realist concept of power includes both actual and potential or latent power resources. Despite low military spending, structural realists argue that Germany is a relatively powerful country given its large population and wealth – factors that can be mobilized quickly and translated into actual military power resources (Waltz 2000). Therefore an indicator solely based upon military expenditures would not measure power as it is used by structural realists. To capture both latent and actual power resources, the standard quantitative structural realist measure of power is the COW composite index of material capabilities, which includes the following components: total population, urban population, iron and steel production, energy consumption, military personnel, and military expenditure of all state members.

Designing your research project: choosing qualitative or quantitative methods

At first glance one might think that the choice between using qualitative and quantitative methods is solely decided by the number of cases to be analyzed; a small number of cases means qualitative methods should be used, whereas a larger number equals quantitative methods. While this does capture some of the rationale behind the choice, there is also a difference in kind between the two different research methods. Some scholars believe that relatively broad generalizations about relationships in the social sciences are possible across a wide range of cases, making relevant quantitative statistical tools that can detect systematic patterns in a large number of cases.

Many qualitative scholars counter that the social world is too complex and contingent for us to make broad generalizations, advocating either case-centric designs or theory-centric designs where theoretical claims are restricted to a very small population of cases (for example the foreign policy of modern parliamentary democracies in Northern Europe instead of the broader population of democratic states).

This does not however mean that qualitative scholars do not have ambitions to generalize findings beyond the single or handful of cases studied. But the argument is often made by qualitative scholars that we should make more limited claims that respect these complexities in order to avoid 'conceptual stretching'. This is the risk that a broad measure lumps together dissimilar cases in order to get a large sample, creating a relatively invalid measure (George and Bennett 2005). Qualitative scholars tend to use bounded conceptualizations of key concepts by placing adjectives such as major/minor or liberal/illiberal in front of them.

One example of this distinction is seen in the indicators chosen to measure the concept 'democracy'. Quantitative scholars use broad measures of democracy like the Polity measure to create a dataset of observations of each country in the world spanning back to 1800 (Marshall *et al.* 2010). In this dataset, the US scores an almost perfect score (9 out of 10) for much of the first half of the 1800s despite the fact that a large minority of the population were slaves and women did not have the right to vote. Qualitative scholars would contend that this broad measure does not capture the way in which democracy has changed over time, and would instead choose to use more contingent measures that capture this complexity (e.g. *liberal* versus *illiberal* democracy) (George and Bennett 2005; Goertz 2006).

The choice between the two methods is a tradeoff, with each method having relative advantages and disadvantages (for discussions, see King *et al.* 1994; Brady and Collier 2004; George and Bennett 2005; Gerring

2007). Qualitative methods are strong as regards capturing the complexity of concepts, operating often with more constrained definitions of concepts such as liberal or parliamentary democracy that restrict the scope of theoretical claims. Qualitative methods also have strong tools to investigate causal mechanisms (X/Y-centered analysis), for example using process-tracing techniques.

On the other hand, quantitative methods are less prone to forms of case selection bias, as they tend to select such a large number of cases that they achieve a representative sample of the whole population, whereas qualitative scholars often select a smaller number of cases that for instance share the same outcome. Quantitative scholars would argue that this non-random sampling of the population can produce significant bias, with the result that the findings are skewed. Qualitative scholars counter that this form of case selection is a conscious choice. If we want to find out if cause X (independent variable) is necessary for war to occur, we should only choose cases where war actually occurred and see whether X was always present (Dion 1998).

You therefore need to ask yourself whether you believe that the phenomenon you are investigating is sufficiently broad that large-*n*, statistical analysis is possible and necessary. Do you believe that broad generalizations across many cases are possible, or is the social world so complex that only limited claims can be made?

There are a range of quantitative data sources available to study foreign policy, with examples including the COW dataset, the Penn State Event Data Project that codes foreign policy events in the Middle East, the Balkans and West Africa for the period 1979 until the present (http://eventdata.psu.edu/index.html), and the CREON dataset for 36 nations in the period 1959–68 (www.icpsr.umich.edu/icpsrweb/ICPSR/studies/5205).

Qualitative methods

Qualitative methods involve a range of methodological tools, ranging from comparative methods, to in-depth case study methods such as process-tracing, to discourse and content analysis. *Comparative methods* usually strive to detect causal relations that involve either necessary or sufficient conditions. *Necessary conditions* are independent variables that always have to be present for an outcome to occur, such as a strong conflict of interest for a war to occur. In Table 10.1, the only variable that is present in both of the cases where Y is present is X1, suggesting that X1 is a necessary variable to produce Y.

However, necessary conditions are often not sufficient on their own to produce an outcome. *Sufficient conditions* are independent variables that on their own are able to produce an outcome, often in combination with each other. For example, a match and combustible material

Table 10.1   *Necessary and sufficient conditions*

Case	Conditions present in case	Outcome present?
1	X1 * X2	Y present
2	X1 * X3	Y present

Note: '*' should be read as 'and'.

together are sufficient to produce a fire, but a match is not a necessary condition for a fire to occur, as lightning, an electrical spark or numerous other causes can also produce fire together with combustible material. The two combinations X1 and X2, and X1 and X3 are both sufficient to produce Y, whereas X1 alone is not sufficient to produce Y.

To test for necessary conditions you need to compare all of the causes of outcome (Y) and investigate whether a hypothesized X (independent variable) was present in all of the cases (Dion 1998). Tests of sufficiency investigate all cases where X has occurred to see whether Y also occurred. If Y occurred in all of the cases, then X is a sufficient cause. Given that qualitative researchers use bounded conceptualizations of concepts (such as *major* international war), the number of cases is usually relatively limited. Hypotheses in comparative studies take the form 'a minimal level of X is necessary for Y', whereas quantitative hypotheses tend to take the form 'the higher the level of X, the more likely Y is to occur'.

If the independent variable survives this method of elimination, it can be *possibly* associated with the outcome as either a necessary or sufficient condition, although we cannot automatically infer that this finding holds for the whole population of cases (Dion 1998). See Table 10.2.

Process-tracing techniques are in-depth, case-study tools that can be used to examine a hypothesized causal mechanism linking an independent variable (or set of variables) and an outcome (Y) (see Beach and Pedersen, forthcoming). Van Evera (1997: 64) defines process-tracing as a method where 'the cause–effect link that connects independent variable and outcome is unwrapped and divided into smaller steps; then the investigator looks for observable evidence of each step'. The promise of process-tracing as a methodological tool is that it enables the researcher to study more-or-less directly the *causal mechanism* linking an independent variable (or set of variables) and an outcome, allowing us to open up the 'black box' of causality. A classic example from medical science is scholarship on the association between smoking and cancer. While a strong empirical correlation had been

Table 10.2 *An example of comparative analysis: Risse-Kappen's comparative study of the impact of public opinion*

Research question	When should we expect societal preferences to matter in foreign policy making?			
Conceptualization phase	Building on existing research, Risse-Kappen theorizes that three factors determine the impact that public opinion have in defining national preferences: 1. Degree of centralization of the political system 2. Degree of polarization and mobilization of domestic society 3. The nature of coalition building			
Operationalization phase	Provides little guidance for how he measures the three factors. In the actual analysis, he puts forward empirical material suggesting high/low values on each of the factors			
Analysis	*USA*	*Germany*	*Japan*	*France*
Political system	Decentralized	Intermediate	Intermediate	Centralized
Society	Heterogeneous, weak organizations	Heterogeneous, strong organizations	Homogeneous, strong organizations	Heterogeneous, weak organizations
Policy network	Society-dominated	Democratic, corporatist	Quasi-corporatist	State-dominated
Impact of public opinion	Ample opportunities to affect policy	Influence through party system	Similar to Germany, but more homogeneous society	Only marginal role

Source: Based on Risse-Kappen (1991).

well established for many years, it was only recently that medical scientists using techniques analogous to process-tracing have provided strong proof that a biological mechanism actually exists that causally links smoking and cancer (Brady 2008).

Causal mechanisms can be defined as 'a complex system which produces an outcome by the interaction of a number of parts' (Glennan 1996: 52; Glennan 2002). Each part of a hypothesized causal mechanism can helpfully be understood as composed of *entities* that undertake *activities* (Machamer *et al.* 2000). Entities are the factors engaging in activities, where the activities are the producers of change or what transmits causal forces through a mechanism. Entities can be individual persons, groups or states depending upon the level of the theory. Entities are described by nouns, while activities are described as verbs expressing action.

Note that it is *not* the independent variable (X) that is producing the outcome per se, but the *mechanism* composed of a series of parts that actually produces the outcome by transmitting causal forces. Figure 10.1 illustrates the logic. In a simple model of the democratic peace, where democracy is the independent variable (X) and peace is the outcome (Y), a simple causal mechanism involves two parts (Rosato 2003: 585). First, liberal groups agitate their government for anti-war policies. Given that democratic governments are dependent upon the support of elite groups for re-election, if the anti-war liberals

Figure 10.1   *A simple example of a 'mechanistic' conceptualization of a causal mechanism*

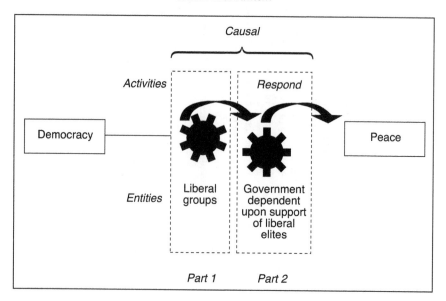

are sufficiently strong their pressure should result in a government responding by adopting more peaceful foreign policies.

A process-tracing test of this mechanism would involve testing whether the hypothesized parts of the mechanism were actually present in a particular case or small set of cases. Here the two parts of the mechanism need to be carefully operationalized, enabling us to answer questions such as: how do we empirically recognize liberal groups agitating for anti-war policies in cases?

Table 10.3 *An example of process-tracing analysis*

Research question	What is the causal mechanism behind the democratic peace?

Conceptualization phase	• Liberal democracy is defined as a state that 'instantiates liberal ideas, one where liberalism is the dominant ideology and citizens have leverage over war decisions' (Owen 1994: 89)
	• A causal mechanism is formulated that links liberal ideas to peace through two causal pathways:
	  1. Liberal ideas → ideology → no wars against democracies → constraints on government → democratic peace
	  2. Liberal ideas → institutions → free debate → constraints on government → democratic peace

Operationalization phase	A set of six testable hypotheses of the observable implications of each of the causal pathways is developed, formulated as a set of questions asked of each historical case 1. Liberals will trust states they consider liberal and mistrust those considered illiberal 2. When liberals observe a foreign state becoming liberal by their own standards, they will expect pacific relations with it 3. Liberals will claim that fellow liberal democracies share their ends, and that illiberal states do not 4. Liberals will not change their assessments of foreign states during crisis unless those states change institutions. 5. Liberal elites will agitate for policies during war-threatening crises 6. During crises, statesmen will be constrained to follow liberal policy
Analysis	• Each of the hypotheses is empirically investigated in four historical cases • For instance, hypothesis five is tested in the Anglo-American crisis of 1895–96 by investigating whether American liberals actually agitated for peace. The sources used are newspapers from the time period

Source: Owen (1994).

Case selection within process-tracing methods that aim to test whether a hypothesized causal mechanism is present/absent should be based upon selecting cases where the hypothesized mechanism potentially is present (both X and Y are present, but we are unsure of whether there is an actual causal mechanism linking the two). This type of study was termed an X/Y centered focus above. Most studies of this type select multiple cases to control for the possibility that a single case is so unique that the findings cannot be generalized beyond the single case. (See Table 10.3.)

Table 10.4   *An example of discourse analysis*

Research question	Analysis of the role that shifts in the discursive representations of Turkish identity and the Soviet 'Other' had in the Turkish foreign policy move away from a cooperative stance with the Soviet Union after World War II toward a close alliance with the West (the US)
Conceptualization phase	• Discourses are defined as structures of signification out of which representations of 'Self' and 'Other' are constructed • Foreign policies are social constructs produced by, and that produce state identity and interests through, 'interpretative labor' by elites
Operationalization phase	• Representations of the 'Other' are to be identified, although the study lacks clearly formulated criteria for what types of sources will be used to measure these representations, and how we can identify an influential representation • Sources that are used to measure representations are primarily speeches by elite actors
Analysis	• Anomalies that cannot be explained with existing accounts (shifts in external threats or domestic politics) are first illustrated • The article then identifies three distinct prevailing identities held at different times in speeches by Turkish foreign policy elites. For example, the Soviet Union was recast as 'USSR, the tsarist expansionist' after World War II • The analysis also illustrates the 'intepretative labor' undertaken by elites in the construction of the Soviet Union as a friend in the interwar years, and the construction of the Soviet Union as a hostile 'imperialist' power in the immediate after war years. Unfortunately, the analysis reflects a lack of clear conceptualization of 'interpretative labor', and little evidence is produced that illuminates how the elites reconstructed discourses through this term

Source: Cos and Bilgin (2010).

Discourse analysis deals with the study of language and its impacts. The fundamental split within discourse analysis is primarily along ontological lines, dealing with the very nature of reality. Positivists investigate questions such as how language is used strategically by leaders or how we can map the content of the beliefs of leaders from their pronouncements (see George 1969; Hermann 2008). Post-structuralists (also termed 'reflectivists' in Chapter 1) believe that it is through language that 'reality' is constructed and reconstructed. As such, there is no 'objective' meaning beyond the linguistic representation that one can refer to (Shapiro 1981). Language is a social construct through which identities are, for instance, built through a series of juxtapositions that value one object over its opposite (the Other) (Hansen 2006: 19). For example, US national identity is seen as constructed in relation to the Other (the rest of the world), resulting in a national identity that emphasizes 'exceptionalism'. In the concluding section of this chapter a brief note on the methodology of post-structuralist foreign policy analysis is included.

In contrast to the theory-testing methods described above, most discourse analysis uses *interpretivist* methods where the focus is upon *understanding* instead of explaining. As such, interpretivists do not frame their analysis in terms of causal relations between independent and dependent variables. Instead, the aim is often to create thick narratives and descriptions of the structures and categorizations that can be detected through a systematic reading of texts. An example of a discourse analysis is provided in Table 10.4.

Quantitative methods

Beyond merely descriptive quantitative methods, such as frequency tables that show for instance what percentage of US voters hold 'internationalist' or 'isolationist' foreign policy views, the primary quantitative methods used in the analysis of foreign policy are methods that analyze statistical correlations between variables. This involves a range of different statistical techniques from simple correlation analysis (bivariate measures of association) to advanced non-linear regression techniques.

Even making sense of hundreds or thousands of observations is virtually impossible without quantitative methods. Finding empirical relationships between variables in large populations is impossible. For example, the results of surveys of thousands of voter attitudes toward foreign policy matters cannot be evaluated without statistical tools.

Beyond making inferences possible for large populations, quantitative methods also have other advantages. One is that the explicit measurement criteria that are necessary to permit the quantification of measurements helps mitigate against the natural human tendency to only notice trends that are consistent with one's own theory (Braumoeller and Sartori 2004). Any benefit is that statistical methods offer tools that can compare the explanatory strength of two or more independent variables, whereas qualitative methods are weaker and more 'subjective' for assessing which explanation provides the biggest 'bang for the buck'.

The basic idea behind statistical analysis is that hypothesized correlations between variables are assessed against the statistical laws of probability to determine whether a found relationship is the product of 'chance' or represents a correlation. Figure 10.2 illustrates the logic. There are two axes that run from 0 to 100. Each x marks individual *observations* and their measures on two different variables (*X* and *Y*). The x-axis is the independent variable and the y-axis is the dependent variable. As can be seen in the figure, there appears to be a linear relationship between *X* and *Y*, with higher values of *X* associated with higher values of *Y*. Whether this relationship is the product of chance or whether we can conclude that it represents a real relationship with a high degree of certainty can then be assessed using statistical laws of probability. In this case, we would run a linear regression that tests whether the relationship is a product of chance or not.

Figure 10.2   *A hypothesized relationship between X and Y*

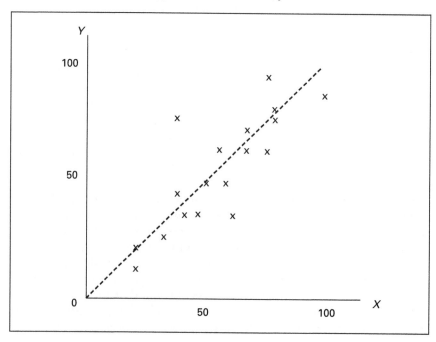

Table 10.5   *An example of a quantitative foreign policy study*

Research question	Explanations of the support of US Senators for Israel
Conceptualization phase	• Four different independent variables are theorized to matter for senatorial support of Israel: (1) partisanship (Republican or Democrat); (2) religious identification; (3) constituency interests; or (4) ideology (conservative or liberal) • Hypothesis 1: Republicans are expected to support Israel more than Democrats • Hypothesis 2: Jewish and evangelical Protestant senators are expected to be more likely to support Israel • Hypothesis 3: Larger state-level evangelical and Jewish populations will result in more support for Israel • Hypothesis 4: More conservative senators will be more likely to support Israel
Operationalization phase	• Senatorial support is measured according to whether a senator has voted in support of Israel in roll call votes • Partisanship and religious identification are measured as either yes or no • State-level percentages of populations are used to measure religion • An existing index (DW-Nominate) is used to measure whether senators are conservative or liberal
Analysis	• Poisson analysis of the correlations between variables are first run, followed by a predicted probability of support analysis that attempts to capture the relative explanatory power of the different independent variables • The findings indicate strong support for Hypotheses 1 and 4, and more qualified support for 2 and 3

Source: Rosenson *et al.* (2009).

It is however important to note that we cannot infer that a *causal* relationship exists between *X* and *Y* merely because we find a statistically significant correlation between the two. Some quantitative scholars claim that we can never prove causality, and therefore we should confine ourselves to studying correlations. Most contend that we can infer causality if additional criteria are fulfilled; the most important being: (1) there has to be a conceptual, theoretical link between *X* and *Y* (i.e. it is plausible that *X* caused *Y*) and (2) *X* must precede *Y* in time and space (i.e. *X* could have been a cause of *Y*). This is also a major source of contention with qualitative scholars, who argue that only process-tracing case studies can actually test causal relationships between variables. Table 10.5 illustrates an example of quantitative, foreign policy scholarship.

Inductive, theory-building research designs

If there has not been much research on a topic a different approach can be called for. Inductive, theory-building research designs attempt to investigate empirically a case or set of cases in a systematic manner that allows the research to develop ideas about general patterns that can become theoretical propositions. Unfortunately, there is little guidance in the methodological literature about how to best proceed with inductive research designs. Therefore, the best suggestion is to seek inspiration in the handful of existing foreign policy studies that engage in more inductive theory-building. Below I offer two different examples. They are selected according to the overall methodology that they utilize. The first example is a qualitative study, using Janis's (1983) case study that he used to develop the theory of Groupthink. Second, I illustrate the use of inductive methods in quantitative analysis, where scholars engage in what can be termed 'data-mining' to detect correlations that can form the basis of theorization based upon a correlation analysis of a plethora of hypothetical causes (Singh and Way 2004).

Janis's inductive analysis in the book Groupthink

Janis utilized a series of case studies to build his theory of Groupthink, investigating which common factors were cases of faulty decision-making processes that resulted in policy fiascoes. The Bay of Pigs debacle is one of these. In the words of Janis:

> Planned by an overambitious, eager group of American intelligence officers who had little background or experience in military matters, the attempt to place a small brigade of Cuban exiles secretly on a beachhead in Cuba with the ultimate aim of overthrowing the government of Fidel Castro proved to be a 'perfect failure'. The group that made the basic decision to approve the invasion plan included some of the most intelligent men ever to participate in the councils of government. Yet all the major assumptions supporting the plan were so completely wrong that the venture began to founder at the outset and failed in the earliest stages. (Janis 1983: 14)

Janis details the core members of the advisory group that took the decisions for the Kennedy administration and the six major miscalculations that the group made. He then evaluates the existing answers to why these miscalculations were made, finding that the existing four explanations do not fully explain why the miscalculations were produced.

Unfortunately, Janis is quite unclear about how he took the next step where he inductively develops his Groupthink hypothesis based upon a detailed reading of the empirical material, including participant recollections such as Schlesinger. He merely states that 'sensitized by my dissatisfaction with the four-factor explanation, I noticed in Schlesinger's account of what policy-makers said to each other during and after crucial sessions numerous signs of group dynamics in full operation. *From studying this material I arrived at the groupthink hypothesis*' (Janis 1983: 34; my italics). He does not tell us how he arrived at the specific hypotheses from reading the material. Hypotheses do not just come from divine inspiration; instead they require a careful grounding in the empirical material along with inspiration from theories that explain related phenomena.

An example of inductive, quantitative analysis

Inductive quantitative analysis is really only possible in purely descriptive statistical analysis of the relative distributions of variables in large populations of cases. For instance, in the study of public opinion in the US much effort went into detecting patterns in the polling data through the use of frequency tables (see Holsti 1996). However, attempts to analyze correlations between independent and dependent variables is not possible unless independent variables have been identified prior to the analysis being undertaken – meaning that all statistical correlation analysis is deductive at least in name.

Yet many quantitative scholars have engaged in statistical analyses of foreign policy that has a more inductive feel. In contrast to deductive, theory-testing quantitative analysis that examines a handful of explicitly theorized explanations, more inductive research designs start with only a brief description of a large number of potential independent variables, with little or no explicit conceptualization of why variable X is a hypothetical cause of Y. The correlation between these explanatory variables and the dependent variable are then tested with multivariable statistical analyses. Critics of this type of design often term it 'data mining', referring to the trawling of datasets in search of robust correlations, after which the scholar reasons backward from the correlation to a plausible theoretical connection between the two.

Singh and Way (2004) engage in what can be termed an inductive quantitative analysis that attempts to detect the 'correlates' of why some 'rogue' states pursue the acquisition of nuclear weapons whereas other disdain. Eleven (!) different potential explanatory variables are tested against each other in a multinomial logistic regression and hazard analysis. They find that the level of economic development and the external threat environment are the best predictors of whether a country will seek to obtain nuclear weapons.

The methodology of post-structuralist foreign policy analysis: a brief guide

Post-structuralists do not believe in causal analysis, as there is no 'objective' reality against which causal claims that 'discourse matter' can be tested (Hansen 2006). Further, there is no such thing as a purely independent or dependent variable in post-structuralist discourse analysis, given that they mutually reproduce each other. Foreign policies are therefore inseparable from identities. As described in Chapter 1, the position here is reflectivistic and critical.

Political discourses produce national identity by linking concepts together in a series of signs (the Self and the Other) that are differentiated from each other. For instance, Hansen (2006: 42–3) argues that two sets of signs regarding the 'Balkans' and 'Europe' exist. A set of interlinked terms including 'barbarian', 'violent', 'underdeveloped' and 'irrational' form the sign 'Balkans', whereas the discourse on 'Europe' is composed of the terms 'civilized', 'controlled', 'developed' and 'rational' that are juxtaposed from the 'Balkan' terms. Differentiation does not only have to have a spatial dimension, but can also have a temporal one. Wæver (1996) for instance refers to the discourse on the 'EU', where the 'Other' is Europe's own bloody past that needs to be avoided.

How do you go about using post-structuralist discourse analysis to study foreign policy discourses? Hansen (2006) suggests four steps when studying national identity and discourses. First, through the reading of a large number of texts you need to establish the 'basic discourses', defined as the 'main structural positions within a debate'. Second, identify the 'key representations' of national identity in these basic discourses, for instance 'evil' in George W. Bush's foreign policy discourse. These representations can include geographical identities, historical analogies or political concepts. Third, use existing conceptual histories to compare current articulations with past discourses, but also to trace the concept back in time to understand when and how it was formed and became dominant. An example could be how 'the Balkans' has historically been understood in the West. Fourthly, investigate how the basic discourses are composed in how the Self and the Other are articulated, in particular how radical the differentiation is in their spatial, temporal and ethical constructions of identity. Taken together, a post-structuralist research design could look like Figure 10.3, where we see Campbell's ideas about how we can critically study discourses of identity, illustrated with what we would need to know when studying US identity.

Figure 10.3 *An example of post-structuralist discourse research design*

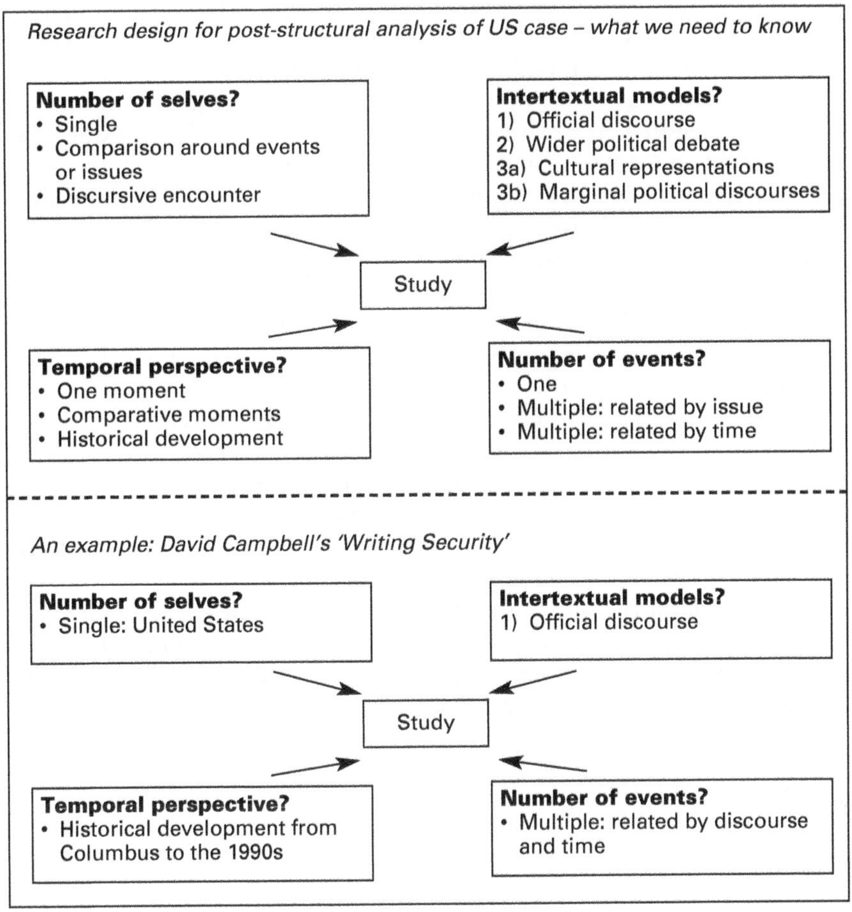

Research design for post-structural analysis of US case – what we need to know

Number of selves?
• Single
• Comparison around events
  or issues
• Discursive encounter

Intertextual models?
1) Official discourse
2) Wider political debate
3a) Cultural representations
3b) Marginal political discourses

Study

Temporal perspective?
• One moment
• Comparative moments
• Historical development

Number of events?
• One
• Multiple: related by issue
• Multiple: related by time

An example: David Campbell's 'Writing Security'

Number of selves?
• Single: United States

Intertextual models?
1) Official discourse

Study

Temporal perspective?
• Historical development from
  Columbus to the 1990s

Number of events?
• Multiple: related by discourse
  and time

Source: Based on Hansen (2006: 81).

Conclusions

Nobody said that studying foreign policy is easy. There are a number of challenges that you will face due to for example the inherent complexity of foreign policy phenomena and the difficulties of collecting accurate empirical material due to the often secret, behind-closed-doors nature of foreign policy-making. That said, this chapter has offered an introduction to how you can use state-of-the-art research methods to study foreign policy phenomena. The two most important things to remember are to be relatively pragmatic and avoid claiming too much.

There are many tradeoffs and choices you will have to make when studying foreign policy that cannot be solved by referring to research methodologies. For example, there is the tradeoff between valuing theoretical parsimony and using more complex, multifactor theories in your research. The choice between using qualitative and quantitative methods is often a choice that is not only determined by the nature of the phenomenon you are researching, but also by beliefs about how generalizable phenomena are in the empirical world. Can we meaningfully compare the foreign policies of European great powers in the 19th century with modern great power foreign policies? This choice relates to one's overall orientation toward an explanatory or understanding position (Chapter 1).

You should strive to be systematic in your research and clearly describe the design that you have chosen. This suggestion applies both to case-centric and theory-centric designs.

It is also important to explain your methodological choices in your work and make your choices transparent. Why did you choose a qualitative case study approach? Describe clearly the existing theorization in the area and how you conceptualize and operationalize the key variables and their relationship with each. Why did you select the case(s) that you chose? What implications do the cases selected have for your ability to generalize your findings? If you are explicit in the description of your research design and the reasoning behind your methodological choices, you will be able to produce research that contributes to our knowledge of foreign policy phenomena.

Bibliography

Achen, Christopher H. and Dunan Snidal (1989) 'Rational Deterrence Theory and Comparative Case Studies', *World Politics*, Vol. 41, No. 2, pp. 143–69.

Adcock, Robert and David Collier (2001) 'Measurement Validity: A Shared Standard for Qualitative and Quantitative Research', *American Political Science Review*, Vol. 95, No. 3, pp. 529–46.

Adler, Emanuel (1997) 'Seizing the Middle Ground: Constructivism in World Politics', *European Journal of International Relations*, Vol. 3, Issue 3, pp. 319–63.

Aldrich, John H., John L Sullivan and Eugene Borgida (1989) 'Foreign Affairs and Issue Voting: Do Presidential Candidates "Waltz Before A Blind Audience?"', *American Political Science Review*, Vol. 81, No. 1, pp. 123–41.

Aldrich, John H., Christopher Gelpi, Peter Feaver, Jason Reifler and Kristin Thompson Sharp (2006) 'Foreign Policy and the Electoral Connection', *Annual Review of Political Science*, Vol. 9, pp. 477–502.

Alesina, Alberto and David Dollar (2000) 'Who Gives Foreign Aid to Whom and Why?', *Journal of Economic Growth*, Vol. 5, No. 1, pp. 33–63.

Allison, Graham (1971) *The Essence of Decision: Explaining the Cuban Missile Crisis.* Boston: Little, Brown.

Allison, Graham and Philip Zelikow (1999) *The Essence of Decision: Explaining the Cuban Missile Crisis.* New York: Longman.

Almond, Gabriel (1950) *The American People and Foreign Policy.* New York: Harcourt Bruce.

Alons, Gerry C. (2007) 'Predicting a State's Foreign Policy: State Preferences between Domestic and International Constraints', *Foreign Policy Analysis*, Vol. 3, No. 2, pp. 211–32.

Anderson, Benedict (1990) *Imagined Communities: Reflections on the Origin and Spread of Nationalism.* London: Verso.

Axelrod, Robert (1984) *The Evolution of Cooperation.* New York: Basic Books.

Axelrod, Robert and Robert Keohane (1986) 'Achieving Cooperation Under Anarchy: Strategies and Institutions', *World Politics*, Vol. 38, No. 1, pp. 226–54.

Baldwin, David A. (1980) 'Interdependence and Power: A Conceptual Analysis', *International Organization*, Vol. 34, No. 4, pp. 471–506.

Baldwin, David A. (1985) *Economic Statecraft.* Princeton: Princeton University Press.

Baldwin, Robert (1986) *The Political Economy of US Import Policy.* Cambridge, MA: MIT Press.

Bapat, Navin A. (2010) 'A Game Theoretic Analysis of the Afghan Surge', *Foreign Policy Analysis*, Vol. 6, Issue 3, pp. 217–36.

Barbieri, Katherine and Gerald Schneider (1999) 'Globalization and Peace: Assessing New Directions in the Study of Trade and Conflict', *Journal of Peace Research*, Vol. 36, No. 4, pp. 387–404.

Barkin, J. Samuel (2010) *Realist Constructivism: Rethinking International Relations Theory*. Cambridge: Cambridge University Press.

Barnett, Michael and Raymond Duvall (2005) 'Power in International Politics', *International Organization*, Vol. 59, Issue 1, pp. 39–75.

Bartels, Larry (1991) 'Constituency Opinion and Congressional Policy Making: The Reagan Defense Build Up', *American Political Science Review*, Vol. 85, No. 2, pp. 457–74.

Baum, Mathew A. and Tim Groeling (2009) 'Shot by the Messenger: Partisan Cues and Public Opinion Regarding National Security and War', *Political Behavior*, Vol. 31, No. 2, pp. 157–86.

Beach, Derek (2005) *The Dynamics of European Integration*. Basingstoke: Palgrave Macmillan.

Beach, Derek and Rasmus Brun Pedersen (forthcoming) *Process Tracing: An Introduction*. Ann Arbor: University of Michigan Press.

Bearce, David H. and Daniel C. Tirone (2010) 'Foreign Aid Effectiveness and the Strategic Goals of Donor Governments', *Journal of Politics*, Vol. 72, No. 3, pp. 837–51.

Bendor, Jonathan and Thomas H. Hammond (1992) 'Rethinking Allison's Models', *American Political Science Review*, Vol. 86, No. 2, pp. 301–22.

Bercovitch, Jacob and Ole Elgström (2001) 'Culture and International Mediation', *International Negotiation*, Vol. 6, No. 1, pp. 3–23.

Berridge, G.R. (1995) *Diplomacy: Theory and Practice*. London: Prentice-Hall.

Blanchard, Jean-Marc F. and Norrin M. Ripsman (2008) 'A Political Theory of Economic Statecraft', *Foreign Policy Analysis*, Vol. 4, Issue 4, pp. 371–98.

Boone, Peter (1996) 'Politics and the Effectiveness of Foreign Aid', *European Economic Review*, Vol. 40, No. 2, pp. 289–329.

Brady, Henry E. and David Collier (eds) (2004) *Rethinking Social Inquiry: Diverse Tools, Shared Standards*. Oxford: Rowman and Littlefield.

Brady, Henry E. (2008) 'Causation and Explanation in Social Science', in Janet M. Box-Steffensmeier, Henry E. Brady and David Collier (eds), *The Oxford Handbook of Political Methodology*, Oxford: Oxford University Press, pp. 217–70.

Braumoeller, Bear F. and Anne E. Sartori (2004) 'The Promise and Perils of Statistics in International Relations', in Detlef F. Sprinz and Yael Wolinsky-Nahmias (eds), *Models, Numbers, and Cases: Methods for Studying International Relations*. Ann Arbor: University of Michigan Press, pp. 129–51.

Brecher, Michael (1972) *The Foreign Policy System of Israel: Setting, Images, Process*. London: Oxford University Press.

Brulé, David J. (2008) 'Congress, Presidential Approval, and U.S. Dispute Initiation', *Foreign Policy Analysis*, Vol. 4, No. 4, pp. 349–70.

Brzezinksi, Zbigniew (1984) 'The Three Requirements for a Bipartisan Foreign Policy', *The Washington Quarterly White Paper*. Washington, DC: Center for Strategic and International Studies, Georgetown University.

Budden, Philip (2002) 'Observations on the Single European Act and the "Relaunch of Europe": A Less "Intergovernmental" Reading of the 1985

Intergovernmental Conference', *Journal of European Public Policy*, Vol. 13, No. 4, pp. 351–80.

Bueno de Mesquita, Bruce and David Lalman (1992) *War and Reason*. New Haven: Yale University Press.

Bueno de Mesquita, Bruce, James D. Morrow, Randolph M. Siverson and Alastair Smith (1999) 'An Institutional Explanation of the Democratic Peace', *American Political Science Review*, Vol. 93, No. 4 (Dec. 1999), pp. 791–807

Bull, Hedley (1977) *The Anarchical Society: A Study of Order in World Politics*. Basingstoke: Macmillan.

Burk, James (1999) 'Public Support for Peacekeeping in Lebanon and Somalia: Assessing the Casualties Hypothesis', *Political Science Quarterly*, Vol. 114, No. 1, pp. 53–78.

Burnside, Craig and David Dollar (2000) 'Aid, Policies, and Growth', *American Economic Review*, Vol. 90, No. 4, pp. 847–68.

Burton, J (1972) *World Society*. Cambridge: Cambridge University Press.

Buzan, Barry (2006) 'Will the "Global War on Terrorism" be the new Cold War?', *International Affairs*, Vol. 82, Issue 6, pp. 1101–18.

Buzan, Barry and Ole Wæver (2009) 'Macrosecuritization and Security Constellations. Reconsidering Scale in Securitisation Theory', *Review of International Studies*, Vol. 35, Issue 2, pp. 253–76.

Buzan, Barry, Ole Wæver and Jaap de Wilde (1998) *Security: A New Framework for Analysis*. Boulder: Lynn Rienner.

Caldwell, Dan (1977) 'Bureaucratic Foreign Policy-Making', *American Behavioral Scientist*, Vol. 21, No. 1, pp. 87–110.

Campbell, David (1992) *Writing Security: United States Foreign Policy and the Politics of Identity*. Minneapolis: University of Minnesota Press.

Carlsnaes, Walter (1986) Ideology and Foreign Policy: Problems of Comparative Conceptualization. Oxford: Basil Blackwell.

Carnevale, Peter J. (2002) 'Mediating from Strength', in Jacob Bercovitch (ed.) *Studies in International Mediation*. Basingstoke: Palgrave Macmillan, pp. 25–40.

Carnevale, Peter J. and Sharon Arad (1996) 'Bias and Impartiality in International Mediation', in Jacob Bercovitch (ed.) *Resolving International Conflicts: The Theory and Practice of Mediation*. London: Lynne Rienner Publishers.

Carter, Ashton B. (2001/2002) 'The Architecture of Government in the Face of Terrorism', *International Security*, Vol. 26, No. 3, pp. 5–23.

Cashman, Greg (1993) *What Causes War? An Introduction to Theories of International Conflict*. New York: Lexington Books.

Checkel, Jeffrey T. (2001) 'Why Comply? Social Learning and European Identity Change', *International Organization*, Vol. 55, Issue 3, pp. 553–88.

Checkel, Jeffrey T. (2004) 'International Institutions and Socialization in Europe: Introduction and Framework', *International Organization*, Vol. 59, Issue 4, pp. 801–26.

Checkel, Jeffrey T. (2005) 'International Institutions and Socialization in Europe: Introduction and Framework', *International Organization*, Vol. 59, Issue 4, pp. 801–26.

Checkel, Jeffrey T. (forthcoming) 'Theoretical Synthesis in IR: Possibilities and

Limits', in Walter Carlsnaes, Thomas Risse and Beth Simmons (eds) *Sage Handbook of International Relations*, 2nd edn. London: Sage Publications.

Christensen, Thomas J. and Jack Snyder (1990) 'Chain Gangs and Passed Bucks: Predicting Alliance Patterns in Multipolarity', *International Organization*, Vol. 44, No. 1, pp. 137–68.

Clark, Cal (2007) 'Economic Integration between China and Taiwan: No Spillover into the Identity and Security Realms', in Shale Horowitz, Uk Heo and Alexander C. Tan (eds) *Identity and Change in East Asian Conflicts: The Cases of China, Taiwan and the Koreas*. Basingstoke: Palgrave Macmillan, pp. 71–90.

Cohen, Raymond (2001) 'Negotiating Across Cultures', in Crocker, Hampson and Aall (eds) *Turbulent Peace: The Challenges of Managing International Conflict*. Washington, DC: United States Institute of Peace Press, pp. 469–81.

Cooper, Robert (1968) *The Economics of Interdependence*. New York: McGraw-Hill.

Cos, Kivanc and Pinar Bilgin (2010) 'Stalin's Demands: Constructions of the "Soviet Other" in Turkey's Foreign Policy, 1919–1945', *Foreign Policy Analysis*, Vol. 6, Issue 1, pp. 43–60.

Craig, Gordon A. and Alexander L. George (1995) *Force and Statecraft: Diplomatic Problems of Our Times*, 3rd edn. Oxford: Oxford University Press.

Crescenzi, Mark J.C. (2003) 'Economic Exit, Interdependence, and Conflict', *Journal of Politics*, Vol. 65, No. 3, pp. 809–32.

Creveld, Martin van (1999) *The Rise and Decline of the State*. Cambridge: Cambridge University Press.

Dacey, Raymong and Lisa J. Carlson (2004) 'Traditional Decision Analysis and the Poliheuristic Theory of Foreign Policy Decision Making', *Journal of Conflict Resolution*, Vol. 48, No. 1, pp. 38–55.

Dahl, Robert A. (1961) *Who Governs? Democracy and Power in an American City*. New Haven, CN: Yale University Press.

Dahl, Robert A. (1971) *Polyarchy: Participation and Opposition*. New Haven: Yale University Press.

Davies, Graeme A.M. (2008) 'Inside Out or Outside In: Domestic and International Factors Affecting Iranian Foreign Policy Towards the United States, 1990–2004.' *Foreign Policy Analysis*, Vol. 4, No. 3, pp. 209–25.

Dawisha, Karen and Bruce Parrott (eds) (1997) *The End of Empire? The Transformation of the USSR in Comparative Perspective*. Armonk: M.E. Sharpe.

DeLaet, C. James and James M. Scott (2006) 'Treaty-Making and Partisan Politics: Arms Control and the U.S. Senate, 1960–2001', *Foreign Policy Analysis*, Vol. 2, No. 2, pp. 177–200.

DeRouen, Karl Jr. and Christopher Sprecher (2004) 'Initial Crisis Reaction and Poliheuristic Theory', *Journal of Conflict Resolution*, Vol. 48, No. 1, pp. 56–68.

Deutsch, Karl, Sidney Burrel, Robert Kann, Maurice Lee, Martin Lictherman, Raymond Lindgren, Francis Loewenheim and Richard van Wagenen (1957) *Political Community and the North Atlantic Area*. Princeton: Princeton University Press.

Deutsch, Karl W. (1968) *The Analysis of International Relations*. Englewood Cliffs: Prentice-Hall.

Dion, Douglas (1998) 'Evidence and Inference in the Comparative Case Study', *Comparative Politics*, Vol. 3, No. 2, pp. 127–45.

Donnelly, Jack (2000) *Realism and International Relations*. Cambridge: Cambridge University Press.

Dorussen, Han and Hugh Ward (2010) 'Trade Networks and the Kantian Peace', *Journal of Peace Research*, Vol. 47, No. 1, pp. 29–42.

Drezner, Daniel W. (2000) 'Bargaining, Enforcement, and Multilateral Sanctions: When Is Cooperation Counterproductive?', *International Organization*, Vol. 54, Issue 1, pp. 73–102.

Drezner, Daniel W. (2011) *International Politics and Zombies*. Princeton: Princeton University Press.

Dueck, Colin (2009) 'Neoclassical Realism and the National Interest', in Steven E. Lobell, Norrin M. Ripsman, and Jeffrey W. Taliaferro (eds) *Neoclassical Realism, The State, And Foreign Policy*. Cambridge: Cambridge University Press, pp. 139–69.

Dunleavy, Patrick. 1991. *Democracy, Bureaucracy and Public Choice*. Harlow: Prentice-Hall.

Dyson, Stephen Benedict (2007) 'Alliances, Domestic Politics, and Leader Psychology: Why Did Britain Stay Out of Vietnam and Go into Iraq?', *Political Psychology*, Vol. 28, No. 6, pp. 647–66.

Easterly, William (2003) 'Can Foreign Aid Buy Growth?', *Journal of Economic Perspectives*, Vol. 17, No. 3, pp. 23–48.

Eckstein, Harry. 1975. 'Case Study and Theory in Political Science'. In Fred I. Greenstein and Nelson W. Polsby (eds), *Handbook of Political Science – Strategies of Inquiry Vol. 7*. Reading: Addison-Wesley Publishing Company, pp. 79–138.

Eichenberg, Richard C. (2005) 'Victory has Many Friends: US Public Opinion and the Use of Military Force, 1981–2005', *International Security*, Vol. 30, No. 1, pp. 140–77.

Elman, Colin (1996) 'Horses for Courses: Why *Not* Neorealist Theories of Foreign Policy?', *Security Studies*, Vol. 6, No. 1, pp. 7–53.

Emirbayer, Mustafa and Ann Mische (1998) 'What is Agency?', *American Journal of Sociology*, Vol. 103, No. 4, pp. 962–1023.

Erlich, Sean D. (2009) 'Constituency Size and Support for Trade Liberalization: An Analysis of Foreign Economic Policy Preferences in Congress', *Foreign Policy Analysis*, Vol. 5, Issue 3, pp. 215–32.

Evans, Peter (1995) Contribution to symposium The Role of Theory in Comparative Politics. *World Politics*, Vol. 48, No. 1, pp. 3–10.

Farber, Henry S. and Joanne Gowa (1995) 'Polities and Peace', *International Security*, Vol. 20, No. 2, pp. 123–46

Faure, G.O. and Gunnar Sjösted (1993) 'Culture and Negotiation: An Introduction', in Faure and Rubin (eds) *Culture and Negotiation*. Newbury Park: Sage, pp. 1–13.

Fearon, James D. (1995) 'Rationalist Explanations for War', *International Organization*, Vol. 49, Issue 3, pp. 379–414.

Finnemore, Martha and Kathryn Sikkink (1998) 'International Norm Dynamics and Political Change', *International Organization*, Vol. 52, Issue 4, pp. 887–917.

Fisher, Roger and William Ury (1991) *Getting to Yes: Negotiating Agreement Without Giving In*, 2nd edn. New York: Penguin Books.

Foyle, Doug (1999) *Counting the Public In: Presidents, Public Opinion, and Foreign Policy*. New York: Columbia University Press.

Frank, Andre Gundar (1969) *Capitalism and Underdevelopment in Latin America*. New York: Modern Reader Paperbacks.

Friedberg, Aaron L. (2005) 'The Future of US–China Relations: Is Conflict Inevitable?', *International Security*, Vol. 30, No. 1, pp. 7–45.

Friedrichs, Jörg and Friedrich Kratochwill (2009) 'On Acting and Knowing: How Pragmatism can advance International Relations Research and Methodology', *International Organization*, Vol. 63, Issue 4, pp. 701–31.

Fuller, Sally Riggs and Ramon J. Aldag (1998) 'Organizational Tonypandy: Lessons from a Quarter Century of the Groupthink Phenomenon', *Organizational Behavior and Human Decision Processes*, Vol. 73, No. 2/3, pp. 163–84.

Gadarian, Shana Kushner (2010) 'The Politics of Threat: How Terrorism News Shapes Foreign Policy Attitudes', *Journal of Politics*, Vol. 72, No. 2, pp. 469–83.

Gaddis, John Lewis (1997) *We Now Know: Rethinking Cold War History*. Oxford: Clarendon Press.

Garrison, Jean (2007) 'Constructing the "National Interest" in U.S.–China Policy Making: How Foreign Policy Decision Groups Define and Signal Policy Choices', *Foreign Policy Analysis*, Vol. 3, Issue 2, pp. 105–26.

Gartner, Scott S. and Gary M. Segura (1998) 'War Causalities and Public Opinion', *Journal of Conflict Resolution*, Vol. 42, No. 2, pp. 278–320.

Gartzke, Erik, Quan Li and Charles Boehmer (2001) 'Investing in the Peace', *International Organization*, Vol. 55, No. 2, pp. 391–438.

Gelpi, Christopher (2010) 'Performing on Cue? The Formation of Public Opinion on War', *Journal of Conflict Resolution*, Vol. 54, No. 1, pp. 88–116.

George, Alexander (1969) 'The "Operational Code": A Neglected Approach to the Study of Political Leaders and Decision-Making', *International Studies Quarterly*, Vol. 13, No. 2, pp. 190–222.

George, Alexander (1989) 'Deterrence and Foreign Policy', *World Politics*, Vol. 41, No. 2, pp. 170–83.

George, Alexander L. and Bennett, Andrew (2005) *Case Studies and Theory Development in the Social Sciences*. Cambridge, MA: MIT Press.

Gerner, Deborah J. (1995) 'The Evolution of the Study of Foreign Policy', in Laura Neack, Jeanne A.K. Hey and Patrick J. Haney (eds) *Foreign Policy Analysis: Continuity and Change in its Second Generation*. Englewood Cliffs: Prentice Hall, pp. 17–32.

Gerring, John (2006) 'Single-Outcome Studies: A Methodological Primer', *International Sociology*, Vol. 21, No. 5, pp. 707–34.

Gerring, John (2007) *Case Study Research: Principles and Practices*. Cambridge: Cambridge University Press.

Giddens, Anthony (1976) *New Rules of Sociological Method: A Positive Critique of Interpretive Sociologies*. London: Hutchinson.

Giddens, Anthony (1984) *The Constitution of Society*. Berkeley: University of California Press.

Gilady, Lilach and Bruce Russett (2002) 'Peacemaking and Conflict Resolution', in Walter Carlsnaes, Thomas Risse and Beth A. Simmons (eds) *Handbook of International Relations*. London: Sage Publications, pp. 392–408.

Gilpin, Robert (1981) *War and Change in World Politics*. Cambridge: Cambridge University Press.

Gilpin, Robert (2000) 'No One Loves a Political Realist', in Robert J. Art and Robert Jervis (eds) *International Politics: Enduring Concepts and Contemporary Issues*. New York: Longman, pp. 348–62.

Gilpin, Robert (2001) *Global Political Economy: Understanding the International Economic Order*. Princeton: Princeton University Press.

Ginsberg, Roy H. (1999) 'Conceptualizing the European Union as an International Actor: Narrowing the Theoretical Capability-Expectations Gap', *Journal of Common Market Studies*, Vol. 33, No. 3, pp. 429–54.

Glarbo, Kenneth (1999) 'Wide-awake Diplomacy: Reconstructing the Common Foreign and Security Policy of the European Union', *Journal of European Public Policy*, Vol. 6, No. 4, pp. 634–51.

Glenn, John (2009) 'Realism Versus Strategic Culture: Competition and Collaboration?', *International Studies Review*, Vol. 11, No. 3, pp. 523–51.

Glennan, Stuart S. (1996) 'Mechanisms and the Nature of Causation', *Erkenntnis*, Vol. 44, No. 1, pp. 49–71.

Glennan, Stuart S. (2002) 'Rethinking Mechanistic Explanation', *Philosophy of Science*, Vol. 69 (Suppl), pp. 342–53.

Goertz, Garry (2006) *Social Science Concepts: A User's Guide*. Princeton: Princeton University Press.

Goldgeier, James M. (1997) 'Psychology and Security', *Security Studies*, Vol. 6, No. 4, pp. 137–66.

Goldgeier, James M. And Michael McFaul (1992) 'A Tale of Two Worlds: Core and Periphery in the Post-cold War Era', *International Organization*, Vol. 46, Issue 2, pp. 467–91.

Goldstein, Judith (1993) *Ideas, Interests and American Trade Policy*. Ithaca: Cornell University Press.

Gordon, Philip (1997/98) 'Europe's Uncommon Foreign Policy', *International Security*, Vol. 22, No. 3, pp. 74–100.

Gourevitch, Peter (1986) *Politics in Hard Times*. Ithaca: Cornell University Press.

Gowa, Joanne (1994) *Allies, Adversaries and International Trade*. Princeton: Princeton University Press.

Gray, Colin S. (2005) 'How Has War Changed Since the End of the Cold War?', *Parameters*, Vol. 35, No. 1, pp. 14–26.

Grieco, Joseph (1988) 'Anarchy and the Limits of Cooperation: A Realist Critique of the Newest Liberal Institutionalism', *International Organization*, Vol. 42, Issue 3, pp. 485–529.

Grieco, Joseph (1990) *Cooperation among Allies: Europe, America, and Non-tariff Barriers to Trade*. Ithaca: Cornell University Press.

Grieco, Joseph (1997) 'Realist International Theory and the Study of World Politics', in Michael Doyle and G. John Ikenberry (eds), *New Thinking in International Relations Theory*. Boulder: Westview Press.

Haas, Ernst B. (1958) *The Uniting of Europe. Political, Social and Economic Forces, 1950–1957*. Stanford: Stanford University Press.

Haas, Ernst B. (1961) 'International Integration: The European and the Universal Process', *International Organization*, Vol. 15, Issue 3, Summer 1961, pp. 366–92.

Haas, Ernst B. (1964) *Beyond the Nation State: Functionalism and International Organization*. Stanford: Stanford University Press.

Habeeb, William M. (1988) *Power and Tactics in International Negotiation*. Baltimore: Johns Hopkins University Press.

Hagan, Joe D. (1993) *Political Opposition and Foreign Policy in Comparative Perspective*. Boulder: Lynne Reiner.

Hagan, Joe D., Philip P. Everts, Haruhiro Fukui and John D. Stempel (2001) 'Foreign Policy by Coalition: Deadlock, Compromise, and Anarchy', *International Studies Review*, Vol. 3, No. 2, pp. 170–216.

Halperin, Morton (1974) *Bureaucratic Politics and Foreign Policy*. Washington, DC: The Brookings Institution.

Hampson, Fen Osler (1995) *Multilateral Negotiations: Lesson from Arms Control, Trade, and the Environment*. Baltimore: Johns Hopkins University Press.

Haney, Patrick J. and Walt Vanderbush (1999) 'The Role of Ethnic Interest Groups in U.S. Foreign Policy. The Case of the Cuban American National Foundation', *International Studies Quarterly*, Vol. 43, No. 2, pp. 341–61.

Hansen, Henrik and Finn Tarp (2001) 'Aid and Growth Regressions', *Journal of Development Economics*, Vol. 64, No. 2, pp. 547–70.

Hansen, Lene (2006) *Security as Practice: Discourse Analysis and the Bosnian War*. Routledge: London.

't Hart, Paul and Marceline B. R. Kroon (1997) Groupthink in Government: Pathologies of Small-Group Decision Making', in J.L. Garnett (ed.) *Handbook of Administrative Communication*, Chicago: Marcel Dekker, pp. 101–41.

Hegre, Håvard (2000) 'Development and the Liberal Peace: What Does it Take to be a Trading State?', *Journal of Peace Research*, Vol. 37, No. 1, pp. 5–30.

Held, David, Anthony McGrew, David Goldblatt and Jonathan Perraton (1999) *Global Transformations*. Stanford: Stanford University Press.

Hermann, Charles F. (1972) (ed.) *International Crisis: Insights from Behavioral Research*. New York: Free Press.

Hermann, Charles F. (1978) 'Foreign Policy Behavior: That Which is to be Explained', in Maurice A. East, Stephen A. Salmore, and Charles F. Hermann (eds) *Why Nations Act: Theoretical Perspectives for Comparative Foreign Policy Studies*. London: Sage Publications, pp. 25–48.

Hermann, Charles F. (1990) 'Changing Course: When Governments Choose to Redirect Foreign Policy', *International Studies Quarterly*, Vol. 34(1): 3–21.

Hermann, Margaret G. (2001) 'How Decision Units Shape Foreign Policy: A Theoretical Framework', *International Studies Review*, Vol. 3, No. 2, pp. 47–81.

Hermann, Margaret G. (2008) 'Content Analysis', in Audie Klotz and Deepa Prakash (eds) *Qualitative Methods in International Relations: A Pluralist Guide*. Basingstoke: Palgrave Macmillan, pp. 151–67.

Hermann, Margaret G., Thomas Preston, Baghat Korany and Timothy M. Shaw (2001) 'Who Leads Matters: The Effects of Powerful Individuals', *International Studies Review*, Vol. 3, Issue 2, pp. 93–131.

Hermann, Charles F., Janice Gross Stein, Bengt Sundelius and Stephen G. Walker (2001) 'Resolve, Accept, or Avoid: Effects of Group Conflict on Foreign Policy Decisions', *International Studies Review*, Vol. 3, Issue 2, pp. 133–68.

Herrmann, Richard K. (2003) 'Image Theory and Strategic Interaction in International Relations', in David O. Sears, Leonie Huddy and Robert Jervis (eds) *Oxford Handbook of Political Psychology*. Oxford: Oxford University Press, pp. 285–314.

Hersman, Rebecca K.C. (2000) *Friends and Foes: How Congress and the President Really make Foreign Policy*. Washington, DC: Brookings Institution.

Herz, John (1950) 'Idealist Internationalism and the Security Dilemma', *World Politics*, Vol. 2, No. 2, pp. 171–201.

Hill, Christopher (2003) *The Changing Politics of Foreign Policy*. Basingstoke: Palgrave Macmillan.

Hill, Christopher (2004) 'Renationalizing or Regrouping? EU Foreign Policy Since 11 September 2001', *Journal of Common Market Studies*, Vol. 42, No. 1, pp. 143–63.

Hill, Christopher and Michael Smith (eds) (2005) *International Relations and the European Union*. Oxford: Oxford University Press.

Hirst, Paul and Grahame Thompson (1999) *Globalization in Question*, 2nd edn. Cambridge: Polity Press.

Holsti, Kalevi J. (1991) *Peace and War: Armed Conflicts and International Order*. Cambridge: Cambridge University Press.

Holsti, Ole R. (1967) 'Cognitive Dynamics and Images of the Enemy: Dulles and Russia', in David Finlay, Ole Holsti and Richard Fagen (eds) *Enemies in Politics*. Chicago: Rand McNally.

Holsti, Ole R (1996) *Public Opinion and American Foreign Policy*. Ann Arbor: University of Michigan Press.

Hopf, Ted (1998) 'The Promise of Constructivism in International Relations Theory', *International Security*, Vol. 23, No. 1, pp. 171–200.

Hopf, Ted (2002) *Social Construction of International Politics: Identities and Foreign Policies*. Ithaca: Cornell University Press.

Hopf, Ted (2005) 'Identity, Legitimacy, and the Use of Military Force: Russia's Great Power Identities and Military Intervention in Abkhazia', *Review of International Studies*, Vol. 31, Supplement 1, pp. 225–43.

Hopf, Ted (2010) 'The Logic of Habit in International Relations', *European Journal of International Relations*, Vol. 16, No. 4, pp. 539–61.

Houghton, David Patrick (2007) 'Reinvigorating the Study of Foreign Policy Decision Making: Toward a Constructivist Approach', *Foreign Policy Analysis*, Vol. 3, Issue 1, pp. 24–45.

Howell, William G. and Jon C. Pevehouse (2005) 'Presidents, Congress and the Use of Force', *International Organization*, Vol. 59, No. 1, pp. 209–32.

Hudson, Valerie M. (2007) *Foreign Policy Analysis: Classic and Contemporary Theory*. Lanham: Rowman & Littlefield.

Humphreys, Adam R.C. (2010) 'The Heuristic Application of Explanatory Theories in International Relations', *European Journal of International Relations*, Vol. 17, No. 2, pp. 257–77.

Huth, Paul, D. Scott Bennett and Christopher Gelpi (1992) 'System Uncertainty, Risk Propensity, and International Conflict Among the Great Powers', *Journal of Conflict Research*, Vol. 36, No. 3, pp. 478–517.

Iklé, Fred Charles (1964) *How Nations Negotiate*. New York: Praeger.

International Institute of Security Studies (2010) *The Military Balance 2010*. London: IISS.

Jackson, Patrick Thaddeus (2011) *The Conduct of Inquiry in International Relations – Philosophy of Science and its Implications for the Study of World Politics*. London: Routledge.

Jackson, Robert and Georg Sørensen (2010) *Introduction to International Relations – Theories and Approaches*. Oxford: Oxford University Press.

Jakobsen, Peter Viggo (2000) 'Focus on the CNN Effect Misses the Point: The Real Media Impact on Conflict Management is Invisible and Indirect', *Journal of Peace Research*, Vol. 37, No. 2, pp. 131–43.

James, Carolyn C. and Özgür Özdamar (2009) 'Modeling Foreign Policy and Ethnic Conflict: Turkey's Policies Towards Syria', *Foreign Policy Analysis*, Vol. 5, Issue 1, pp. 17–36.

James, Patrick and Enyu Zhang (2005) 'Chinese Choices: A Poliheuristic Analysis of Foreign Policy Crises, 1950–1996', *Foreign Policy Analysis*, Vol. 1, No. 1, pp. 31–54.

Janis, Irving L. (1983) *Groupthink: Psychological Studies of Policy Decisions and Fiascoes*. Boston: Houghton Mifflin.

Jentleson, Bruce W. and Christopher A. Whytock (2005/06) 'Who "Won" Libya? The Force-Diplomacy Debate and Its Implications for Theory and Policy', *International Security*, Vol. 30, No. 3, pp. 47–86.

Jervis, Robert (1976) *Perception and Misperception in International Politics*. Princeton: Princeton University Press.

Jervis, Robert (1989a) 'Rational Deterrence: Theory and Evidence', *World Politics*, Vol. 41, No. 2, pp. 183–207.

Jervis, Robert (1989b) *The Meaning of the Nuclear Revolution*. Ithaca: Cornell University Press.

Jervis, Robert (1991/92) 'The Future of World Politics: Will it Resemble the Past?', *International Security*, Vol. 16, No. 3, pp. 39–73.

Jervis, Robert (1992) 'Political Implications of Loss Aversion', *Political Psychology*, Vol. 13, No. 2, pp. 187–204.

Jervis, Robert (1994) 'Leadership, Post-Cold War Politics, and Psychology', *Political Psychology*, Vol. 15, No. 4, pp. 769–77.

Jervis, Robert (2009) 'Unipolarity: A Structural Perspective', *World Politics*, Vol. 61, No. 1, pp. 188–213.

Jervis, Robert (2010) *Why Intelligence Fails: Lessons from the Iranian Revolution and the Iraq War*. Ithaca: Cornell University Press.

Johnston, Alastair Iain (1995) 'Thinking about Strategic Culture', *International Security*, Vol. 19, No. 4, pp. 32–64.

Johnston, Alastair Iain (2003) 'Is China a Status Quo Power?', *International Security*, Vol. 27, No. 4, pp. 5–56.

Johnston, Alastair Iain and Paul Evans (1999) 'China's Engagement with Multilateral Security Institutions.' in Alastair Iain Johnston and Ross (eds), *Engaging China: The Management of an Emerging Power*. New York: Routledge, pp. 235–72.

Jönsson, Christer (2002) 'Diplomacy, Bargaining and Negotiation', in Walter Carlsnaes, Thomas Risse and Beth A. Simmons (eds) *Handbook of International Relations*. London: Sage Publications, pp. 212–34.

Jørgensen, Knud Erik (2004a) 'European Foreign Policy: Conceptualising the Domain', in Walter Carlsnaes, Helene Sjursen and Brian White (eds) *Contemporary European Foreign Policy*. London: Sage Publications, pp. 32–56.

Jørgensen, Knud Erik (2004b) 'Theorising the European Union's foreign policy', in Ben Tonra and Thomas Christiansen (eds) *Rethinking European Union Foreign Policy*. Manchester: Manchester University Press, pp. 10–25.

Jørgensen, Knud Erik (2010) *International Relations Theory*. Basingstoke: Palgrave Macmillan.

Kahneman, Daniel and Amos Tversky (1979) 'Prospect Theory: An Analysis of Decision Under Risk', *Econometrica*, Vol. 47, No. 2, pp. 263–92.

Kant, Immanuel (2006) *Toward Perpetual Peace and Other Writings on Politics, Peace, and History*. New Haven: Yale University Press.

Katzenstein, Peter and Nobuo Okawara (1993) 'Japan's National Security: Structures, Norms and Policies', *International Security*, Vol. 17, No. 1, pp. 84–118.

Kennedy, Paul (1987) *The Rise and Fall of the Great Powers*. New York: Random House.

Keohane, Robert O. (1984) *After Hegemony: Cooperation and Discord in the World Political Economy*. Princeton: Princeton University Press.

Keohane, Robert O. (1986) 'Theory of World Politics: Structural Realism and Beyond', in Robert O. Keohane (ed.) *Neo-Realism and Its Critics*. New York: Columbia University Press, pp. 158–203.

Keohane, Robert O. (1988) 'International Institutions: Two Approaches', *International Studies Quarterly*, Vol. 32, No. 4, pp. 379–96.

Keohane, Robert O. (1989) *International Institutions and State Power: Essays in International Relations Theory*. Boulder: Westview Press.

Keohane, Robert O. (2002) *Power and Governance in a Partially Globalized World*. London: Routledge.

Keohane, Robert O. and Joseph S. Nye (2001) *Power and Interdependence*, 3rd edn. New York: Longman.

Keshk, Omar M.G., Brian M. Pollins and Rafael Reuveny (2004) 'Trade Still Follows the Flag: The Primacy of Politics in a Simultaneous Model of Interdependence and Armed Conflict', *Journal of Politics*, Vol. 66, No. 4, pp. 1155–79.

Keukeleire, Stephan and Jennifer MacNaughtan (2008) *The Foreign Policy of the European Union*. Basingstoke: Palgrave Macmillan.

Khong, Yuen Foong (1992) *Analogies at War: Korea Munich Dien Bien Phu and the Vietnam Decisions of 1965*. Princeton: Princeton University Press.

Kim, Woosang and James D. Morrow (1992) 'When Do Power Shifts Lead to War?', *American Journal of Political Science*, Vol. 36, No. 4, pp. 896–922.

Kindleberger, Charles (1973) *The World in Depression, 1929–1939*. Berkeley: University of California Press.

King, Gary, Robert Keohane and Sidney Verba (1994) *Designing Social Inquiry*. Princeton: Princeton University Press.

Kissinger, Henry (1994) *Diplomacy*. New York: Simon & Schuster.

Klare, Michael T. (2002) *Resource Wars: The New Landscape of Global Conflict*. New York: Henry Holt and Company.

Knecht, Thomas and M. Stephen Weatherford (2006) 'Public Opinion and Foreign Policy: The Stages of Presidential Decision Making', *International Studies Quarterly*, Vol. 50, Issue 3, pp. 705–27.

Koremenos, Barbara, Charles Lipson and Duncan Snidal (2001) 'The Rational Design of International Institutions', *International Organization*, Vol. 55, Issue 4, pp. 769–99.

Kramer, Roderick M. (1998) 'Revisiting the Bay of Pigs and Vietnam Decisions 25 Years Later: How Well Has the Groupthink Hypothesis Stood the Test of Time?', *Organizational Behavior and Human Decision Processes*, Vol. 73, No. 2/3, pp. 236–71.

Krasner, Stephen D. (1978) *Defending the National Interest: Raw Material Investments and US Foreign Policy*. Princeton: Princeton University Press.

Krasner, Stephen D. (1991) 'Global Communications and National Power: Life on the Pareto Frontier', *World Politics*, Vol. 43, No. 2, pp. 336–66.

Kratochwil, Friedrich V. (1989) *Rules, Norms and Decisions: On the Conditions of Practical and Legal Reasoning in International Relations and Domestic Affairs*. Cambridge: Cambridge University Press.

Kreps, Sarah (2010) 'Elite Consensus as a Determinant of Alliance Cohesion: Why Public Opinion Hardly Maters for NATO-led Operations in Afghanistan', *Foreign Policy Analysis*, Vol. 6, Issue 3, pp. 191–215.

Kubálková, Vendulka (2001) 'Foreign Policy, International Politics, and Constructivism', in Vendulka Kubálková (ed.) *Foreign Policy in a Constructed World*. Armonk, NY: M.E.Sharpe, pp. 15–37.

Kupchan, Charles A. (1994) *The Vulnerability of Empire*. Ithaca: Cornell University Press.

Larsen, Henrik (2009) 'A Distinct FPA for Europe? Towards a Comprehensive Framework for Analysing the Foreign Policy of EU Member States', *European Journal of International Relations*, Vol. 15, No. 3, pp. 537–66.

Larson, Deborah (1985) *Origins of Containment: A Psychological Explanation*. Princeton: Princeton University Press.

Lax, David A. and James K. Sebenius (1986) *The Manager as Negotiator*. London: The Free Press.

Layne, Christopher (1993) 'The Unipolar Illusion: Why New Great Powers Will Rise', *International Security*, Vol. 17, No. 4, pp. 5–51.

Layne, Christopher (1994) 'Kant or Cant: The Myth of the Democratic Peace', *International Security*, Vol. 19, No. 2, pp. 5–49.

Layne, Christopher (1997) 'From Preponderance to Offshore Balancing: America's Future Grand Strategy', *International Security*, Vol. 22, No. 1, pp. 86–124.

Layne, Christopher (2006) *The Peace of Illusions: American Grand Strategy from 1940 to the Present*. Ithaca: Cornell University Press.

Lebow, Richard (1981) *Between Peace and War: The Nature of International Crisis*. Baltimore: Johns Hopkins University Press.

Lebow, Richard and Janice Gross Stein (1989) 'Rational Deterence Theory: I Think, Therefore I Deter', *World Politics*, Vol. 41, No. 2, pp. 208–24.

Legro, Jeffrey W. (1996) 'Culture and Preferences in the Cooperation Two-Step', *American Political Science Review*, Vol. 90, No. 1, pp. 118–37.

Legro, Jeffrey W. and Andrew Moravcsik (1999) 'Is Anybody Still a Realist?', *International Security*, Vol. 24, No. 2, pp. 5–55.

Levy, Jack S. (1983) 'Misperceptions and the Causes of War: Theoretical Linkages and Analytical Problems', *World Politics*, Vol. 36, No. 1, pp. 76–99.

Levy, Jack S. (1992a) 'An Introduction to Prospect Theory', *Political Psychology*, Vol. 13, No. 2, pp. 171–86.

Levy, Jack S. (1992b) 'Prospect Theory and International Relations: Theoretical Applications and Analytical Problems', *Political Psychology*, Vol. 13, No. 2, pp. 283–310.

Levy, Jack S. (2003) 'Political Psychology and Foreign Policy', in David O. Sears, Leonie Huddy and Robert Jervis (eds) *Oxford Handbook of Political Psychology*. Oxford: Oxford University Press, pp. 253–84.

Levy, Marc A. (1995) 'International Co-operation to Combat Acid Rain', in Helge Ole Bergesen, Georg Parmann, and Øystein B. Thommessen (eds) *Green Globe Yearbook of International Co-operation on Environment and Development 1995*. Oxford: Oxford University Press, pp. 59–68.

Lindberg, Leon N. (1963) *The Political Dynamics of European Economic Integration*. Stanford: Stanford University Press.

Lindberg, Leon N. (1966). 'Integration as a Source of Stress on the European Community System', *International Organization*, Vol. 20, Issue 2, pp. 233–65.

Lindberg, Leon N. and Stuart A. Scheingold (1970) *Europe's Would-Be Polity: Patterns of Change in the European Community*. Englewood Cliffs: Prentice-Hall.

Lippmann, Walter (1955) *Essays in the Public Philosophy*. Boston: Little, Brown.

Lobell, Steven E. (2009) 'Threat Assessment, the State, and Foreign Policy: A Neoclassical Realist Model', in Steven E. Lobell, Norrin M. Ripsman, and Jeffrey W. Taliaferro (eds) *Neoclassical Realism, the State, and Foreign Policy*. Cambridge: Cambridge University Press, pp. 42–74.

Löfstedt, Ragnar E. (1996) 'Risk Communication: The Barsebäck nuclear plant case', *Energy Policy*, Vol. 24, No. 8, pp. 689–96.

Machamer, Peter, Lindley Darden and Carl F. Craver (2000) 'Thinking about Mechanisms', *Philosophy of Science*, Vol. 67, No. 1, pp. 1–25.

Mansfield, Edward D. (1988) 'The Distribution of Wars Over Time', *World Politics*, Vol. 41, No. 1, pp. 21–51.

Mansfield, Edward (1994) *Power, Trade, and War*. Princeton: Princeton University Press.

Mansfield, Edward and Jon C. Pevehouse (2000) 'Trade Blocs, Trade Flows and International Conflict', *International Organization*, Vol. 54, Issue 4, pp. 775–808.

Mansfield, Edward, Helen Milner and B. Peter Rosendorff (2000) 'Free to Trade: Democracies and International Trade Negotiations', *American Political Science Review*, Vol. 94, No. 2, pp. 305–21.

Mansfield, Edward and Brian M. Pollins (2001) 'The Study of Interdependence and Conflict: Recent Advances, Open Questions, and Directions for Future Research', *Journal of Conflict Resolution*, Vol. 45, No. 6, pp. 834–59.

March, James G. and Johan P. Olsen (1998) 'The Institutional Dynamics of International Political Orders', *International Organization*, Vol. 52, Issue 4, pp. 943–69.

Marshall, Monty G, Ted Robert Gurr and Keith Jaggers (2010) *Polity IV – Datauser's Manual.* Available at: www.systemicpeace.org/polity/polity4.htm.

Martin, Garret (2011) 'The 1967 Withdrawal from NATO – a Cornerstone of de Gaulle's Grand Strategy?', *Journal of Transatlantic Studies*, Vol. 9, No. 3, pp. 232–43.

Marx, Karl (1959) *Basic Writings on Politics and Philosophy.* Edited by Lewis S. Feuer. Garden City: Doubleday Anchor.

Mastanduno, Michael, David A. Lake and G. John Ikenberry (1989) 'Toward a Realist Theory of State Action', *International Studies Quarterly*, Vol. 33, No. 4, pp. 457–74.

Mattli, Walter (1999) *The Logic of Regional Integration: Europe and Beyond.* Cambridge: Cambridge University Press.

Mayer, Frederick W. (1992) 'Managing Domestic Differences in International Negotiations: The Strategic Use of Internal Side-payments', *International Organization*, Vol. 46, Issue 4, pp. 793–818.

Mayer, Wolfgang (1984) 'Endogenous Tariff Formation', *American Economic Review*, Vol. 74, Issue 5, pp. 970–85.

McCauley, Clark (1998) 'Group Dynamics in Janis's Theory of Groupthink: Backward and Forward', *Organizational Behavior and Human Decision Processes*, Vol. 73, No. 2/3, pp. 142–62.

McDermott, Rose (1992) 'Prospect Theory in International Relations: The Iranian Hostage Rescue Mission', *Political Psychology*, Vol. 13, No. 2, pp. 237–63.

McDonald, Matt (2008) 'Securitization and the Construction of Security', *European Journal of International Relations*, Vol. 14, No. 4, pp. 563–87.

Mearsheimer, John J. (2001) *The Tragedy of Great Power Politics.* New York: W.W. Norton.

Mearsheimer, John J. (2009) 'Reckless States and Realism', *International Relations*, Vol. 23, No. 2, pp. 241–56.

Mearsheimer, John J. and Stephen M. Walt (2007) *The Israel Lobby and US Foreign Policy.* London: Penguin Books.

Meernik, James (1994) 'Presidential Decision Making and the Political Use of Military Force', *International Studies Quarterly*, Vol. 38, No. 1, pp. 121–38.

Meernik, James (1995) 'Congress, the President, and the Commitment of the US Military', *Legislative Studies Quarterly*, Vol. 20, No. 3, pp. 377–92.

Merolla, Jennifer and Elizabeth Zechmeister (2009) *Democracy at Risk: How Terrorism Threats Affect the Public.* Chicago: University of Chicago Press.

Michaud, Nelson (2002) 'Bureaucratic Politics and the Shaping of Policies: Can We Measure Pulling and Hauling Games?', *Canadian Journal of Political Science*, Vol. 35, No. 2, pp. 269–300.

Milner, Helen (1991) 'The Assumption of Anarchy in International Relations Theory: A Critique', *Review of International Studies*, Vol. 17, No. 1, pp. 67–85.

Milner, Helen (1997) *Interests, Institutions, and Information: Domestic Politics and International Relations*. Princeton: Princeton University Press.

Milner, Helen and B. Peter Rosendorff (1997) 'Democratic Politics and International Trade Negotiations: Elections and Divided Government As Constraints on Trade Liberalization', *Journal of Conflict Resolution*, Vol. 41, No. 1, pp. 117–46.

Minoiu, Camelia and Sanjay G. Reddy (2010) 'Development Aid and Economic Growth: A Positive Long-run Relation', *The Quarterly Review of Economics and Finance*, Vol. 50, No. 1, pp. 27–39.

Mintz, Alex (1993) 'The Decision to Attack Iraq: A Noncompensatory Theory of Decision Making', *Journal of Conflict Resolution*, Vol. 37, No. 4, pp. 595–618.

Mintz, Alex (2004) 'How Do Leaders Make Decisions? A Poliheuristic Perspective', *Journal of Conflict Resolution*, Vol. 48, No. 1, pp. 3–13.

Mintz, Alex and Nehemia Geva (1997) 'The Poliheuristic Theory of Decision', in Nehemia Geva and A Mintz (eds) *Decision Making on War and Peace: The Cognitive Rational Debate*. Boulder: Lynne Reinner, pp. 81–101.

Mintz, Alex, Nehemia Geva, Steven Redd and Amy Carnes (1997) 'The Effect of Dynamic and Static Choice Sets on Political Decision-making: An Analysis Using the Decision Board Platform', *American Political Science Review*, Vol. 91, No. 3, pp. 553–66.

Mitchell, David and Tansa George Massoud (2009) 'Anatomy of Failure: Bush's Decision-Making Process and the Iraq War', *Foreign Policy Analysis*, Vol. 5, Issue 3, pp. 265–86.

Modelski, George (1978) 'The Long Cycle of Global Politics and the Nation-State', *Comparative Studies in Society and History*, Vol. 20, No. 2, pp. 214–38.

Monten, Jonathan (2005) 'The Roots of the Bush Doctrine: Power, Nationalism, and Democracy Promotion in US Strategy', *International Security*, Vol. 29, No. 4, pp. 112–56.

Moravcsik, Andrew (1993) 'Introduction: Integrating International and Domestic Theories of International Bargaining', in Peter B. Evans, Harold K. Jacobson and Robert D. Putnam (eds) *Double-edged Diplomacy*. Berkeley: University of California Press, pp. 3–42.

Moravcsik, Andrew (1997) 'Taking Preferences Seriously: A Liberal Theory of International Politics', *International Organization*, Vol. 51, No. 4, pp. 513–53.

Moravcsik, Andrew (1998) *The Choice for Europe*. Ithaca: Cornell University Press.

Moravcsik, Andrew (1999) 'A New Statecraft? Supranational Entrepreneurs and International Cooperation', *International Organization*, Vol. 53, No. 2, Spring 1999, pp. 267–306.

Morgenthau, Hans (1951) *Politics Among Nations*. New York: Alfred A. Knopf.

Mueller, John E. 1973. *War, Presidents, and Public Opinion*. New York: John Wiley & Sons.

Neustadt, Richard E. (1969) *Presidential Power: The Politics of Leadership*. New York: John Wiley & Sons.

Nincic, Miroslav (2010) 'Getting What You Want: Positive Inducements in International Relations', *International Security*, Vol. 35, No. 1, pp. 138–83.

9/11 Commission (2004) The 9/11 Commission Report. Washington, DC: Government Printing Office.

Øhrgaard, Jakob C. (2004) 'International Relations or European Integration: is the CFSP *sui generis?*', in Ben Tonra and Thomas Christiansen (eds) *Rethinking European Union Foreign Policy*. Manchester: Manchester University Press, pp. 26–45.

Olson, Mancur (1965) *The Logic of Collective Action*. Cambridge, MA: Harvard University Press.

Oneal, John R. (1988) 'The Rationality of Decision Making During International Crises', *Polity*, Vol. XX, No. 4, pp. 598–622.

Oneal, John R., Bruce Russett and Michael L. Berbaum (2003) '*Causes of Peace: Democracy: Interdependence, and International Organizations, 1885–1992'*, *International Studies Quarterly*, Vol. 47, No. 3, pp. 371–93.

Onuf, Nicholas (1989) *World of Our Making: Rules and Rule in Social Theory and International Relations*. Columbia: University of South Carolina Press.

Onuf, Nicholas (1998) 'Constructivism: A User's Manual', in Vendulka Kubálková (ed) *Foreign Policy in a Constructed World*. Armonk: M.E.Sharpe, pp. 77–98.

O'Sullivan, Meghan L. (2003) *Smart Sanctions: Statecraft and State Sponsors of Terrorism*. Washington, DC: Brookings Institution.

Ougaard, Morten (2004) *Political Globalization: State, Power and Social Forces*. Basingstoke: Palgrave Macmillan.

Owen, John M. (1994) 'How Liberalism Produces Democratic Peace', *International Security*, Vol. 19, No. 2 (Fall 1994), pp. 87–125.

Page, Benjamin I. and Robert Y. Shapiro (1983) 'Effects of Public Opinion on Policy', *American Political Science Review*, Vol. 77, No. 1, pp. 175–90.

Pape, Robert A. (1997) 'Why Economic Sanctions Do Not Work', *International Security*, Vol. 22, No. 2, pp. 90–136.

Phillips, David L. (2005) *Losing Iraq: Inside the Postwar Reconstruction Fiasco*. Boulder: Westview Press.

Posen, Barry R. (1984) *The Sources of Military Doctrine : France, Britain, and Germany Between the World Wars*. Ithaca: Cornell University Press.

Polachek, William Solomon (1980) 'Conflict and Trade', *Journal of Conflict Resolution*, Vol. 24, No. 1, pp. 55–78.

Powell, Robert (1991) 'Absolute and Relative Gains in International Relations Theory', *American Political Science Review*, Vol. 85, No. 4, pp. 1303–20.

Preston, Thomas and Paul t'Hart (1999) 'Understanding and Evaluating Bureaucratic Politics: The Nexus Between Political Leaders and Advisory Systems', *Political Psychology*, Vol. 20, No. 1, pp. 49–98.

Price, Richard (1998) 'Reversing the Gun Sights: Transnational Civil Society Targets Land Mines', *International Organization*, Vol. 52, No. 3, pp. 613–44.

Price, Richard and Christian Reus-Smit (1998) 'Dangerous Liasons? Critical International Theory and Constructivism', *European Journal of International Relations*, Vol. 4, Issue 3, pp. 259–94.

Pruitt, Dean G. (1991) 'Strategy in Negotiations', in Victor A. Kremenyuk (ed) *International Negotiation*. San Francisco: Jossey-Bass, pp. 78–89.

Pruitt, Dean G. and Sung Hee Kim (2004) *Social Conflict: Escalation, Stalemate, and Settlement*, 3rd edn. Boston: McGraw-Hill.

Putnam, Robert (1988) 'Diplomacy and Domestic Politics', *International Organization*, Vol. 42, Issue 3, pp. 427–60.

Reinicke, Wolfgang H. (1998) *Global Public Policy: Governing without Government?* Washington, DC: Brookings Institution.

Reinicke, Wolfgang H. (2000) 'The Other World Wide Web: Global Public Policy Networks', *Foreign Policy*, Issue 117, Winter 1999/2000, pp. 44–57.

Ripsman, Norrin M. (2002) *Peacemaking by Democracies: The Effect of State Autonomy on the Post-World War Settlements*. University Park: The Pennsylvania State University Press.

Ripsman, Norrin M. (2009) 'Neoclassical Realism and Domestic Interest Groups', in Steven E. Lobell, Norrin M. Ripsman, and Jeffrey W. Taliaferro (eds) *Neoclassical Realism, The State, And Foreign Policy*. Cambridge: Cambridge University Press, pp. 170–93.

Ripsman, Norrin M. and T.V. Paul (2005) 'Globalization and the National Security State: A Framework for Analysis', *International Studies Review*, Vol. 7. Issue 2, pp. 199–227.

Ripsman, Norrin M. and T.V. Paul (2010) *Globalization and the National Security State*. Oxford: Oxford University Press.

Risse-Kappen, Thomas (1991) 'Public Opinion, Domestic Structure, and Foreign Policy in Liberal Democracies', *World Politics*, Vol. 43, No. 4, pp. 479–512.

Roberts, Clayton (1996) *The Logic of Historical Explanation*. University Park: Pennsylvania State University Press.

Robinson, Piers (2002) *The CNN Effect: The Myth of News, Foreign Policy and Intervention*. London: Routledge.

Rodrik, Dani (1995) 'Political Economy of Trade Policy', in G. Grossman and K. Rogoff (eds) *Handbook of International Economics*, Vol. 3. Netherlands: Elsevier Science Press, pp. 1457–94.

Rogowski, Ronald (1987) 'Trade and the Variety of Democratic Institutions', *International Organization*, Vol. 41, Issue 2, pp. 203–23.

Rogowski, Ronald (1989) *Commerce and Coalitions*. Princeton: Princeton University Press.

Rosati, Jerel A. (1981) 'Developing a Systematic Decision-Making Perspective: Bureaucratic Politics in Perspective', *World Politics*, Vol. 33, No. 2, pp. 234–52.

Rosati, Jerel A. (2000) 'The Power of Human Cognition in the Study of World Politics', *International Studies Review*, Vol. 2, Issue 3, pp. 45–75.

Rosati, Jerel A., Martin W. Sampson III and Joe D. Hagan (1994) 'The Study of Change in Foreign Policy.' In: Jerel A. Rosati, Joe D. Hagan and Martin W. Sampson III (Ed.) *Foreign Policy Restructuring: How Governments Respond to Global Change*. Columbia: University of South Carolina Press, pp. 3–21.

Rosato, Sebastian (2003) 'The Flawed Logic of Democratic Peace Theory', *American Political Science Review*, Vol. 97, No. 4, pp. 585–602.

Rose, Gideon (1998) 'Neoclassical Realism and Theories of Foreign Policy', *World Politics*, Vol. 51, No. 1, pp. 144–72.

Rosecrance, Richard (1986) *The Rise of the Trading State: Commerce and Conquest in the Modern World*. New York: Basic Books.

Rosecrance, Richard and Chih-Cheng Lo (1996) 'Balancing, Stability, and War: The Mysterious Case of the Napoleonic International System', *International Studies Quarterly*, Vol. 40, No. 4, pp. 479–500.

Rosenau, James N. (1961) *Public Opinion and Foreign Policy: An Operational Formulation*. New York: Random House.

Rosenau, James N. (1967) *The Domestic Sources of Foreign Policy*. New York: The Free Press.

Rosenau, James N. (1971) *The Scientific Study of Foreign Policy*. New York: The Free Press.

Rosenau, James N. (1974) 'Comparing Foreign Policies: Why, What, How', in James N. Rosenau (ed.) *Comparing Foreign Policies: Theories, Findings, Methods*. New York: Sage Publications, pp. 3–24.

Rosenau, James N. (1987) 'Introduction: New Directions and Recurrent Questions in the Comparative Study of Foreign Policy.' In: Charles F. Hermann, Charles W. Kegley, Jr and, James N. Rosenau (eds) *New Directions in the Study of Foreign Policy*. Winchester: Allen & Unwin, pp. 1–12.

Rosenau, James N. (2003) *Distant Proximities: Dynamic Legal Globalization* Princeton: Princeton University Press.

Rosenson, Beth A., Elizabeth A. Oldmixon and Kenneth D. Wald (2009) 'U.S. Senators' Support for Israel Examined Through Sponsorship/Cosponsorship Decisions, 1993–2002: The Influence of Elite and Constituent Factors', *Foreign Policy Analysis*, Vol. 5, No. 1, pp. 73–91.

Ross, Robert S. (1999) 'The Geography of the Peace: East Asia in the Twenty-First Century', *International Security*, Vol. 23, No. 4, pp. 81–118.

Rousseau, D., C. Gelpi, D. Reiter and P.K. Huth (1996) 'Assessing the Dyadic Nature of the Democratic Peace', *American Political Science Review*, Vol. 90, No. 3, pp. 512–33.

Russett, Bruce and Steve Oneal (2001) *Triangulating Peace: Democracy, Interdependence, and International Organizations*. New York: Norton.

Sarkees, Meredith Reid and Frank Wayman (2010) *Resort to War: 1816–2007*. Washington, DC: CQ Press.

Schroeder, Paul (1994) 'Historical Reality vs. Neo-Realist Theory', *International Security*, Vol. 19, No. 1, pp. 108–48.

Scott, James M. and Ralph G. Carter (2002) 'Acting on the Hill: Congressional Assertiveness in U.S. Foreign Policy', *Congress and the Presidency*, Vol. 29. No.2, pp. 151–70.

Schelling, Thomas C. (1960) *The Strategy of Conflict*. Cambridge, MA: Harvard University Press.

Schelling, Thomas C. (1966) *Arms and Influence*. New Haven: Yale University Press.

Scheve, Kenneth and Mathew Slaughter (2001) 'What Determines Individual Trade-policy Preferences?', *Journal of International Economics*, Vol. 54, Issue 2, pp. 267–92.

Schmitter, Philippe (1971) 'A Revised Theory of European Integration', in Lindberg, Leon N. and Stuart A. Scheingold (eds) *Regional Integration:*

Theory and Research. Cambridge, MA: Harvard University Press, pp. 232–64.

Schimmelfennig, Frank (2001) 'The Community Trap: Liberal Norms, Rhetorical Action, and the Eastern Enlargement of the European Union', *International Organization*, Vol. 55, No. 1, pp. 47–80.

Scholte, Jan Art (1997) 'Global Capitalism and the State', *International Affairs*, Vol. 73, No. 3, pp. 427–52.

Scholte, Jan Art (2000) *Globalization: A Critical Introduction*. Basingstoke: Palgrave Macmillan.

Schroeder, Paul (1994) 'Historical Reality vs. Neo-realist Theory', *International Security*, Vol. 19, No. 1, pp. 108–48.

Schultz, Kenneth (1998) 'Domestic Opposition and Signalling in International Crises', *American Political Science Review*, Vol. 92, No. 4, pp. 829–44.

Schweller, Randall L. (1994) 'Bandwagoning for Profit: Bringing the Revisionist State Back In', *International Security*, Vol. 19, No. 1, pp. 72–107.

Schweller, Randall L. (1996) 'Neo-realisms Status-Quo Bias: What Security Dilemma?', *Security Studies*, Vol. 5, No. 3, pp. 90–121.

Schweller, Randall L. (2003) 'The Progressiveness of Neoclassical Realism,' in Colin Elman and Miriam Fendius Elman (eds) *Progress in International Relations Theory: Appraising the Field*. Cambridge: MIT Press, pp. 311–48.

Schweller, Randall L. (2004) 'Unanswered Threats: A Neoclassical Realist Theory of Underbalancing', *International Security*, Vol. 29, No. 2, pp. 159–201.

Sebenius, James K. (1983) 'Negotiation Arithmetic: Adding and Subtracting Issues and Parties', *International Organization*, Vol. 37, Issue 2, pp. 281–316.

Sebenius, James K. (2002) 'International Negotiation Analysis', in Victor A. Kremenyuk (ed.) *International Negotiation*. San Francisco: Jossey-Bass, pp. 229–55.

Sewell, William H. Jr. (1992) 'A Theory of Structure: Duality, Agency, and Transformation', *American Journal of Sociology*, Vol. 98, No. 1, July 1992, pp. 1–29.

Shafer, Mark and Scott Crichlow (2002) 'The Process-Outcome Connection in Foreign Policy Decision Making: A Quantitative Study Building on Groupthink', *International Studies Quarterly*, Vol. 46, No. 1, pp. 45–68.

Shapiro, Michael J. (1981) *Language and Political Understanding: The Politics of Discursive Practices*. New Haven: Yale University Press.

Sil, Rudra and Peter J. Katzenstein (2010) *Beyond Paradigms: Analytical Eclecticism in the Study of World Politics*. Basingstoke: Palgrave Macmillan.

Simon, Herbert A. (1997) *Administrative Behavior: A Study of Decision-making Processes in Administrative Organizations*, 4th edn. New York: Free Press.

Singer, J. David, Stuart Bremer and John Stuckey (1972) 'Capability Distribution, Uncertainty, and Major Power War, 1820–1965', in Bruce Russett (ed) *Peace, War, and Numbers*. Beverly Hills: Sage, pp. 19–48.

Singh, Sonali and Christopher R. Way (2004) 'The Correlates of Nuclear

Proliferation: A Quantitative Test', *Journal of Conflict Resolution*, Vol. 48, No. 6, pp. 859–85.

Sjursen, Helene (1998) 'Missed Opportunity or Eternal Fantasy', in John Peterson and Helene Sjursen (eds) *A Common Foreign Policy for Europe?* London: Routledge, pp. 95–112.

Slaughter, Anne-Marie (2004) *A New World Order*. Princeton: Princeton University Press.

Smith, Steve (2002) 'The End of the Unipolar Moment? September 11 and the Future of World Order', *International Relations*, Vol. 16, No. 2, pp. 171–83.

Smith, Steve, Amelia Hadfield and Tim Dunne (2008) *Foreign Policy: Theories, Actors, Cases*. Oxford: Oxford University Press.

Snidal, Duncan (1985) 'The Limits of Hegemonic Stability Theory', *International Organization*, Vol. 39, Issue 4, pp. 579–614.

Snyder, Jack (1991) *Myths of Empire: Domestic Politics and International Ambition*. Ithaca: Cornell University Press.

Snyder, Richard, H.W. Ruck and Burton Sapin (2002) *Foreign Policy Decision-Making (Revisited)*. Basingstoke: Palgrave Macmillan.

Sobel, Richard (2001) *The Impact of Public Opinion on US Foreign Policy Since Vietnam: Constraining the Colossus*. Oxford: Oxford University Press.

Sprinz, Detlef F. and Yael Wolinsky-Nahmias (eds) (2004) *Models, Numbers, and Cases: Methods for Studying International Relations*. Ann Arbor: University of Michigan Press.

Steinbruner, John (2002) *The Cybernetic Theory of Decision*, 2nd edn. Princeton: Princeton University Press.

Sterling-Folker, Jennifer (1997) 'Realist Environment, Liberal Process, and Domestic-Level Variables', *International Studies Quarterly*, Vol. 41, No. 41, Issue 1, pp. 1–25.

Sterling-Folker, Jennifer (2009) 'Neoclassical Realism and Identity: Peril Despite Profit Across the Taiwan Strait', in Steven E. Lobell, Norrin M. Ripsman and Jeffrey W. Taliaferro (eds) *Neoclassical Realism, the State, and Foreign Policy*. Cambridge: Cambridge University Press, pp. 99–138.

Stern, Eric (2004) 'Contextualizing and Critiquing the Poliheuristic Theory', *Journal of Conflict Resolution*, Vol. 48, No. 1, pp. 105–26.

Stoessinger, John G. (1998) *Why Nations Go to War*, 7th edn. New York: St Martin's Press.

Stone, Diane (2002) 'Knowledge Networks and Policy Expertise in the Global Polity', in Morten Ougaard and Richard Higgott (eds) *Towards a Global Polity*. London: Routledge, pp. 125–44.

Stone Sweet, Alec and Wayne Sandholtz (1998) 'Integration, Supranational Governance, and the Institutionalization of the European Polity', in Wayne Sandholtz and Alec Stone Sweet (eds) *European Integration and Supranational Governance*. Oxford: Oxford University Press, pp. 1–26.

Strange, Susan (1996) *The Retreat of the State*. Cambridge: Cambridge University Press.

Sørensen, Georg (2001) *Changes in Statehood: The Transformation of International Relations*. Basingstoke: Palgrave Macmillan.

Sørensen, Georg (2004) *The Transformation of the State: Beyond the Myth of Retreat*. Basingstoke: Palgrave Macmillan.

Taber, Charles S. and Milton Lodge (2006) 'Motivated Skepticism in the Evaluation of Political Beliefs', *American Journal of Political Science*, Vol. 50, No. 3, pp. 755–69.

Taliaferro, Jeffrey W., Steven E. Lobell, and Norrin M. Ripsman (2009) 'Introduction: Neoclassical Realism, the State, and Foreign Policy', in Steven E. Lobell, Norrin M. Ripsman and Jeffrey W. Taliaferro (eds) *Neoclassical Realism, the State, and Foreign Policy*. Cambridge: Cambridge University Press, pp. 1–41.

Tallberg, J. (2006) *Leadership and Negotiation in the European Union*. Cambridge: Cambridge University Press.

Tannenwald, Nina (1999) 'The Nuclear Taboo: The United States and the Normative Basis of Nuclear Non-Use', *International Organization*, Vol. 53, No. 3, pp. 433–68.

Taureck, Rita (2006) 'Securitization Theory and Securitization Studies', *Journal of International Relations and Development*, Vol. 9, No. 1, pp. 53–61.

Tonra, Ben (2003) 'Constructing the Common Foreign and Security Policy: The Utility of a Cognitive Approach', *Journal of Common Market Studies*, Vol. 42, No. 4, pp. 731–56.

Touval, Saadia (1989) 'Multilateral Negotiations: An Analytical Approach', *Negotiation Journal*, Vol. 5, No. 2, pp. 159–73.

Touval, Saadia and I. William Zartman (1985) 'The Context of Mediation', *Negotiation Journal*, Vol. 1, Issue 4, pp. 373–78.

Touval, Saadia and I. William Zartman (1989) 'Mediation in International Conflicts', in Kenneth Kressel and Dean Priutt (eds) *Mediation Research: The Process and Effectiveness of Third-Party Intervention*. San Francisco: Jossey-Bass, pp. 115–37.

Tsebelis, George (1995) 'Decision Making in Political Systems', *British Journal of Political Science*, Vol. 25, No. 3, pp. 289–326.

Turner, Marlene E. and Anthony R. Pratkanis (1998) 'Twenty-Five Years of Groupthink Theory and Research: Lessons from the Evaluation of a Theory', *Organizational Behavior and Human Decision Processes*, Vol. 73, No. 2/3, pp. 105–15.

Vanderbush, Walt (2009) 'Exiles and the Marketing of U.S. Policy toward Cuba and Iraq', *Foreign Policy Analysis*, Vol. 5, No. 3, pp. 287–306.

Van Evera, Stephen (1997) *Guide to Methods for Students of Political Science*. Ithaca: Cornell University Press.

Vasquez, John (1993) *The War Puzzle*. Cambridge: Cambridge University Press.

Vasquez, John (1998) *The Power of Power Politics. From Classical Realism to Neotraditionalism*. Cambridge: Cambridge University Press.

Vasquez, John and Marie T. Henehan (2001) 'Territorial Disputes and the Probability of War: 1816–1992', *Journal of Peace Research*, Vol. 38, No. 2, pp. 123–38.

Wæver, Ole (1996) 'European Security Identities', *Journal of Common Market Studies*, Vol. 34, No. 1, pp. 103–32.

Wæver, Ole (1997) 'Concepts of Security'. PhD dissertation submitted to the University of Copenhagen.

Wagner, R. Harrison (2000) 'Bargaining and War', *American Journal of Political Science*, Vol. 44, No. 3, pp. 469–84.

Walker, Stephen G. (1995) 'Psychodynamic Processes and Framing Effects In Foreign Policy Decision-making: Woodrow Wilson's Operational Code', *Political Psychology*, Vol. 16, No. 4, pp. 697–717.

Walker, Stephen G. (2003) 'Operational Code Analysis as a Scientific Research Program: A Cautionary Tale', in Colin Elman and Miriam Fendius Elman (eds) *Progress in International Relations Theory: Appraising the Field*. Cambridge, MA: MIT Press, pp. 245–76.

Walker, Stephen G. and Lawrence F. (1984) 'The Operational Codes of U.S. Presidents and Secretaries of State: Motivational Foundations and Behavioral Consequences', *Political Psychology*, Vol. 5, No. 2, pp. 237–66.

Walker, Stephen G., Mark Schafer and Michael D. Young (1999) 'Presidential Operational Codes and Foreign Policy Conflicts in the Post-Cold War World', *Journal of Conflict Resolution*, Vol. 43, No. 5, pp. 610–35.

Wallerstein, Immanuel (1974) *The Modern World System*. New York: Academic Press.

Wallerstein, Immanuel (1980) *The Modern World System II: Mercantilism and the Consolidation of the European World-Economy*. New York: Academic Press.

Wallerstein, Immanuel (1989) *The Modern World System III: The Second Era of Great Expansion of the Capitalist World-economy*. New York: Academic Press.

Walt, Stephen M. (1985) 'Alliance Formation and the Balance of World Power', *International Security*, Vol. 9, No. 4, pp. 3–43.

Walt, Stephen M. (1988) 'Testing Theories of Alliance Formation: The Case of Southwest Asia', *International Organization*, Vol. 42, No. 2, pp. 275–316.

Walt, Stephen M. (1991) 'The Renaissance of Security Studies', *International Studies Quarterly*, Vol. 35, No. 2, pp. 211–39.

Walt, Stephen M. and John Mearsheimer (2007) *The Israel lobby and U.S. Foreign Policy*. London: Penguin Books.

Waltz, Kenneth N. (1970) 'The Myth of Interdependence', in Charles Kindleberger (ed) *The International Corporation*, Cambridge: MIT Press, pp. 205–23.

Waltz, Kenneth N. (1979) *Theory of International Politics*. New York: McGraw-Hill.

Waltz, Kenneth N. (1990) 'On the Nature of States and their Recourse to Violence', *US Institute of Peace Journal*, Vol. 3, No. 2, pp. 6–7.

Waltz, Kenneth N. (1991) 'America as a Model for the World? A Foreign Policy Perspective', *PS: Political Science and Politics*, Vol. 24, No. 4, pp. 667–70.

Waltz, Kenneth N. (1993) 'The Emerging Structure of International Politics', *International Security*, Vol. 18, No. 2, pp. 44–79.

Waltz, Kenneth N. (1996) 'International Politics is not Foreign Policy', *Security Studies*, Vol. 6, No. 1, pp. 54–7.

Waltz, Kenneth N. (2000) 'Structural Realism after the Cold War', *International Security*, Vol. 25, No. 1, pp. 5–41.

Wang, Kevin H. (1996) 'Presidential Responses to Foreign Policy Crises:

Rational Choice and Domestic Politics', *Journal of Conflict Resolution*, Vol. 40, No. 1, pp. 68–97.

Weart, Spencer R. (1998) *Never at War: Why Democracies Will Not Fight One Another*. New Haven: Yale University Press.

Weiss, Stephen (1994) 'Negotiating with Romans, Part I', *Sloane Management Review*, Vol 35, No. 2, pp. 51–61.

Welch, David A. (1992) 'The Organizational Process and Bureaucratic Politics Paradigms: Retrospect and Prospect', *International Security*, Vol. 17, No. 2, pp. 112–46.

Weldes, Jutta (1999) *Constructing National Interests: The United States and the Cuban Missile Crisis*. Minneapolis: University of Minneapolis Press.

Wendt, Alexander (1992) 'Anarchy is What States Make of it: The Social Construction of International Politics', *International Organization*, Vol. 46, No. 2, pp. 391–425.

Wendt, Alexander (1999) *Social Theory of International Politics*. Cambridge: Cambridge University Press.

White, Brian (1989) 'Analysing Foreign Policy: Problems and Approaches', in Michael Clarke and Brian White (eds) *Understanding Foreign Policy: The Foreign Policy Systems Approach*. Aldershot: Edward Elgar, pp. 1–26.

White, Brian (2004a) 'Foreign Policy Analysis and European Foreign Policy', in Ben Tonra and Thomas Christiansen (eds) *Rethinking European Union Foreign Policy*. Manchester: Manchester University Press, pp. 45–61.

White, Brian (2004b) 'Foreign Policy Analysis and the New Europe', in Walter Carlsnaes, Helene Sjursen and Brian White (eds) *Contemporary European Foreign Policy*. London: Sage, pp. 11–31.

Wight, Colin (2006) *Agents, Structures and International Relations: Politics as Ontology*. Cambridge: Cambridge University Press.

Wintrobe, Ronald (1998) *The Political Economy of Dictatorship*. Cambridge: Cambridge University Press.

Wittkopft, Eugene R. (1990) *Faces of Internationalism. Public Opinion and American Foreign Policy*. Durham: Duke University Press.

Wivel, A. (2005). Explaining why state X made a certain move last Tuesday: The promise and limitations of realist foreign policy analysis. *Journal of International Relations and Development*, Vol. 8, No. 4, pp. 355–80.

Wohlforth, William C. (1994/95) 'Realism and the End of the Cold War', *International Security*, Vol. 19, No. 3, pp. 91–129.

Wohlforth, William C. (1999) 'The Stability of a Unipolar World', *International Security*, Vol. 24, No. 1, pp. 5–41.

Ye, Min (2007) 'Poliheuristic Theory, Bargaining, and Crisis Decision Making', *Foreign Policy Analysis*, Vol. 3, No. 4, pp. 317–44.

Yergin, Daniel (1977) *Shattered Peace: The Origins of the Cold War and the National Security State*. Boston: Houghton Mifflin.

Yetiv, Steve A. (2004) *Explaining Foreign Policy: U.S. Decision-Making & the Persian Gulf War*. Baltimore: Johns Hopkins University Press.

Young, Helen and Nicholas Rees (2005) 'EU Voting Behavior in the UN General Assembly, 1990–2002: the EU's Europeanising Tendencies', *Irish Studies in International Affairs*, Vol. 16, pp. 193–207.

Young, John W. and John Kent (2004) *International Relations since 1945: A Global History*. Oxford: Oxford University Press.

Young, Oran R. (1991) 'Political Leadership and Regime Formation: on the Development of Institutions in International Society', *International Organization*, Vol. 45, No. 3, Summer 1991, pp. 281–308.

Zakaria, Fareed (1992) 'Realism and Domestic Politics: A Review Essay', *International Security*, Vol. 17, No. 1, pp. 177–98.

Zakaria, Fareed (1998) *From Wealth to Power: The Unusual Origins of America's World Role*. Princeton: Princeton University Press.

Zartman, I. William (2003) 'Conclusion: Managing Complexity', *International Negotiation*, Vol. 8, No. 1, pp. 179–86.

Index

Printed and bound in Great Britain by
CPI Group (UK) Ltd, Croydon, CR0 4YY